Sex and thugs and rock 'n'roll

Sex and thugs and rock 'n' roll

Billy Thorpe

PAN

Pan Macmillan Australia

*This book is dedicated to my mother, who is
90 years old this year, bless her heart, and to
the memory of my dear old Dad, who passed
away at the age of 89 during my writing it.
I love you both.*

First published 1996 in Macmillan by Pan Macmillan Publishers Australia Pty Ltd
First published 1997 in Pan by Pan Macmillan Australia Pty Limited
St Martins Tower, 31 Market Street, Sydney

Reprinted 1997, 1998 (twice), 1999

National Library of Australia
cataloguing-in-publication data:

Thorpe, Billy, 1946– .
Sex and thugs and rock 'n' roll : a year in Kings Cross 1963-1964.
ISBN 0 330 35992 4

1. Thorpe, Billy, 1946– 2. Aztecs (Musical Group).
3. Rock musicians – Australia – Biography. 4. Kings Cross
(N.S.W.) – Social life and customs. I. Title.

782.42166092

Printed in Australia by McPherson's Printing Group

I want to thank Lynn, my wife of twenty-five years and soul mate for life, without whose love, enthusiasm, advice, patience and encouragement this book would never have been written. I love you. If I hadn't heard you laughing hysterically when you read my first drafts of some of the funny chapters, I don't think I would have gone any further.

In looking at my life I realised that I am only a small part of my own story—the characters, places and events that moulded me being the truly fascinating elements. I owe whatever success I've had, and my ability to survive, to the smarts I learned on the streets of the Cross and inside the doors of Surf City in those early days.

To the Aztecs, Vince, Col, Bluey and Tony, for their talent, respect, friendship, hard work and humour. To John and Ma Harrigan. To Pepper and Natalie for sharing their lives and love with me. To Jean-Pierre, Sammy and dear old Dulcie. To Candy, Jimmy and Laz for the great music they introduced me to. To all our fans and most importantly to the Surf City fans who believed in us, encouraged and supported us, helped choose our songs and bought our records in the beginning when nobody else wanted to know. Thank you all from the bottom of my heart.

Without you this story would have never have happened.

Contents

Introduction

HAVING lived primarily in the United States for the past twenty years I had not spent a great deal of time in Australia. Although returning almost every year, my first extended trip home wasn't until June of 1994. During that visit something in my perception of Australia, the people, and my part in its musical history hit me in a way I'd never experienced before.

Characters, places, and events that I'd either filed away or taken for granted for over thirty years suddenly sprang magically back to life in a form that transcended memories. Particularly while visiting and staying in Kings Cross in Sydney, where I had first lived as a teenager after leaving home at sixteen, and where my musical career got its launch. While walking its historically charged streets, I was confronted daily by vivid images of my past there, and of events that shaped my life forever.

This is my first attempt at writing, and although most

certainly autobiographical in nature, it is by no means an autobiography in the strict sense of the word. It is instead a reflection, through my eyes, of a time long gone, of a red-light district in a place called Kings Cross, and in particular of the experiences of a young teenager during his quest for the grail on the streets of the Cross in 1963 and 1964.

If you were there please forgive me if occasionally some of the events are slightly out of chronological order. Outside of statistics, so little has been documented about this crucial twelve-month period in Australia, that apart from the scant information I've received from a few people who were there, and a few magazine and newspaper articles, I've had to rely solely on my memory to fill in the gaps.

Had I attempted a work of fiction I couldn't have invented characters and situations more bizarre and hilarious than those documented in this book. It's hard even for me to believe that some of the events actually took place, let alone happened to me, but I assure you, no matter how bizarre they may seem at times, they did.

Certain names and places have been changed, both out of respect for the privacy of others and to protect the innocent and guilty alike, including myself. These otherwise factual elements have been included to enable me to write about this magical period in my life in the form of an adventure, as opposed to a traditional autobiography, and to enhance the reader's ability to feel, hear, smell, taste, see, understand, and experience a truly unique place and time.

This is a true story about Australian humour, attitudes, musicians, fashion, hookers, strippers, street life, history, love, murder, sex and thugs and rock 'n' roll. It's my story.

Billy Thorpe
Los Angeles, 1996

I
The Cross

'THAT suit is sharper than shark shit, my son,' was the first thing Little Sammy said to me the first night we met. The year was 1963. The place, Kings Cross, in Sydney, New South Wales. The country, Australia.

The Cross, the 'Irish Moss'—or just the 'Irish' in 'Steak and Kidney' to those of us who lived there. And I did, right smack-dab in the middle of it in Victoria Street, just a few doors down from a whorehouse.

I left home and moved into the Canberra Oriental Hotel in June 1963. I'd been singing and performing professionally since I was a child, playing dances, rock gigs and hotels in my home town of Brisbane and around Queensland. My professional debut at the Railway Hotel, Woolloongabba, at the age of ten, had been a raging success. After my performance the cheering audience had showered the stage with coins. Crawling around on my hands and knees in my short pants, I collected the staggering amount of ten pounds, which was a fortune to a ten-year-old, considering the basic wage in those days was about three quid a week.

Ah this is the game, I thought.

I was eleven years old when I first signed with QTQ Channel 9 and the Channel Nine Television Network, appearing up to four nights a week on local Brisbane television, with the odd appearance on interstate shows. Now here I was in Sydney, ready for the big time, looking for the big break and determined to make it. Having visited Sydney a couple of times in the past to perform, I sort of knew my way around, and the Cross was my chosen hang. I *loved* it.

That June of '63 Kings Cross was music, musicians, poets, painters, dips' joints, brothels, hookers, pimps, hoons, charity molls, spruikers, toffs, chats, mooks, lairs, mugs, phizgigs, drag queens, straights, shines, bent cops, street gangs, armed robbers, killers, tea-leaves, neon, glitz, Surf City, the Chevron Hotel, the Rex, the Mansions, the Hampton Court, the Mayfair, the Pink Pussycat, the Paradise, Angelo's Spaghetti Bar, the Kellett Club, Les Girls, Italian, Hungarian, Thai and Indian food, and the best bloody schnitzels on the planet. God, I loved it.

The sounds and smells. And the night!

The night takes on a different feel and meaning to anyone who has spent any real time working the night shift in a place like the Cross. You not only become part of the night community, a local, but part of the night itself. Part of its fabric. Part of what the straights come out of their boring little lives to spend their hard-earned getting a fix of.

It's magic and I don't mean starlight and moonbeams. It's electric, neon, blue and red. The other side of the door that closes when the sun goes down, no strings linking it to the straight and real world of the day. It has texture, angles, geography, both physical and psychological. Within its walls dwells the embodiment of the dichotomy of those two great con artists, pleasure and pain. It's a territory unto itself, where all who pay are welcome, but those who can't are not. There's a line that can only be crossed by another 'night-shifter', that invisible line with an invisible sign that warns, 'no straights allowed'. It's the chatter of the strippers and handlers as they move along the street from club to club. The silent language of nods and body signs as night-shifters pass each other on their rounds.

'Hi, mate . . . what's doing? . . . Sweet? . . . Don't get none on ya!' all contained in the flick of a lapel, the wink of an eye or tap of the nose.

It's the muffled sounds of bar music coming up from the basement joints as it underscores the spruiker's pitch. The colour and aroma of cigar and cigarette smoke as it mixes and ferments with the cheap perfume of the night ladies in the bars. The pace, the pulse, the crystal-clear unambiguity of its purpose. *Good times, good times, good times, here and now!* It's just knowing your way around it when you're accepted as a night-shifter. Getting home safe at sunrise every morning, wobbly or sober. Getting up at 3 p.m. and not being able to wait for the sun to go down and that neon door to open so it can start all over again. *Good times, good times, good times, here and now!* This is my life twenty-four, seven . . . I am in heaven!

Sammy was a little guy in his early twenties, no more than five six, porky and round, with no discernible angles to his body. With his curly black hair and beard, laughing, black eyes, fat belly and short, powerful arms and legs, he's the spitting image of a young Dom De Luise. Like his body, his face is round, his features formed as if someone had bunched their fingers and dipped them in the mix while it was still wet. His cheeky grin gives him the appearance of a mischievous schoolboy who's just shit in the teacher's drawer and can't contain himself while he waits for the pong to hit. Ready to crack a new joke every minute, which he usually does, he's got the best wit and quickest repartee of anyone I've ever known. A cabaret-style performer, Sammy's a fine singer and natural comic whose on-stage antics are simply an effortless extension of his everyday demeanour. He's a great friend, one of the funniest men on the planet, and a joy to be around. Lebanese by descent, real name Nebil Gaha, Sammy is also into disguises, playing roles, screwing with people's heads, but in a cool, hilarious way. And he was wearing a preacher's bib and back-to-front collar under his black jacket that first night we met . . .

I had wandered into the Pink Pussycat at the top of William Street, just across from my hotel. I'd only been in town a few days and every night on my way home I'd noticed it. I didn't know much about the place, other than it was obviously a strip joint. Then I met some old dear in her eighties named Dulcie Maysberry in a pub on William Street. Dulcie had lived around the Cross all her life and after shouting her a few Scotches, which she dropped like a wharfie, she eagerly filled me with gems of information about the Cross and Darlinghurst.

She told me that she'd slept with actor Peter Finch when he lived in Victoria Street in the '30s, and that Bill Dobell— later Sir William Dobell, the great Australian artist—had once lived above the ANZ bank in Darlinghurst Road and for a time in the spot now occupied by the Pussycat.

'Even though 'e was an old poof, 'e'd 'ave been there pervin' every night, the dirty old bastard,' Dulcie said, throwing back another shot of Cutty and chasing it with a pony of beer. 'Jeeesus Chariist, life's as bony as a dingo's dick, ain't it, darl? Naked tits 'n' arse dancin' round in Dobell's fuckin' living room, who'd ever 'ave believed it, eh?' She coughed and wheezed as she spoke. ''E'd've fuckin' loved it.' She cackled through a near-toothless grin, pissed rotten. Dulcie was classic!

It was nothing as deep as Sir William Dobell that had drawn me to the Pussycat that night, just the hot music floating down from the windows and the funky, pink neon sign on the street below. They both seemed to have the right kind of 'come in and get some' appeal . . . so I did. It was about 1.30 a.m. on a cool Thursday morning in June.

I was seventeen years old.

The Pink Pussycat was on the third floor of an old building at the T-intersection of Darlinghurst Road and William Street. It was directly above a greasy-spoon restaurant eloquently named the Hasty Tasty by its original owners in the 1930s. My first night in the Cross I'd wandered in for a graze and ate the biggest and best mixed grill I'd had in my life. It cost me the princely sum of two bob. No wonder the place had survived for so long.

Walking through a glass door to the left of the old restaurant, I climbed a set of rickety wooden stairs and paid my money to some bloke at the top. A moose in a funky black dinner suit and bow tie gave me the once-over twice, asked no questions, took my ticket, gave me a voucher saying I was a bona fide Pussycat 'Top Cat' and opened the door. *I was in.* I looked like I could pay and that's all that mattered in those days. Sure I was under age, but I was dressed expensively, sharp. From my years as a performer, I had a great wardrobe, the best of which I'd brought with me to Sydney. You know . . . Edward

Mellor, triple-D point, spit-polished brown brogues and Clive Cook, cream linen suit kinda shit.

I'd been performing and hanging around with musicians twice my age since I was ten years old. I knew the rap, knew how to act, and I could easily pass for twenty or twenty-one, or so I thought. Anyway, it seemed to work. At least enough to get me into the bars, strip joints and nightclubs around Sydney and the Cross in 1963 and not get thrown out.

Once inside the door, I was greeted by a spunky young bleached blonde wearing pink high heels and about four square inches of black silk bikini. Ninety per cent of it was straining to contain and support about a forty-inch set. The other 10 per cent looked more like Long John Silver's eye patch than a bikini bottom and it barely covered her shaved babooey which stuck out like a camel toe with a black bandaid on it.

'Welcome to the Pussycat, sir,' she said. 'Would you prefer to sit at a table or by the stage?'

'Er, a table will be OK,' I managed to reply.

'Fine,' she said. 'Walk this way, please.'

Holy shit, if I ever walked that way they'd lock me up, I thought, following her naked arse as it swung through two black curtains and into the club. The place was full, jammed with the usual contingent of late-night strip-joint aficionados, men of every size, age and persuasion. Some were expensively dressed, some down at the heel, some young, some old, but all horny as a bull in springtime. And all there for a little taste of what they knew wasn't waiting for them at home. Pure unadulterated naked young pussy.

The hostess sat me down at a table about halfway along the room and I noticed someone already sitting there watching the show.

'That suit is sharper than shark shit, my son,' he said to me, nodding a hello as I sat down. I smiled and nodded back, then did a double-take. What the fuck was a priest doing in a strip joint? Then I checked out the room. My table was one of about thirty placed around a black, velvet-draped catwalk that started just inside the front door and ran the length of the room. As well as tables and chairs, there were vinyl-covered, studded booths around the walls and single bar stools around the edge of the catwalk. These stools catered to the hard core, seriously discriminating, up close, ta-ta snifters and crotch perves. Mainly servicemen and Orientals who, by their hypnotic gaze, seemed to have some secret, mystical, communication going with the dancing pussy. It definitely spoke to them.

They were so close and into it that I expected them to lose control at any minute, dive in head-first and disappear. But the girls knew how to work them and they rarely got groped. These catwalk Casanovas were usually regulars. Tittie-whipped into believing they had a personal, intimate relationship going with some of the strippers, they spent all night drinking hard and tipping their favourite girl. She usually knew him by name and had the poor sucker convinced she was head over heels in love with him, 'cause she didn't flash her twang like that for just anyone. He believed he was her knight in shining armour, the one mug in the whole wide world who could whisk her away from all this, and he should jump ship, desert, or go home immediately, sell his car, empty his bank account, and leave a note telling the cheese 'n' kisses and tin lids that he was leaving them for true love with a pair of big tits.

Like all joints, the Pussycat was minimum on charm and

maximum on glitz. Silver wallpaper was big everywhere in those days and the Pussycat had more than its share. To the right of the catwalk sat a small bar and along the opposite wall was a floor-to-ceiling mirror which made the club seem a lot bigger than it really was. For some reason strippers seem to get some innate pleasure out of watching themselves get their gear off, and one or two of them usually enjoyed watching their girlfriends get their gear off too. I guess doing the same ol' same ol' night after night, watching themselves in the mirror is the only thing that gets them off.

Three single red, blue and white spotlights beamed from a booth above the entrance. Along with the colour wheel and glitter ball hanging in the middle of the room above the catwalk, these seemed to be the joint's total investment in production. But punters don't come to look at lights. It's tits and arse that parted them from their hard-earned cash and kept them drooling, cockeyed, while the establishment plied them with liquor at premium prices.

Cigarette smoke sat in a thick blue mist in the spots that night, hanging there like nimbus clouds, dancing and changing direction with every movement in the room. It was hot, sweaty hot, but it's always hot in joints because 'cool don't sell drinks'. Even the music was hot and it was funky and loud! The first stripper I saw should have won Miss World that year as far as I was concerned. She was gorgeous.

'Less tits and more crotch!' some old guy shouted from out of the dark behind me at the sweet young thing doing her all-but-naked best to ease all the angst in the world.

'Jesus, she's a winner, my son,' the priest shouted to me across the table. 'Look at that lemon. Whoa!' He gestured toward her and nodded like a proud trainer admiring a thoroughbred.

'Her what?' I asked, not having any idea what the fuck he was talking about.

'Her lemon! . . . Her lemon and sarse my son! Her arse!' he said, shaking his head and smiling, not taking his eyes off her.

Who the hell is this maniac? I thought. Then I looked at her lemon and realised he wasn't that crazy after all.

'Her name's Helgar, my son,' he yelled over the music. 'She's German or Austrian or some fuckin' thing. Anyway, it would take a Panzer division and Hitler himself to get into her fuckin' bunker. Nobody's been there yet, my son, but veer tryink . . . veeer tryink!' He shielded his mouth with a cupped hand, faking a high-pitched German accent.

I watched her do her thing and she was *hot*. Bare-arse naked except for a tiny black patent leather G-string, a black patent leather SS officer's peaked cap and a pair of six-inch patent leather spike heels. She was slowly grinding herself against a pole in the centre of the catwalk to the beat of some James Brown number and moving like she knew exactly what ol' James was wailing about. A tall, lean, young fraulein with bright red lipstick and blonde, shoulder-length hair, maybe eighteen and extremely beautiful. A drunken sailor sitting on a stool directly in front of her nearly screwed his head off his neck trying to get the perfect view of her golden gate, but she ignored him and danced over in our direction. She nodded at my crazy friend the priest, then turned around, bent over with her legs wide apart, put her face between them, and gave me a big, deliberate smile. Licking her lips, she moved her tongue slowly from one side of her mouth to the other, blew me a kiss and winked.

'Jeeezus Chariist, I'm viss you, mine Fuehrer!' the priest yelled at me.

He stood up, clicked his heels together and saluted me Nazi style, yelling 'Sieg Heil!' at the top of his lungs. I had no idea who he was, but in his vicar's bib and collar he was as funny as a hat full of arseholes. Loud, but somehow not offensive.

The stripper cracked up and so did half the people in the joint. I wasn't surprised. After all, it wasn't every day you'd see a priest get up and give a Sieg Heil in the middle of a stripper's act. And things were getting weirder by the minute. Now the big fraulein was on her knees directly in front of me, grinning and squeezing her boobs, grinding her hips back and forth in my direction, pretending to screw me from six feet away.

'Jesus, look at those brace 'n' bits, will ya!' the priest yelled in a raspy voice, squeezing his eyes shut like he was in pain.

'Those what?' I yelled.

'Her brace 'n' bits, my son! Her tits! Her fuckin' tits! Christ, where you from, my son, Brisbane?'

'Well, er, yes mate,' I said. 'As a matter of fact I am.'

'Shit, son, I won't hold that against you. You can still buy me a drink. What am I having?'

The priest laughed and waved over a long-legged waitress who looked like she should be the star of the show, not waiting tables. She must have been about the same age as the stripper. Even in the electric red and blue of the club lights, the first thing I noticed as she came towards me was her short, natural, bright red hair. All natural redheads seem to have the same skin tone and complexion, an Irish look, and she had it. Her hair colour was definitely not store-bought. She was wearing one of those one-piece, strapless, black satin, bustier costumes, like the Playboy bunnies wear, and sheer black stockings with high heels. Her shoulders and arms were bare, but on each wrist she wore a large white starched shirt cuff with shining pink cufflinks. This girl was a stunner, with a pair of legs that didn't quit, and tits so firm you could balance a tray full of shot glasses on them without spilling a drop. She came around to my side of the table and I felt the blood rush to my face. For a second I was struck dumb by the sheer beauty of her.

'What would you gentlemen like?' she asked politely, smiling at me. I was still mapping her geography and she caught me letching. 'To drink, I mean,' she added through clenched teeth, scolding me with a look.

'Er, yes please, miss. Can I . . . er, have . . . umm . . .'

Mumbling like a fool, I managed to order two double OP rum and Cokes, paid her with two crisp pound notes, told her to 'er, keep the change' and watched her arse wiggle away from the table. If it had been any tighter, I swear it would have squeaked.

'God, who's *that*?' I asked the priest.

'You're shweet as a fuckin' nut there, my son,' he said. 'Jesus, look at that lemon. Eet-fucking-shwa as an ut-na. Her bracens 've got a hard-on for you, my son, no wuckin' furries. I got the drum.'

He got up and came around to my side of the table, sat down and put his arm around me, then raised his glass in a toast.

'Adolf, my son, you're a winner! As your spiritual adviser and attorney, I strongly advise you to take me with you wherever you go for the rest of your life.'

He threw back his head and laughed uproariously at his own joke. It was one of those throaty, raspy laughs that comes from deep down in the gut. The kind that sounds like you have to smoke six packs of Gauloise a day to perfect. It was instantaneously infectious and the second I heard it I liked him a lot. In about ten seconds we were both rolling around crying, tears running down our cheeks.

I've always been a sucker for a good laugher, male or female. It hooks me, it's hypnotic, sucks me in. I get caught up in it and can't stop. It takes me to a point where I laugh so hard I cry and can't remember what the fuck made me laugh in the first place. It just feels good to be laughing.

'What's your name, china?' he asked at last, his arm still round my shoulders.

'What?' I replied, not understanding.

'China . . . me old china plate. You know . . . *mate*. What's your name, mate?' he asked again, taking his arm off me and offering his hand. 'I'm Sammy, Sammy Gaha, my son, Little Sammy to my friends. You can call me Bruce.'

'Oh, Billy, Billy Thorpe,' I said, shaking his hand and my head.

'Ah, so it's William, is it?' He rubbed the point of his beard between his thumb and forefinger as he contemplated the ceiling. 'In that case, my son . . . in that case I will dub thee Sir Gil, and you will address me as Sir Ponson. From this moment on we are brother Knights of the Royal Order of the Shalamanikee, forever shworn to protect the secret code of the Zippee Qua Quandeye Nacktie Whoopie Crash Malik with a Crrrap handle on top. If you ever reveal the sacred secret of the code, Sir Gil . . . your arse will drop off!'

Another instant round of laughter.

'I don't know the secret of the code,' I laughed.

'Then you're safe as a schoolgirl with no knickers in the dressing room at Les Girls, Sir Gil, my son.'

More outrageous laughter. Les Girls was a drag club just off Darlinghurst Road.

By this time several people at adjacent tables were being infected with Sammy's laugh and started to break up. When the red-headed waitress brought our drinks, Sammy gestured to me saying, 'Sir Gil, this is my very good friend, Pepper. She's the best sort this side of the moon and, Pepper, this is my good friend Sir Gil, from Bris-a-baine, but don't hold that against him, he's a real good bloke. He's also been known to answer to the names Herr Adolf and Billy.'

Pepper's smile was big and warm and she put her hand out, leant in close to my ear and said, 'Pleased to meet you, Sir Gil.' She smelt fantastic!

'Pleased to meet you too, my lady,' I said, taking her hand as I stood up. I gently turned it over, politely kissing the back, which made her smile and blush at the same time. Her scent was incredible. I don't mean her perfume, I mean her natural scent. The combination of her sweet breath, hair, skin, and body. Way back in the cave, that's what originally attracted. It's the primal scent, the original aphrodisiac, and Pepper had my flavour.

Without realising it, I was still standing there holding her hand. There was a pause as we just stood and looked at one another, then she leant in close to me again.

'Can I please have it back?' she asked timidly. 'I need it for work tonight.'

'Ah, eet's a love shweet love,' Sammy sang at the top of his voice and the three of us cracked up. I let go of Pepper's hand and she walked away smiling as Sammy and I continued to laugh. He had me going now and I couldn't stop.

People at other tables started laughing again, hooked by the hypnotic quality of Sammy's laughter. Pretty soon half the joint was breaking up without knowing what the hell they were laughing at.

'Fuckin' turn it up, Sammy!' said the bloke in the sharp suit as he leant over the table. 'What d'ya think this is, South Sydney fuckin' Leagues Club? The sheilas are trying to make a living up there, I'm trying to sell drinks, and you've got half the fuckin' joint goin', you little goose. Turn it up!'

He spoke out of the corner of his mouth in a conspiratorial way and something in his voice told me they knew each other well. He was about thirty-five years old, short, with black curly hair and a huge grin full of teeth. From what I could see in the dim light, his dark blue suit was immaculately cut and made out of some sort of mohair, probably Ganier by the sheen. His shirt, a white cotton polo neck. As he sat down next to Sammy, he checked out my threads and nodded hello to me approvingly. I nodded back and he and Sammy went into a huddled conversation.

Shouting through a microphone that distorted his voice, an announcer spruiked the next girl on, carny style:

'And nowww, *ladeez* and *gentlemennah*, the Pink a-Pussycat *paroudlee preesents* our next attraction. She's got more curves than a geometry class. She's a girl who *deefies* Newton's law of *garavitee* . . . the one *everee* teacher wants to spank . . . She'll make you harder than Chinese 'rithametic . . . the *paride* of the student body, *aaal* thee *waaaeey* from *Pariiis Farance*, *paleese* give a big Pussycat *welcome* to the *loverlee* . . . *Briiigitte!*'

Out through the curtains and down the catwalk, to rousing howls and wolf-whistles, looking like every schoolboy's wet dream, skipped a spunky young brunette in pigtails. The *loverlee* Brigitte was almost dressed in a skimpy black schoolgirl's uniform, black lace garter belt, black stockings, high heels and frilly black see-through panties. In her hand she held a big red lollypop which she licked seductively as she skipped on in time to Chuck singing 'up in the morning and off to school'. She was every bit as beautiful as the big German blonde, and so were her brace 'n' bits. I started to realise that this was a hot club, not some armpit. The girls were class, the drinks were thick and the vibe was definitely happening . . .

'Sir Gil, my son, this is Sir Wayne Martin,' said Sammy. 'He and Last Card Louie run the joint.'

'G'day, Wayne, Billy Thorpe,' I said, shaking his hand. 'Pleased to meet you.'

'G'day, me old,' he replied. 'So Sammy tells me yer from Brisbane. My condolences.' He smiled. 'What brings you to the Cross, my son?'

I explained about being a singer, my background in Brisbane and how I'd just come down to Sydney to try and crack the big time. 'I'm going to get a contract, make some records,' I shouted across the table. 'I'm staying here in the Cross. Only been here a few days.'

'A singer, eh. You any good?' he asked, just a small touch of smartarse in his tone.

'As good as it gets in this country, mate!' I yelled, a bag full of get fucked in mine.

Just at the instant I yelled, the record stopped playing. Everybody in the room heard my statement and the whole place politely applauded.

'Oh, shit!' I said, embarrassed as hell.

Both Sammy and Wayne fell about laughing. As the next

record started, Wayne waved over the red-headed waitress. My eyes followed her as she walked across the room and over to our table. She must have heard my blunder too, because she was looking at me and grinning as she walked up.

'Yes, sir,' she said to Wayne. 'What can I get for you?'

Gesturing to me, he said, 'Pepper, my love, please get my mate Billy here whatever he wants. On me. This kid's going to be a star.'

2
The Golden Pagoda

WHEN I woke up the first thing I saw was this beautiful naked arse bending over a table trying to reach something. I couldn't tell what. I didn't much care.

The sight of that beautiful quim smiling at me was more than enough for my brain to handle at one time. I didn't know where I was and I had the hangover from hell. As I tried to sit up and look around the room, the arse shot out of focus. I felt like somebody had pushed a pencil in each ear, like my head had exploded. I went to say something but all that came out was gibberish. My tongue was as thick as carpet and my mouth tasted like a dog had shit in it. I wanted to die!

'You OK, baby?' the arse seemed to say. 'I'm trying to find somefing. I fink it's here somewhere. You know, Aspros or somefing, uverwise we'll have to walk up the Cross for a draft at the chemist. You want some coffee, mate? I just made some fresh.'

'Uughsklosut,' I heard myself reply, 'uughsklosut, goffee pleashe . . . Aaaahh!' Every time I tried to speak a lightning bolt shot through my head.

'How do you take it?' the arse asked again.

'Uuugh . . . blaaag,' I mumbled. 'Blaaagnoshug.'

During all this my eyes were shut tight, trying to shut out the pain, but it was no use. Some maniac was inside my cranium pounding a forty-four gallon drum with two feet of steel pipe and my head felt as if it was about to cave in. Pain or no pain, my curiosity got the better of me and I slowly forced my eyes open to see if the arse had a face. What I saw was worth all the pain in hell, which is where I thought I might be.

Next to the bed, about a foot from my face, was a beautiful silky bush which curled into the whitest skin I had ever seen. As I looked up it only got better. Satin skin flowed over a tight belly, up and over her ribs, then rose, forming a pair of the most magnificent breasts I had ever seen. They stood out as firm and cheeky as the grin on the beautiful young face above them. Her eyes were big, green and smiling and she just stood there looking down at me, grinning the grin, cup in one hand and, I hoped, pain-killers in the other.

The only item of clothing she was wearing was a man's olive-green Kangol cap, which she wore with the peak cocked down towards the right side of her face like a street urchin. She wasn't at all embarrassed by the fact that she was standing there totally naked, one knee on the bed, with her pussy in my face. For a second I had the urge to lean out and bite it, but I didn't know who the hell she was, where I was, or how I got there, so I contained myself. The last thing I could remember from last night was 'Father

Samuel' blessing the Pussycat and all the strippers from the catwalk, wailing like a crazed monseigneur: 'My father beat your father at dominos!'

'Where am . . .?' I tried to ask.

'Jesus, mate, I know you were pissed last night, but you didn't seem that out of it a while ago.' She giggled, still smiling down at me. 'Maybe this will help.'

Whipping the cap off her head, she doffed it to me politely. For a second I couldn't work it out, then it started to come back. She had bright red hair. I hadn't noticed, even though some of it was almost in my face.

'Red hair . . . the club, from the, ah . . . Pussycat,' I mumbled. 'What's your name? I know, Pamela. No. No, Pat . . . no no . . . it's, um?'

'Pepper,' she said, mocking outrage with her hands on her hips. 'It's Pepper Walker, you cheeky young bugger!' She cuffed me hard on the top of my head with her cap, which she then sent skimming through the air across the room like a frisbee, landing it perfectly on the top of an old empty birdcage in the far corner.

'Ah yes, Pep . . . I remember. How did . . .'

'Sshhsh,' she said. 'First fings first. Plenty of time for that when you've had this.'

Pepper sat on the edge of the bed, gently giving me Aspros and sips of coffee like she was nursing her dying mother. I was hoping I'd never get better. A week in the Cross and here I am with a fucking goddess nursing me back to life. I *am* in heaven.

She gently stroked my forehead as she administered her cure, but I couldn't get my brain and mouth in sync and I just lay there with my mouth open like a stunned mullet without uttering a single word. It took about five minutes for the Aspros and coffee to have any effect, then I finally got it together and spoke.

'What happened? Where am I? How did . . .'

'Shhh,' she said, stroking my cheek. 'First fings first.'

She stood up and as I watched her walk naked across the room, my brain took in the full majesty of her body. God she was beautiful. Long legs, but not real tall, about five seven or eight from the soles of her feet to the top of her carrot-coloured head. She was perfectly proportioned, with long, strong, lightly muscled legs, arms, shoulders and back, her slim waist tapering into the most gorgeous arse I had ever seen. Pepper had the body of an athlete and must have trained at some stage to have that cut and detail. The Pepper I'd met in the Pussycat was a stunner, but she was coiffed and made-up. If I'd seen her on the street without it, I would have never recognised her. The real Pepper was walking across the room totally naked and she was magnificent. In fact she didn't walk as much as prowl, like a big cat, a lioness. She didn't hurry, and from the way she moved I got the distinct impression that she enjoyed her nakedness and me looking at her.

'I've got just the fing to fix you up. Umm, let me see, where is it? Ah here it is,' she said, reaching up to take something off a shelf.

Her back was to me as she stretched up to reach whatever she was looking for. My eyes were still glued to her beautiful bum and at first I didn't notice what she had in her hand. Then she turned around and I saw it was a bottle of something. A bottle of cognac. Cognac? Oh Jesus no! If I had another drink I'd die!

'No, I couldn't drink any. I, er, really I couldn't! I'd be sick as a dog,' I pleaded, feeling nauseous at the thought.

'Relax, mate,' she said, with a grin on her face. 'Trust me.'

Walking seductively back over to me, she took a large swig from the bottle but didn't swallow it, just held it in her mouth and put the bottle on the table next to the bed. Kneeling down on the floor beside me with this big grin on her face, she winked and let a little of the cognac trickle from her mouth, purring 'mmmmm'. As she leant over me, I went to put my arms around her, expecting a big cognac kiss, but she gently pulled back the sheets, took my dick in her hand and put it in her mouth. It felt like she'd wrapped it in cool, electrically charged silk and the unbelievable sensation crept slowly through me like a tingling current until it reached the outer extremities of my body. The rush was ridiculous.

It wasn't until that moment that I realised I was stark naked. It was also right then and there that I gained a firm belief there was a God, and reincarnation, because something religious was happening and I was certainly coming back to life. All pain left me. I swear my headache went in an instant. The combined sensations of watching and feeling this gorgeous young girl performing her magic on me, and the cool electric tingling sensation from the cognac in her mouth, gave me a hard-on that Superman couldn't have bent. It was incredible. After about ten minutes of taking me to the edge and bringing me back, she stopped and brought her face up to mine. She still had her mouth full of cognac and that cheeky grin still on her face. 'Mmmmm,' she purred again and swallowed the lot. By this time my dick felt like a Titan missile about to launch.

Pepper got up on the bed and stood over me, smiling, with one foot either side of my body. Looking into my eyes she began swaying her hips seductively. Every inch of her body was exposed to my gaze and I just lay there looking up at her, incredibly aroused, transfixed by her beauty, drinking her in. Without taking her eyes from mine, she slowly lowered herself onto me and I entered her. I slid straight in and she went straight off. At first her movements were slow and deliberate. She gently rode up and down on me, rocking slowly back and forth, staring into my eyes, quietly moaning as the pleasure moved through her. She was completely uninhibited, but there was nothing vulgar about her. It felt right. She wasn't just fucking me, she was making love, and she could tell I was loving every second of it.

Christ, I was just a seventeen-year-old kid! I'd never experienced anything like Pepper in my life. She was gentle, but completely in control. I just went with her movements until our rhythms were completely in sync and we became one. Slowly increasing the intensity of our movement, our bodies became drenched with perspiration and we got higher and higher. Thrusting herself against me, she sat with her hands resting on the bed to steady herself and rode me like a champion show jumper for the next half an hour. A dozen times she brought me to the edge of an enormous climax, only to ease off, bringing me slowly back down before effortlessly taking me up again to the edge. Everything in my sexual experience before this could only be described as fucking. This was euphoria.

Reaching forward, she gently took my hands, lacing her fingers in mine. I felt her knees grip my sides, her body tightened, and I knew she was about to explode. Suddenly she stopped moving and went rigid. Sitting there on top of me with her back arched and head back shuddering uncontrollably, Pepper came. She made no sound, just sat there trembling on top of me for a full minute as the climax took her.

It took me too. She had brought me to an enormous climax and I came so hard I thought I was going to pass out, completely overwhelmed by the intensity of the experience. Shivers ran all through my body like shock waves and I had an overwhelming urge to cry. To my surprise, when I looked at Pepper I saw tears of pleasure running down her cheeks. She leaned forward, took my face in her hands and kissed me passionately on the lips. Then she sat up, sighed a big sigh and with a grin on her face, said 'Oh God' and fell straight back with her arms out like she had died, but with me still inside her, hard as a rock.

I swear I thought she'd snapped the fucker clean off at the base. Amazing things, dicks, when you think of the pounding they take in a lifetime and they never wear out or snap off. Anyhow, with closer scrutiny and some gentle, soothing massage therapy, she convinced me it wasn't damaged at all, just in need of a little coaxing. And coax she did.

After about another hour and a half of epic lovemaking, Pepper decided to take a shower. As she closed the bathroom door behind her, I thought it was the perfect opportunity to get out of there before she ended my career on the spot. I felt like I'd just played fifteen straight quarters of footy and the first time I got up I just collapsed back on the bed.

Oh please God fix me up or let me die, I thought as I tried it again, mumbling and farting around on my hands and knees trying to find my clothes. I could only find one sock and Christ knows where my underpants were. *Ah fuck it, I gotta get outta here before she nails me again*, I thought, and somehow managed to get dressed. I was just about to stick my head into the bathroom and say goodbye when she came out, half-wrapped in a towel.

'Where you going, mate?' she asked coyly. 'Why don't you stay and I'll make us some dinner or somefing. There's no need to rush.'

She smiled at me, let the towel drop to the floor, and stood there naked and wet, tempting me. Her beauty got me again. She threw her arms around me and kissed me. Oh shit, she was turning me on again. This girl was determined to fuck me to death. *I have to get out of here quick*, I thought.

'You don't have to go just yet. The Oriental's only round the corner,' she whispered as she kissed and nibbled my ear, but I knew if I wanted to live, now was the time to make a run for it.

'Er, I've got a big audition coming up,' I told her, 'and I'll blow it if I don't get some sleep.' It sounded like a lame excuse, even though it was the truth.

She stuck her bottom lip out, faking a little girl hurt look.

'Aw, c'monnn, just come and have a quick shower wiv me before you go.'

I saw my life passing before my eyes. Not only was she the horniest girl I'd ever seen in my life, but the way she pronounced, or should I say couldn't pronounce 'th' made everything she said that much more sexy . . . and that much harder to say no to. It was an unbelievable turn-on.

'I can't, mate,' I said, 'I really can't. I'd drown. I'm dead and I've got to get some sleep. It's real important that I'm fresh, or I'll sing like shit. This audition is very important to me.'

Pepper stood there a while, looking into my eyes like a lost puppy peeping through the fence of the dog pound, waiting for a friend. She looked so beautiful and yet so lonely, so vulnerable.

'Oh, OK,' she said with a big sigh. 'But in case you change your mind later, let me give you my phone number.'

'Of course, mate,' I said. 'I was going to ask you for it anyway.'

This seemed to make Pepper happy again and she beamed a huge, loving smile at me. Without bothering to wrap herself in the towel, she walked over to a small table.

God, there's that arse again. Unbefuckinglievable! said a voice. My dick must be thinking on its own now, because I know that wasn't my brain.

Pepper scribbled her number on a piece of paper, then came over and stuck it in the breast pocket of my jacket, kissing me softly on the cheek at the same time. She still smelt fantastic and the memory of experiencing her scent for the first time in the club came flashing back for an instant.

'Bye,' she said, and sighed, kissing me again on my forehead.

Jesus, you must be crazy to leave this! that voice said. *Look at her, she's magic.* Then my brain tried to seize control of my senses from my dick.

'OK, umm . . . thanks for everything,' I mumbled. 'Er, er . . . bye.'

I kissed her on the cheek, opened the door and left. I walked down about five flights of stairs to the street and the warm fresh evening air. The sun was down but there was still a faint, light blue glow to the evening sky and for a moment I just stood there looking up at it, lost in the bliss.

As I walked up the hill on Bayswater Road towards the Cross, I looked back and saw Pepper's building for the first time. It was a green, modern apartment block, about ten storeys, with a slightly Asian flair to the design. There was a Chinese restaurant at street level and as I stood there a huge, yellow, neon sign on top of the building flashed into life for the first time that night, embossing the name 'The Golden Pagoda' in big Chinese-style letters onto the dimming sky. For a second I felt a wave of pleasure shoot through my body. I shivered, then turned, smiling as the beauty of Pepper's face came to me again. The neon door had opened welcoming another night, and I walked contentedly up the hill to my new home in the Irish Moss.

3
The Bet

THE Canberra Oriental Hotel was across the road from the back of an old theatre on the site now occupied by the Crest Hotel. It had been known as the Kings Cross Theatre since it opened in 1936 and was one of the place's landmarks, having gone through many successful incarnations from theatre to movie house to music venue. In its golden days it had been one of the favourite haunts for Sydney's fashionable set, when, in between champers and martinis, Chips Rafferty and Peter Finch kicked their heels up on Kings Cross dance floors, partying until dawn with the likes of Laurence Olivier, Vivien Leigh and Noel Coward. In the folk music boom the legendary Pete Seeger sang there. By 1963 it was the Australian home of surf music and became known as Surf City.

With all the amazing surf beaches in and around Sydney, surf music and dances, known as 'stomps', were huge. Surf clubs all over Australia, and particularly those around

Sydney, were havens for live music and bands. Some of the local surf groups, such as Roland Storm and the Statesmen, had big local followings on this circuit. The Atlantics, another Sydney instrumental band, had a No. 1 hit with 'Bombora' earlier in the year. They were a big draw and a regular attraction at the Surf City Stomps. By the time I hit the Cross the surfing craze had started to wane, but there were many surf bands and venues still catering to the enthusiastic surf music crowds.

Several months before I made the permanent move, I'd been down in Sydney doing a television show and performed at a number of surf gigs on the bill with such surfing stars as Little Pattie, who had a massive hit later that year with her song, 'He's My Blond-Headed Stompie Wompie Real Gone Surfer Boy'. Fuck, what a title! As a result of hanging in the surfing scene I found out about a talent quest which I entered and won. First prize was a trip to Auckland to sing at the new Surf City there. The only down side was I had to demonstrate the latest surf dance craze, 'the stomp', to the fledgling New Zealand surfing crowds, but what the hell, it was a free trip, all expenses paid, and 150 pounds a week for three weeks.

What could possibly go wrong? I thought. *What could possibly go fucking wrong?*

In a nutshell, the whole thing turned into a disaster. The Kiwis didn't give a shit about the stomp or surf music and the new venue was a complete bomb.

Surf City Auckland was an old cavernous, converted movie theatre and I performed there for about two weeks with some local musicians, billed as Billy Thorpe and the Surf City Surf Boys. The one up side of the experience was that they all played great. I didn't realise till I was back in Sydney that the Surf Boys were actually members of one of

New Zealand's top bands, Ray Columbus and the Invaders. Most of them came to Australia with Ray in 1964 and, as fate would have it, we all ended up touring together and both had No. 1 records.

Tuesday through Sunday nights I sang about five half-hour sets a night and gave two stomp demonstrations to the amazed crowd. The audience generally consisted of about 200 people, usually made up of young surfer girls with bare feet, drunk Maoris with bare feet and drunks off the street who had wandered in, also with bare feet. Here I was in an immaculately pressed, pure white cotton suit and white boots, leaping around the floor of this gigantic old theatre, stomping my little arse off, followed by an assortment of surfing chicks with no time, clapping drunks with no teeth, and drunk, stomping, eighteen-stone Maoris who looked like they wanted to eat someone, shouting 'the pakeha's cool' and 'fucking neat, eh boy'.

I *had* arrived!

The place closed after about a fortnight and I was stranded. Back in Sydney I had been too wound up by the win and too green to have insisted on a return ticket. Like the young mug that I was, I accepted the assurances that it would be supplied by the Auckland promoter upon my arrival. Of course it wasn't! I'd spent a week rehearsing in Auckland prior to the opening, and with two weeks playing this made three weeks in all. I had only been paid one week in advance, so the maths just didn't add up. All this time I was staying at Auckland's leading hotel, the Great Northern. My bill was supposed to be covered. It wasn't!

Here I am, not yet seventeen years old, 2300 miles from home, with a 300-pound hotel bill, no air ticket and fifty quid in my pocket. I have to say the hotel management were great. The manager and his wife were sympathetic to my predicament and took pity on me. I did a little work around the place and had to switch rooms a few times, but they pretty much let me stay free until I could get things sorted out. Of course the Sydney contest organisers had gone bush and the New Zealand promoters were nowhere to be found.

I was fucked! After being stuck in Auckland for six weeks, things were getting desperate.

As luck or fate would have it, I met two Dutch brothers from Sydney who were also staying at the Great Northern. Max Werkendam and his brother Jacky were really great people. They weren't millionaires, but by my standards they were well heeled. On hearing of my plight from the management, they lent me money to pay some bills and to live on.

At first I thought they were a couple of shirtlifters on the make, but I couldn't have been more wrong. They proved to be that real and rare thing—genuine good Samaritans who wanted nothing but the pleasure they got from helping. Business went very well for them in New Zealand. With their Karma, I'm not surprised. So well in fact that Max and Jacky ended up staying on longer than expected and rented an apartment. They offered me a room, which I gladly accepted. Although they were both in their late twenties and I was still a kid, we became great mates. The apartment turned into party central and we turned into the three fuckscateers. No sheep was safe!

I started to really dig Auckland and the people were great. I had been hanging out at a great local club called the Shiralee, getting to know some of the local players. This led to my meeting a girl from the local television station and before I knew it I was singing on a national TV show and starting to get offered gigs. Talk about arse!

As I started to settle into my life in Auckland I learned how much Max and Jacky loved a bet. They'd bet on two flies crawling up a wall. As luck would have it, their gambling fetish eventually gave me an unexpected chance to get the money I needed to square myself and for a plane ticket home.

One Sunday morning about 1 a.m. the three of us were about to have a greasy graze at the White Lady Wagon, which is a late-night pie and hamburger cart. For want of a better description, it was Auckland's version of Sydney's world-famous Harry's Cafe de Wheels. While waiting to place my order I think I said something along the lines of, 'I'm so hungry I could eat six burgers with egg, no problem.'

Well, that's how it all got started. The statement became a challenge, and it soon went from six burgers with egg to a dozen burgers with egg and the lot, no bacon, for a 200 to 10 pound bet my way. And that was Aussie pounds. Max and Jacky were just having fun, thinking there was no way someone my size could eat that much, but twenty to one are good odds by any standard.

Now when I was a little kid, I could eat and I mean EAT! My parents owned food shops in Brisbane and my mother packed a fresh school lunch for me every day. On average it consisted of half a loaf of sliced bread made up into sandwiches. After school there was always a fresh baked apple pie, the size of a dinner plate, with a tin of Nestlés milk on the side, and I mean *every day* after school! Two hours later I would eat dinner! My mother near killed me with love and I was a fat little fuck, but I learned how to eat! I swear it gave me hollow legs.

'A dozen burgers with egg and the lot, no bacon. No wuckin' furries, getcha money out.'

There we were early on a Sunday morning surrounded by the usual pie-cart crowd of clubbies, molls, drunks and taxi drivers. By the time I had effortlessly eaten my way through my seventh burger, Max and Jacky knew they were in deep shit, and the crowd was starting to grow. The White Lady was doing a roaring trade, punters were making bets on the side and bored cabbies were calling the event on their radios. The only ever contender in the New Zealand Hamburger Stakes, I was coming screaming down the home stretch and my little arse was burnin' Jack!

By the end of the ninth burger the crowd was getting loud, people were still making bets, beer bottles were being passed around and it was becoming a serious event. By this stage I had this twenty-something stone Maori who answered to Big Mick massaging my shoulders like I was Cassius Clay and talking to me like he was my second.

'Come on, fella, you gonna make it. Take your time boy, eh? Take your time.' He obviously had money on me, bless him.

Just as I was about to rip into my tenth burger, Max called time out.

'Sshh! Sshh everybody,' he said. 'Ve vant to increase da bet!'

I was all ears. 'Increase the bet to what?' I asked.

'Beelly, Beelly,' he laughed. 'Hotfradummer, you're a farking eating machine. I tell you vaat, how about ve make et double or nossing? I tell you vaat. Double or nossing if you eat a can of peaches ant drink a boddle of milg ven you finish der burgers.'

A hush went round the pie cart. Nobody spoke.

Then Max said, 'One more sing. If you trow up, you're disqualified ant you lose. OK?'

The fucker was trying to psych me out by planting the idea of vomiting in my head.

Double or nothing, I thought. *That's four hundred quid.*

I knew I had the original bet in my pocket and I was starting to get that queasy feeling in my belly, but 400 quid! That could solve a lot of problems.

'Ah, fuck it! You're on!'

A cheer went up and so did the odds. Money was changing hands, the taxi radios were running hot and I was eating like a threshing machine. The vibe was electric. I got through the burgers and was now into the peaches. I still don't know where they came from. Suddenly it was not going to be the shoe-in that I thought. The sweet syrup, meat and eggs were definitely not getting along together. My stomach was rumbling ominously and felt like it was somewhere near the back of my throat. I had an outrageous gas build-up but was terrified to fart in case I shit my pants in front of my adoring fans.

A shit! Now Max didn't say anything about taking a shit. Shitting was definitely legal! *Ah-ha!! A way to some relief . . . buy some time.*

I asked for a time out and pressed my case for a third-quarter dump.

After much haggling over the rules between Big Mick, Max, Jacky and several drunk punters, it was decided that shitting was OK. As long as someone was there to make sure I didn't throw up. It was agreed that Max, as the main better against, and the pie-cart assistant, as the referee, would accompany me to the public toilet and supervise my 'shit out'. So off we went.

It's now about two-thirty in the morning in downtown Auckland and I'm in the last stretch of eating my way back to Australia. The three of us, followed by about a dozen or so onlookers, crossed the damp, deserted streets. We clambered noisily down the stairs into the toilet and I took the most horrendous crap of my lifetime.

I no sooner had my pants down than *Briip, Whoosshh, Kaplooosh!* A cable worthy of an honorary mention in *The Guiness Book of Records* hit the shitter bowl. The sound was bad enough, but the stench was fucking staggering. The assembled group of shitting inspectors seemed to groan in unison.

'Jesus Chariist!' somebody moaned. 'Fuck me,' said another, then 'Payooo!'

It was hilarious and the whole team, including me, started laughing out of control. There was only one problem. The pong was getting to me too and I was starting to gag. If I didn't get out fast, it would be all over. I got myself cleaned up, pulled up my pants and bolted up the stairs, followed by my moaning cheer squad. Back outside again I felt some temporary relief in my stomach and the cool, clean, moist air of the early Auckland morning made me feel better. I was now ready for the final stretch. The dairy. The dreaded bottle of milk.

The excitement in the stands was palpable. 'Give 'im room! Give the pakeha some fuck'n room!' shouted Big Mick.

'Twenty quid says he spews his guts out,' a voice said.

An elegant-looking middle-aged woman in a black satin evening gown stood next to me, her shoes in hand. 'You're on, mate,' she said.

I cracked the top of the bottle of milk and once again a

respectful silence fell over the pie-cart crowd. Slowly I started to drink. At first the cool liquid tasted and felt refreshing. For about the first third of the bottle I was sweet.

No worries here.

It was about the halfway point that I started to lose it. I couldn't get the milk down! Every time I swallowed, it would come back up into my throat along with pieces of meat, bun or peach and I had a mouthful that I'd have to swallow all over again. It was making me gag and I couldn't control it.

Oh shit, shit! I thought, *I'm fucked!*

I was sweating like a turd in a fog and fighting the technicolour yawn. It's a dreadful, helpless feeling and there is none in this world harder to suppress.

'Four hundred. C'mon, four hundred quid,' I heard myself saying. 'Four hundred, four hundred.'

Some of the crowd started to pick it up. 'Four hundred, four hundred, four hundred,' they chanted.

Big Mick was giving me fast and furious expert advice. By his 300-pound frame, of which no more than seventy pounds were muscle, I figured he knew what he was talking about. Anyway, by this stage I was too far gone to argue. His shoulder massage was getting harder and faster and I felt like an old pair of socks he was trying to wring out. However, I was grateful to this big Maori. This great humanitarian. This Angelo Dundee of the pie-cart ring. Glad he was there on my team and for the fact that he had put twenty quid on my arse to win. There was no doubt he was helping me. Slowly, confidently, I raised the bottle of milk for the final assault.

'Just one swallow at a time, boy,' Big Mick coached.

'One more . . . That's it, fella, now rest. That's it, big deep breaths. In, out, in, out.' Massage, massage, massage.

'Now one more, fella, just one more . . . You can do it, boy.' More massage.

'Four hundred, four hundred, four hundred,' went the crowd. Even Max and Jacky had joined in the chant by this time. It was insanity!

Then came the final moment of truth. Big Mick was still coaching me, telling me when to breathe, and I was surrounded by a group of chanting fans, one swallow away from the world championship. Gulp! 'Uuurrpp!' It was down.

And it stayed down!

I was home. I'd done it. A mighty cheer went up, Max and Jacky were both laughing so hard, so caught up in the moment, that I don't think they realised that they'd lost their money. People were clapping and patting each other on the back, toasting each other and collecting from Wal, the pie-cart owner who had held all bets. Big Mick lifted me a foot off the ground in a bear hug and danced me around, kissing and hugging me so hard I could hardly breathe. I thought I was going to lose it all right then and there. He squeezed me so hard I ripped off this enormous fart, that echoed through the early-morning air.

'Jeeezus, mate! Payoooo!' Mick yelled as the pong hit him.

He dropped me like a sack of shit and started fanning the air. 'Payoo, pakeha, you stink bad, boy!' he mumbled and moved to the other side of the ring. I landed on my arse on the pavement, laughing so hard I didn't feel a thing. But he was right. I'd gassed myself too and moved to the other side.

'Don't come over 'ere, boy. You're rotten!' Mick said in disgust, moving away again. 'You've brought the bastard with ya!'

Now I joined in the celebration. Max gave me about 450 New Zealand pounds for a start, which was all he had on him, and I felt great. If I'd won a gold medal at the Olympics it couldn't have felt any better. I was Champion of the Great New Zealand Hamburger Stakes, 400 pounds richer and headed back home to Aussie . . .

All of a sudden I didn't feel right. Something was horribly wrong. I couldn't breathe! I couldn't catch my breath! It felt like somebody was holding something over my mouth, preventing me from breathing. Christ, I'm choking!

Oh no! I thought, *the bet! . . . the fucking bet! . . . The money!* Then, *Fuck the bet, you're choking!*

What's that scent, like perfume? I'm falling. Down, dowwwn. Ooh I'm sick and I'm falling. It's dark in here. Some sort of tunnel. This is weird! . . . I can see shapes! What's that scent? . . . I can't breeeathe. Heeeelp!

What's that? Is it a face? I can see a face ahead! It's smiling, but I'm choking, why is it smiling? Now the face is over me, smiling down at me. It's my mother's face. No it's a girl's face. Pepper's face!

I'm smothering! Somebody's smothering me! Pepper's trying to smother me! The crazy redheaded bitch is trying to kill me! Gotta get her off me! Somebody get her off meeeee!

I reached up with both hands and pushed with all my strength.

Thud! 'Owww! Shit!' a voice cried. 'What the fuck are you doing?'

I realised with a start that I was in bed in my hotel room

back in the Cross and I must have been dreaming. Lifting herself up off the floor next to the bed was Pepper.

'What the fuck are you doing?' I yelled.

'What the fuck are *you* doing?' she whimpered.

Pepper was kneeling next to me, her head in her hands. I could see a tiny trickle of blood running down her forehead.

'You OK?' I asked.

'No I'm not fucking OK, you goose! I hit my head. What the fuck did you do that for?'

'I thought somebody was trying to . . . It was just reflex, mate. I'm sorry . . .'

'I hit my head on the night stand and it hurts!' she blubbered. God she looked beautiful, even when she was upset.

'What the hell are you doing, Pepper? What happened?'

'Well I came in, and and you were fast asleep,' she said. She sounded like a little girl who'd just been spanked for something she didn't do. 'You looked like you were having a real good dream. You were really into it, you know, laughing, moaning and stuff.' She sniffed. 'I didn't want to wake you up and spoil it, so I just fort . . .'

'Just thought what?' I asked.

'Just fort I'd, you know.'

'What?'

'You know, join in,' she giggled. A bubble came out of her nose and popped against her cheek.

Jesus Christ, no wonder I couldn't breathe! Pepper was sitting on my face while I was asleep. *This girl is a fucking maniac!*

Sure enough, when she stood up, there was that unmistakable sweet red bush staring at me again. Pepper was fully dressed from the waist up, but from the waist down she was naked except for her high heels.

Where the hell did I find this one? Whoever named her Pepper was way off. The way she goes off, she should be called Dinah Mite.

'Mate, I thought someone was smothering me,' I said, trying to explain my dream. 'Let me see your head. Come here. Come over here next to me.'

She came and sat on the bed and I put my arm around her. She had a small cut above her left eye, just below the hair line, and it was bleeding a little. I dipped the corner of the sheet in my water glass and gently dabbed the cut until the bleeding stopped. Pepper was still sniffling and she looked so beautiful and vulnerable, both at once. The combination of her half-naked body, the little-girl face and the tears had me as hard as a rock.

Oh no you don't, you low mongrel, my brain said. *She's hurt. Now's not the time! It's taking advantage.*

Look at those legs, that other voice replied. *She's gorgeous. Look at her, go for it!*

Jesus, my dick is thinking for itself again. Like I'm not even in the room! Well shit, I'm only a kid. What do I know? Go for it. Don't go for it. What?

Pepper caught the look and I swear she caught the thought before it finished forming in my head. She whipped her top and bra off and, whoosh, went straight for my old boy. She was relentless.

OK, OK, I thought. *If you insist. After what I did only a senseless, unfeeling cad would resist.*

Pepper's radar was definitely tuned in and the signal was coming straight from my eight-day. You know, eight-day clock. Where are you from, Brisbane?

It wasn't until after things relaxed and I watched her getting dressed that it dawned on me. Pepper was in my room.

'Pepper, how'd you get in here?' I asked.

'Well, you see, I, er, sort of know the guy on the front desk. His name's Joey. Comes in the Pussycat a bit. Always tips me big. He wants to get into my pants but there's no way.'

She was speaking in this little-girl voice again.

'I came over to see you and asked him for a key to your room. Said I wanted to surprise you. He wouldn't cop to it, so I told him you owed me money and I fort I might be able to get some of it . . . you know? Anyway, he hummed and aahed for a bit, but he gave in in the end.' She giggled, her voice sort of singing the last few words.

'It's amazing how far a little flash goes,' she added cheekily, slowly raising her skirt just enough to show the crotch of her white lace panties. God, she was a turn-on.

'I fink he came in his pants right there at the desk.' She laughed. 'His eyes nearly popped out of his head.'

'Pepper, you case . . . you little case. That's going to get you in big trouble one day.'

She stood there seductively, wiggling her bum as she slowly lowered her skirt. All the while her eyes never left mine and she grinned that grin. Pow! That feeling had never happened to me before. The silence between us was deafening. It was undeniable and we both felt it. Pepper was beautiful, totally uninhibited and a true-to-life waif. Even though I was just a kid I knew she was someone special. Pepper was so alive and I simply sat there staring at her, taking her in.

'Come on,' she said, 'when you look at me like that it makes my bum go funny. Anyhow, you're going to be late for your audition at Surf City.'

'That's not till Saturday arvo,' I said.

'It *is* Saturday arvo, you goose. Now get in the shower.' Pepper hustled me out of bed and out the door to the shower like a mother hen.

Saturday! Shit, I couldn't believe it. The Pussycat was two nights ago? I had slept for nearly twenty hours.

On the way out of the hotel we passed the front desk. Joey was still sitting there. He acted like he didn't see us and right away I knew something was wrong. Even a gay blind man would have noticed Pepper's arse wiggle by. He was not looking, but trying too hard! Just as we got to the front door I saw his reflection in the glass and caught the look he was giving us. Who knows what it is or where it comes from, if it's primal instinct or what, but once you've spent any time around heavy people, your survival radar or whatever it is gets fine-tuned and immediately reacts to bad signals. There's a voice that says 'danger'.

Joey was trouble!

4
The Audition

LIFE, it seems, all seventy or eighty years of it if you're lucky, comes down to a handful of moments. Magic times when either the gods are smiling, you get out of bed on the right side, or it's simply your turn. No matter the cause, the effect and ramifications of chance can take on cosmic proportions. As I walked into Surf City there was no way of knowing the events of that day, no matter how bizarre, would set the direction of my life. Wheels would be set in motion that would spin out of control, taking me places I'd never even dreamed of going, tuning the frequency of my life for years to come.

The entrance to Surf City fronted onto Darlinghurst Road, which is the main artery running roughly east to west through Kings Cross, or west to east, depending on how you look at it. The building sat right at the main intersection of the Cross, where Darlinghurst Road, Bayswater Road and Victoria Street meet. It came to a slight point on the corners of Darlinghurst Road and Victoria Street, then fanned out like a pizza slice. Ten huge, brass-trimmed, glass theatre doors and a ticket box took up at least 50 per cent of the 180 feet or so of frontage. As I entered, the first thing I noticed was the smell.

All old theatres have it, like old classic cars. It's the smell of romance, adventure, old leather and velvet. To me it's like an aphrodisiac. If I stand alone in an old theatre for long enough, it always becomes a sensual experience. I am guaranteed to become sexually aroused. It's inevitable, involuntary. I feel connected to the fantasy and romance the place represents. Connected to the mystery, sensuousness and eroticism it seems to contain. It's a feeling outside of time, existing as a space in which I absolutely feel I belong. The old Theatre Royal in Brisbane was the horniest building I've ever been in. I loved to go there to see shows and perform there as a child, but it wasn't the stars, the applause, or the lights. It was the building itself. So majestic and full of ghosts and spirits I expected the Phantom of the Opera to come creeping through at any minute.

'There's John Harrigan over there,' Pepper said.

'Who?' I asked.

'Harrigan. You know, he owns the place or runs it. He's come up to the Pussycat a couple of times. He's OK. Come on, I'll introduce you.'

We walked over to where he was talking to a middle-aged lady.

'G'day, John, how ya goin'?' said Pepper, like she had shares in the joint. 'John, this is Billy Forpe. I don't fink you've met.'

The man standing in front of me was about thirty years old. In his grey business suit, blue shirt and red and black striped tie, he had the feel of a private-school boy. Probably King's or some other snotty academy of refined higher education. All private-school boys seemed to have an air of superiority. I guess it's a defence mechanism, a backlash from all that buggery they have to endure at the hands of some of the horny, twisted masters. It doesn't necessarily come across as arrogance, it's more a patina, a gloss. It's there in the shirts and the ties they wear, and in the grey suits and black oxfords.

As if on a continuation of their school days, most of them seem to go through life still dressed in uniform, rising through a succession of forms until reaching the big graduation day in the sky, upper lip still stiff as a board. Someone must give them lessons in how not to dress. Their pants always seem to fit badly and be slack in the crotch. Maybe that's a result of the buggery too, who knows, but it's definitely daggy. John Harrigan was a short stocky man with dark brown curly hair that needed a trim. He had a pleasant smiling face and was quite handsome, with the most piercing blue eyes I've ever seen.

'Hello, Billy, I'm John Harrigan. And this is my mother, Irene.'

'How do you do.' I shook his hand. 'I'm here for the talent show. Who's on today? Is it a good band or what? Can they play?'

'My, you get right to the point, young man,' said Mrs Harrigan.

'Well, I don't mean any disrespect, but I didn't come here for the view.'

They both laughed.

'Well, Billy,' John said, 'seeing you're so keen to *know*, the band plays here quite a bit and I think they're fine. They wouldn't be here otherwise. I'm looking for a new lead singer and you get three songs if you're good. One if your not. The audition starts in fifteen minutes. There are four other people trying out this afternoon *and*,' he said, pausing, 'you'll be going on third. That OK?'

'Fine with me,' I said. 'Is it all right if I go and talk to the band about three of my songs?'

'Yes, no problem, but please excuse me for now.' John Harrigan turned to his mother and they walked away, laughing and shaking their heads.

'They like you,' said Pepper. 'Can I come in and hear you sing? I won't put you off or laugh or anyfing, really. I promise.'

'It'll be bad luck if you don't,' I told her. 'Come on, mate, let's go!'

This Surf City was at least twice the size of the one in Auckland. The only remaining seats from its days as a theatre were in the balcony on the second floor. As I walked through the curtain from the foyer into the theatre itself, I noticed the floor sloped down to the dance floor at the front of the room some 150 feet away. This dance floor was approximately fifty feet deep, running some 150 feet across the width of the theatre. The place was gigantic. With the upstairs balcony full, I guessed it could hold up to 4000 people, maybe more.

The main stage stood in front of the theatre screen which was hidden by two gold-trimmed burgundy drapes that were at least forty feet high. Ornate plaster-cast cherubs and angels decorated the star-encrusted ceiling some seventy feet from the floor, and from its centre, high above the room, hung a large chandelier. Boing! Instant boner! The band stage extended out at a right angle from the main one. It was about twenty-five feet deep, thirty feet across and fifteen above the theatre floor. The back and side walls of the room were painted flat black and covered in luminescent, white, cartoon-like paintings of surfers on boards in varying poses, some fifteen to twenty feet high. Tables and chairs were scattered around the edges of the room, but this place wasn't meant for sitting. It was set up for mondo stomping.

The whole place was lit with fluorescent, purple-black light, the kind that makes the lint on your clothes glow white and bleached hair look green. As weird as the decor was, the room felt electric and exciting. It grabbed me and I knew at once it was a great place for rock 'n' roll. Staring through the half-light, I could see a band in the last stages of setting up.

'I'm going up to meet the band,' I told Pepper. 'Why don't you grab a chair and I'll be right back.'

'OK.' She smiled at me and I headed off.

I was halfway up the steps beside the band stage when I saw a bouncer wearing black pants and a white T-shirt coming down them. He was roughly the size of an ox and he grabbed my arm in a ham-sized hand.

'Where the f-f-f-fuck do you th-th-think you're going, you little f-f-flip?'

'Up on the stage,' I told him. 'I'm auditioning with the band.'

'B-b-b-bull shshit!' he said and hit me with a left rip to the stomach that was so hard my Mum and Dad in Brisbane fell over. Every ounce of air in my body shot out of my mouth and I sailed backwards. I don't even remember hitting the ground . . .

I woke up lying on a musty old green velvet couch, with

Pepper standing over me yet again. This time she had her pants on, thank God, because there were other people there too, including Mrs Harrigan. It was a dressing-room of some sort and, although I didn't know it at the time, I was directly below the main stage in the Surf City dressing-rooms. The wood-panelled room smelled of old shows and show people, with just the right touch of tobacco and sweat thrown in. The walls were fitted with reproduction antique candle-holders, each one holding a bare flickering light-bulb. Above me was a cobweb-laden chandelier with half the bulbs blown out. Any minute I expected to see the Phantom come creeping through the room, grab Pepper and run. On the walls hung movie and show posters from all eras. One banner read, 'The greatest movie of them all. The greatest feat in motion picture history. Cecil B. De Mille's "The Ten Commandments".' Another, 'Chad Morgan, that Sheik from Scrubby Creek. Appearing August 17 for two great nights. Tickets one and six at the box office or two shillings at the door.'

There were many others, but my brain finally slowed down and allowed me to focus on what the fuck I was doing here. The place seemed to be buzzing with people. Seems my knockout had drawn quite a crowd. Somehow Sammy was there too and the first thing I heard was, 'Come on, my friend Sir Gil, it is I, Sir Ponson, and together we can kick this big cunt's arse. He is a mere mortal, not a God like you and I!'

Someone said, 'Easy, Sammy, easy.'

'Ah fuck him, he's a big goose,' Sammy replied. 'Why'd he have to hit him? He's five times his size, the fuckin' big goose. Oh sorry, Mrs Harrigan.'

'What are you doing here, Sam?' I asked.

'Ah just came over to sprinkle some Naktie Malik dust around for good luck, my son.' He smiled.

Over his shoulder I could just make out John Harrigan paying out on the bouncer who had king-hit me.

'I've told you before, Ivan, no hitting. Don't hit! There's no bloody need to hit. He's only a kid!'

You didn't have to be a brain surgeon to work out that Ivan's shoe size was bigger than his IQ. He just stood there like a kid, shuffling his feet, his hands in his pockets and his head down. He kept saying, 'Er, OK, Mr H-H-Harrigan . . . er, I, er, didn't m-m-mean any harm, Mr H-Harrigan.'

Mrs Harrigan came over to the couch where I was lying. She sat on the edge next to Pepper and took my hand in hers. 'You all right, boy?' she asked. 'Are you hurt? Can you hear me?' She was obviously a kind woman and I liked her.

The back of my head hurt like crazy and I could feel an egg-sized bump, but no blood. Apart from that, a giant bellyache, and the clanging submarine 'Dive . . . Dive' signal sounding in my ears, I seemed fine.

'I'm OK, thank you,' I assured her. 'Yes, I think I'll be OK.'

'Oh good, oh that *is* good to hear,' she said. She sounded genuinely relieved. 'You just stay there until I can have someone make sure. Would you like a drink or anything, son?'

'A Coke or something would be fine, thank you.'

'Coming right up,' she said cheerfully. 'One ice-cold Coke coming right up.'

Shit, I should have been dead! Ivan the Ox's punch should have broken every bone in my body, but somehow it hadn't. I'd been hit before but never that hard. My stomach and head were still hurting but I knew I wasn't *hurt*. I felt like I'd been hit by a bus but I was fine. Didn't feel much like auditioning, but I knew I'd be OK in about twenty-four years . . . er, hours! Waking up with Pepper leaning over me seemed to be becoming a habit. Once again she was fussing over me like a nurse, and while she gently dabbed my face with a wet towel she was unconsciously stroking the inside of my left thigh with her free hand.

This girl is a natural born healer, I thought.

I just wanted to get out of there but when Mrs Harrigan returned with the Coke she insisted that the local doctor take a look at me. Given the circumstances, this was probably the right thing to do. He arrived about ten minutes later and was told what had happened. I later found out his name was Dr Jahil, the 'Doctor Feel Good' of the Cross. If you needed it, he had it. His main clientele were the molls.

'Oh very, very bad . . . very bad. Such ruffians, very, very bad,' he said in as thick an Indian accent as I'd ever heard. 'The poor boy. He must be in pain. I will give him something for the pain. Are you in pain, boy? I will give you something for the pain.'

'No, I'm OK,' I tried to say. 'I'm OK, *really*!'

Jesus Christ, now I'm in a fucking Peter Sellers movie, I thought, and before I knew it there's a syringe in my arm. Dr Feel Good had shot me full of morphine. Whoa boy!

Now I definitely was not feeling any pain. In fact I wasn't feeling anything much at all. I know I didn't feel much like singing right then. In fact I felt more like playing three or four games of football . . . *as the ball*. Boing! Boing! Pepper insisted she take me back to her place until she went to work and I had the distinct feeling that she was going to revive me by sitting on my face again, but the way

I felt right then she would have killed me. Fortunately Mrs Harrigan insisted I go to my hotel and that Sammy go with me. Ah, the sweet old thing. She probably saved my life, but before I left she wanted Ivan the Ox to apologise to me.

'Now come on, Ivan dear,' she said. 'Say you're sorry to this nice boy.'

By this time the morphine had kicked well in and I couldn't find my arse. But I was compos mentis enough to know what was happening around me me meee—heee. I could also see the humour of big Ivan trying his best to say the one word he'd never learned to say, to someone he couldn't remember hitting in the first place.

'Er, I'm, I mean, I d-d-didn't . . . Wha-wha-what happened?'

'Just say "sorry", Ivan,' said Mrs Harrigan.

'Er, all r-right. Are you, er, you all r-r-right? I, er, d-d-didn't mean, I, er . . .'

With that someone led mumbling Ivan away. Although I was held firmly in the arms of morpheus, I could hear him going 'W-w-what ha-happened? Er, I d-d-didn't mean, Mrs Harrigan . . .'

'It's OK, Ivan, just don't hit, all right? It's not nice to hit,' she chided.

'O-O-OK,' I heard him say as I drifted off.

And that's the last thing I remember of my first big audition at Surf City. The funny thing is that if Ivan the Ox hadn't hit me, I would have auditioned with the band there that day, whoever they were, and not the following weekend with a young bunch of blokes called the Aztecs. In fact we may have never met.

Shit, talk about fate!

5
Recovering from Ivan

AS I floated out of my coma my mind danced to the sounds of 'Big Girls Don't Cry'. I had no idea what time it was. The coloured neon outside the window flashed on and off, bouncing its electric messages off the walls and ceiling of my room, dancing with the shadows in an ever-changing surrealistic painting that told me it was night. For a moment I thought I was alone, then a beautiful redhead leaned over my bed.

'You alive, mate?' asked Pepper. 'God I was worried. You've been out for a whole day. I've been sitting here listening to the radio, waiting for you to wake up.'

With the gargantuan hit of morphine the good doctor had given me it's amazing I ever regained consciousness. And the way I felt at the time, I hadn't really cared if I did or not. This was the third time I'd woken up with Pepper standing over me and I instinctively looked to see if she was wearing any panties. She was. And a bra. Both black lace. The luminous hands on the bedside clock glowed 8.30.

My stomach ached, my head pounded, the submarine dive signal was still ringing in my ears, and my mouth tasted as dry as a two-week-old, double-decker camel-turd sandwich.

'Oh shit,' I groaned. 'Water, pleeease.'

Pepper switched on the bedside lamp and the light hit my brain like a million glass needles. I lay there moaning, eyes covered by the sheets, listening to the soothing sound of water tumbling into a glass.

'Here you go, mate.'

I groped for the water like a blind man, spilling half of it over myself before downing the remainder in one swallow.

'Ooh,' I said, rubbing the back of my head as I tried to get the room in focus. 'What day is it?'

'It's Sunday night,' she answered. 'You've been asleep all day, you know. I've been here since last night. I've got to go to work in a little while, but if you need anyfing from the chemist's I'll duck out and get it. I've got about half an hour before I start.'

'Mmmm nuurse, nuuurse,' I whined. 'It hurts. I'm in pain and it hurts bad. Can you take a look?'

'Where?' Pepper asked, concern in her voice.

'Right here,' I laughed, whipping back the sheets.

'Oh I say, Mr Forpe, I *can* see your *problem*.' She smiled. 'Well well, we'll just have to do somefing about that, won't we?'

She was running late when she went off to work at the Pussycat. As she left she said, 'Mr Forpe, you'll probably be needing some additional ferapy later. I'll be making my next rounds at about 2 a.m., so why don't you get some rest, you're going to need it.'

This therapy went on for the next four days. Although I felt 100 per cent better, Nurse Pepper insisted she knew best and came around every day and after work to give me some of her specialised 'ferapy'. I had no desire whatsoever to recover. Friday evening she knocked on the door with her usual tap, tap, ter-tap, bang!

'Who is it?' I called out anyway.

'Oh, Mr Forpe, Mr Forpe, it's Nurse Pepper. I have somefing for you. It's a surprise.'

I opened the door to find Pepper dressed in an ankle-length tan mackintosh and white high heels. She had her hands in her pockets and this cheeky grin on her face.

'What kind of surprise?' I asked suspiciously as she walked in the room.

'This kind!' She whirled around and let the coat fall to the floor, revealing a short, tight, white nurse's uniform. The skirt was so short I could see the top of her white stockings and her suspenders. A stethoscope hung around her neck and pinned on one of her uniform pockets was an identification tag with 'Head Nurse' on it in big red letters. She looked so horny I nearly lost it on the spot.

'Are you feeling any pain, Mr Forpe?' she asked seductively, ''cause if you are, just let me know. I've probably got a remedy here somewhere. Mmmm, let me see, where could it be?' She raised the front of her skirt, revealing that she wasn't wearing any panties.

Oh how I love the colour red, I thought as she stood there, rotating her hips at me like a stripper.

'Ooooooh nurse, I think I feel something fatal coming.'

'Don't worry, Mr Forpe, this cure is guaranteed to revive the dead.' We both broke into hysterical laughter and fell into each other's arms.

'Where the hell did you get that outfit?' I asked, pushing her gently away so I could take another look at her.

'Oh, I told one of the girls at the club that you called me Nurse Pepper and she let me borrow it. Do you like it?' she asked, turning slowly around, giving me a three-sixty view.

'Haaaate it,' I replied, grinning like a Cheshire cat. 'Wait a minute. Did you walk all the way here dressed like that?'

'Of course. Nobody noticed. All they could see was the raincoat, not what I didn't have on underneaf. Now, Mr Forpe,' she said, 'You wanna play doctors or somefing?'

I moaned in mock pain, picked her up and carried her over to the bed.

'Oh no, Mr Forpe, no, no. You wouldn't take advantage of an innocent young nurse, would you? Fink of my uvver patients.' She was using that helpless little girl voice I loved so much.

'Fuck 'em! Let 'em all die!'

The voice on the radio announced in an American accent: 'Yes sireee, you're listening to Sydney's greatest radio, Twoo Sss Mmm. This is the craziest man alive, your favourite jock, Mad Mel, with another gareeeeat song by Roy Orbison.'

Pepper got up off the bed and began teasing me, stripping slowly to the feel of 'Dream Baby'. She undid the buttons on the front of her uniform and as she slowly slipped it off her shoulders, her erect nipples told me I wasn't the only one being turned on by her performance.

'Oh Nurse Pepper, are you cold?'

Taking a boob in each hand, she cheekily rubbed the nipples between her thumb and fingers.

'Oh no, Mr Forpe, this is a permanent condition. I always have it when I'm around you.'

Christ, I'm not going to make eighteen at this rate, I thought. *I'll have to go into training to keep this up.*

What a turn-on Pepper was. She was stunning. I'd never seen anybody this beautiful before, let alone have them letch over me like I was Cary Grant. Even though I'd met her less than two weeks ago, she felt so comfortable to be with. She had such a great uninhibited sense of humour and knew exactly how to push my button.

I grabbed her arm and pulled her onto the bed.

Bang, bang, bang! went the knock on the door. Then a woman's voice said, 'Hello, Billy. Billy, are you in?' Bang! bang! bang! 'There's a phone call for you downstairs, son. It's someone from Surf City.'

Oh shit! I heard my dick say.

'OK, I'll be right down, Mrs Kennedy,' I heard myself reply.

Now I wasn't losing it or anything. You know, imagining my dick was actually talking, but something was definitely happening beyond my control. And I'd realised there was no point in trying to shut it up. Anyhow, whatever he'd been saying had put me in my present situation, so I figured he must know what he was talking about. When he talked, I listened. There didn't seem to be any point arguing. So where was I? Oh yeah. The knock on the door.

Mrs Kennedy sometimes looked after the front desk of the Canberra Oriental. She was a bit weird but seemed like any friendly old thing in her sixties, and had a tendency to talk to all the guests like we were kids, no matter our age. She snooped a bit and was a bit bossy at times, but she was OK.

'Come on then, son,' she said through the door. 'Are you coming?'

'He was just about to,' Pepper yelled, laughing, and pushed me onto the floor.

'Shh,' I said.

'Oh, she's all right,' Pepper said as I climbed up off the floor. 'She saw me come in and we had a good old mag. In fact she told me what a nice young man you are.'

'Shows you what she knows.' I laughed and grabbed the bedcover with both hands, shooting Pepper into the air and off the other side of the bed.

'You bugger!' Pepper yelled as I got to the door, and one of her shoes came sailing through the air. I ducked and it went through the open door, hitting Mrs Kennedy flush in the right eye, which must have been the one she'd had pressed against the key hole.

'Oooh fuck!' she yelled and fell flat on her arse in the hallway. I picked up the shoe and threw it back at Pepper. She was standing by the bed making no attempt to cover herself, frozen in place with both hands over her mouth, her eyes as big as saucers. Her shoe came back at her like a boomerang and she shot down behind the bed with a thud and an 'owwww' as it clipped her.

Mrs Kennedy sat on the floor, rubbing her eye and moaning. 'Oohwaah that hurt! . . . Shit, did that hurt,' she whined. I got the definite impression it hurt. She was in pain, but also embarrassed as hell because she'd been busted perving. I picked her up, helped her to the stairs and asked if she needed a doctor.

'No! No doctors,' she said emphatically. 'Just a bit of blood, that's all. I'll be sweet.'

Her eye had started to puff up and looked like someone had given her a serious serve, but apart from the odd groan she didn't complain or get angry about what had happened.

As we went down the stairs I heard Pepper call out, 'Sorry, Mrs Kennedy,' just like a little kid. God, she was a case.

The phone call was from Mrs Harrigan. She wanted to know if I could pop over to Surf City for a tick. Something about another audition.

'Give me about ten minutes,' I told her.

'I'll be waiting for you,' she said happily.

'Are you sure you're all right?' I asked Mrs Kennedy again.

'Who? Oh yeah, I'll be right. I've got some lint and disinfectant here. I'll fix it meself. You go on.'

I'd really learned to like Mrs Harrigan. After Ivan the mumbling Ox's first-round knockout, she called the hotel every day to see how I was going. It was something she didn't have to do, but she only stopped when I assured her I would either call her, or stick my head into Surf City to let her know I was fine. A couple of times she brought me things like soup and fresh baked bread and sat there like my mother, making sure I ate every last bit.

I told her some of my child performer stories and she talked proudly about her son John and a little about herself. She'd been quite a well-known actress in her day and had even made some films in the '30s. Although her face was lined from a combination of too much sun and the good life, I could tell she must have been a beauty when she was young. As we talked, Irene chain-smoked Rothmans like her life depended on it, and from her deep voice and occasional braaack of a cough, I knew she hadn't just started on the fags yesterday. By the end of the week she insisted I call her Irene and I told her she felt like a second mother to me.

'Then why don't you call me Ma?'

'Are you sure?' I asked her.

'I'd be honoured, son,' she replied, and from that day on Pepper and I called her Mum Harrigan, Mum or just Ma and she loved it.

When I got back to the room Pepper was still lying on the bed, both feet against the wall above the bed head.

'I've got to go over to Surf City for a minute,' I told her.

'Aw mate,' she said. 'I was just getting myself in gear for anuvver treatment. Can't it wait?'

''Fraid not. It sounds important, but it shouldn't take long.'

'Well I've got to leave for work in an hour. If you're not back soon I'm gonna start wivout ya.' She laughed. 'If you get tied up and I'm not here when you get back, just come over to the club,' she added, winking. 'I've got a little surgery in the back and I'll stay open just for you.'

She swung her legs over the bed and purposely took an X-rated shot of me, got up, vamped over and gave me a big kiss as she pushed me out the door.

'See ya soon,' she yelled through the door.

What with sticking my head in to see Ma Harrigan a few times and going over to watch some of the local bands, Surf City started to feel like familiar territory to me. Ivan the Ox was on the front door as I walked up. When he saw me, he came lumbering up to me.

'G-g'day Billy. It's, er, ger-g-good to see you. Is everything, er, OK? I m-m-mean . . .'

'Fit as a fiddle, Ivan,' I said. 'Don't worry about me. Everything is fine, mate.'

Ivan was like something out of a Warner Brothers cartoon. Like that big dumb bear or moose with the big bottom lip I'd seen when I was a kid. He didn't walk, just kind of loped along beside me and I felt good about him for some reason. Although he towered over me he didn't feel at all menacing. Ivan was really just a harmless kid in a giant's body and as long as you didn't piss him off he was just fine. If I gave him a bag of lollies, he'd probably sit right down on the pavement and start separating the reddies from the greenies. We walked through into Surf City, up the old marble staircase and through to Ma Harrigan's office in the back.

'Er, Mrs . . . er, Harrigan,' Ivan said obediently, 'I-I w-waited f-f-f-for him l-like you, er, ta-ta-told me to.'

I realised right then who Ivan reminded me of. It was big Lenny from John Steinbeck's *Of Mice and Men*. I'd read it at school a couple of years before and Ivan didn't just fit the description of Lenny, he *was* big Lenny.

'Er, i-i-is that, er, all right, Mrs Harrigan?' he asked sheepishly. 'I ga-gotta, er, go back and l-look after the, the fa-fa-front door.'

'OK, my boy,' she said, all five foot of her, like a mother to her 300-pound six-year-old. Big Ivan went loping off through the upper lobby with a big 'I done good' grin all over his massive face.

'He's a nice boy,' she said to me as I sat down. 'Just doesn't know his own strength sometimes, that's all. His look usually scares people enough for them not to cause trouble, but sometimes when he's not sure what he's supposed to do, he poleaxes people then works it out later.'

'I'll remember that in future.'

'You know he was real upset that he hurt you,' she told me. 'Wanted to go over to your hotel but I told him you were all right. He's a nice boy really,' she said again.

I bet that's how Genghis Khan's mother thought of her son, I thought. I also felt that Mrs Harrigan saw good in everybody and that's what made her so endearing to people.

'I'm sorry to disturb you on Friday night,' Ma said, 'but John said he saw a clip of you on television the other day. On "Saturday Date". And he said you were really good and there was no need for an audition. There's a young band playing here tomorrow night. We thought you might like to get up and have a sing with them.'

I couldn't believe it. I'd come down from Brisbane about six months before as part of a duo with another singer, Peter James. As well as doing our own solo gigs, Peter and I occasionally got booked on the same shows and would double up and do things like the Isley Brothers' 'Shout'. I was still signed to the Nine Network, performing weekly on a Brisbane show called 'Teenbeat' with a band called the Planets, who often backed international rock acts and people like Col Joye and Johnny O'Keefe. Somebody from Channel 9 saw Peter and me performing together and asked if we'd do it on the show one week. As luck would have it, Jimmy Hannan, the host of the popular Sydney show 'Saturday Date', was a guest that week. He invited us both to come down and perform on his show.

It was during that visit to Sydney that I won the competition that took me on my epic adventure to New Zealand. 'Saturday Date' had been very good for us both and we decided to stay in Sydney for a while and work on our solo careers as well as doing the duo thing. I stayed with Peter and his family in Mascot, near Sydney airport. As a result of the first performance, Peter and I had been offered another booking on 'Saturday Date' and had both been offered solo work around Sydney. It looked like things were starting to happen. Unfortunately because of my saga in Auckland, I didn't get back to Sydney until almost three months later and when I finally did I went straight to

Peter's parents' house, where all my clothes were. His mother met me at the front door and immediately got into me with an atrocious verbal. She accused me of manipulating the circumstances in New Zealand and deliberately extending my stay. She said I'd ruined her son's big chance and had purposely split up the act.

They had known full well I was stuck in New Zealand, but didn't have the money themselves to help me out. I tried again to explain what had happened, but Peter's mother wanted none of it. 'Anyway, Peter doesn't need you,' she said. 'He's the one with all the talent!' She told me to get my stuff and threw me out of the fucking house. Peter James went back to Brisbane all pissed off, and that was the end of both the act and our friendship. It was then and there I decided no more duos. I also decided to go back to Brisbane and tell my folks I was leaving for good to take a shot at the big time in Sydney.

' "Saturday Date",' I said to Mrs Harrigan. 'How fantastic John should see that. No audition, eh? Well, that's great.'

'The band has played here a couple of times on Saturday and Sunday afternoons,' she told me. 'This will be their first time on a Saturday night. They're a bit of a surf band. You know, lots of instrumentals, but the kids seemed to like them. They live in Hornsby on the north shore. Their lead singer's name is Johnny Noble. He's pretty good, but John thought with two good singers it might add something special. So, what do you think?'

'Two singers, eh?' I replied. 'Well I don't really want to get into another duo. The last one turned out to be a bit of a bummer. I really want to do it as a soloist, you know? But if John's willing to give me a shot in front of a Saturday night crowd, then what have I got to lose?'

'That's the spirit, son,' she said. 'What have you got to lose, eh?'

'Nothing, Ma, nothing at all. By the way, do they have a name?'

'They're called the Aztecs.'

The Aztecs? I thought. *Shit, they must be a bloody Mexican mariachi band or something!*

'What sort of music did you say they play?' I asked, a little confused.

'Oh, rock 'n' roll and stomp,' she said. 'They had an album out a while back with instrumentals on one side and some real songs on the other, they're professional and all that. Why don't you wait until tomorrow night and you can see for yourself.'

'OK, tomorrow night then. About what time?'

'They'll start around nine, play one bracket, then the main act comes on. Why don't you come over and meet them at eight-thirty and then you can get up with them in their second show after the main act at around eleven. That sound OK?'

'Fine with me, I'll be here with bells on, Ma,' I replied. 'And thanks for the chance. Please thank John for me, won't you. By the way, who's the main act tomorrow night?'

'Oh, it's the Atlantics.'

'Thanks again,' I said.

'Now you get some sleep, son.' She winked as she said it. 'It's a big day for you tomorrow and you don't want to be tired.'

'OK, I will. See you tomorrow.' I got up, gave her a peck on the cheek and headed home.

The Aztecs, I thought as I walked back to the hotel. *The Aztecs? What a shitty name for a band.*

6
Jackie Marsh

I GUESSED Pepper had already left for work so I decided I'd pop over to the Pussycat and tell her about tomorrow night. Let her know I needed to get a good night's sleep and be fresh. I needed a shower so I thought I'd go back to the hotel, take one, get a feed, then go over and see her. I noticed the police paddy-wagon outside the Canberra Oriental when I walked up, but they were a common sight in the Cross and I didn't give it any thought. It wasn't until I got inside that I noticed the three uniformed coppers. One of them, a big bloke, was talking to Mrs Kennedy at the front desk. She was still moaning and nursing her swollen black eye.

'That's him,' she yelled as I walked across the lobby to the stairs. 'He's the one that bashed me. Just look at me eye. Look at what he did to me.'

I couldn't believe my ears. 'I'm the one who what?' I said in disbelief.

The big copper talking to her turned around and I saw the sergeant's stripes on his dark blue police jacket. He was a big man, somewhere around six foot plus, and although he was pushing sixty he had an extremely fit upper body and barrel chest.

'Wait a minute, you!' the sergeant snarled at me. 'Just hold it right there.'

I stopped dead in my tracks and he came lumbering over to me. 'I want a bloody word with you,' he snarled.

'What's this all about, sergeant?' I asked him politely. 'I didn't . . .'

Whaaack! The back of his right hand smashed across my face and I stumbled backwards over a small table, smashing a lamp as I fell.

'I'll ask the bloody questions here, you young mug. So you like to hit old ladies do you, eh? Get up off the floor, you bludger.'

The slap hadn't hurt that much but the surprise of it knocked the wind out of me and I just lay there, gasping for air.

'Constable Hicks, Constable Myers,' the sergeant barked at the other two coppers, 'get this mug on his feet so I can knock him down again. I'll give you bash old women. GET HIM UP!' he screamed.

The coppers came straight at me and one of them yanked me to my feet by my hair. The other one grabbed my left arm and twisted it up behind my back, putting his right arm across my throat in a choke hold. I'd done nothing wrong and I knew it, but I also knew I was about to get a major hiding. *Ah, fuck it!* I thought.

I reached over my left shoulder and grabbed the front of the copper's collar with my right hand. Dropping down slightly at the knees, I forced myself up sharply, bending forward at the same time, and brought him flying over my head in a perfect shoulder throw. He landed at the sergeant's feet with an 'uurrrghh' as all the air shot out of his lungs. The other young copper was on my right and I caught a movement out of the corner of my eye as his truncheon came at my face. My right hand instinctively went up in a block and I took the force of the blow on my forearm, grabbing his truncheon at the same time with my left hand. I stepped inside him with my arse against his groin, put my right arm under his left armpit, lifted and threw him across the lobby in a hip throw.

He landed on his back at the foot of the stairs.

Back in Brisbane I'd been doing judo and jujitsu since I was ten years old, but I'll get into that later.

During all this Mrs Kennedy was screaming at the top of her lungs. 'Aaaagh! Aaaagh! Aaaagh!'

Both the young coppers were out cold. 'Now you've done it, yer mug,' the sergeant yelled at me. 'You're fuckin' gone!'

The look on his face was insane and he was shaking with rage. The veins on his neck stood out like a weight lifter's. He pulled out his gun, shoving it in my face with the barrel an inch from my nose. For a moment we both stood there without a sound. Me staring down the barrel of his thirty-eight, thinking *Goodbye cruel world*. Him thinking *Jesus I'd like to do this old lady-beating turd!*

Just then another young copper came panting down the stairs, truncheon in hand, and the sergeant snapped at him, 'Where's the moll?'

'She . . . she . . .' the young copper started to explain.

At the same instant Pepper burst through the front door of the hotel, followed by Ivan and a gasping Ma Harrigan.

'That's her!' yelled the constable pointing at Pepper.

'What's going on here, sergeant?' Ma Harrigan snapped. 'Put that silly gun away before somebody gets hurt. Put that gun away, I said!' she ordered.

To my amazement the sergeant obediently lowered his arm and holstered his thirty-eight.

'What's this all about, Sergeant O'Malley?' she asked, her voice now quiet and motherly.

I blurted out, 'Mum, I just walked in after seeing you and this big copper here was about to bash me because that old bitch over there told him I'd given her a hiding!'

'What absolute rubbish!' Ma Harrigan said disgustedly. 'Sergeant, I know this boy well. As a matter of fact he just spent the last twenty minutes with me over at Surf City. Bashing? What rubbish!'

'Mum?' The sergeant mumbled incredulously, taking off his cap to reveal a full head of wavy, snow-white hair. 'Mum?' He scratched his head.

The coppers on the floor started to come back to life and the one who'd come barrelling down the stairs pointed at Pepper. 'That's the moll there, Sergeant,' he yelled. 'That's her in the raincoat. I was bringing her down and she took off out the fire escape.'

'All right, all right, all right. What the fuck's going on here?' said the sergeant.

Ma Harrigan cleared her throat loudly.

'Oh, sorry Mrs Harrigan,' said the sergeant apologetically.

Mrs Harrigan? What the fuck is going on here? Everything seemed to have taken a turn for the better, so I kept my mouth shut.

But then Mrs Kennedy started a neurotic tirade. 'She's been hawking it upstairs all week and this young mug's hooning for her,' she yelled, pointing at each of us. 'I went up and told them to get out and he hit me in the face and ran out. I was bathing my eye when your young constable here walked by and saw me bleeding all over the desk top.'

'Constable James,' the sergeant said, 'can you please tell me what occurred?'

'Well, Sergeant, I was walking by the hotel when I looked in and saw this lady. She seemed to be in some sort of trouble, so I came in to see if she needed any assistance. At first she told me that she'd had an accident or something and didn't need the police involved, but it didn't sound right so I kept up my inquiries until she broke down and told me about these two mugs here. When I asked her why she hadn't called the police, she said she was too scared, because the moll was still upstairs and he was coming back and would bash her again. I called for assistance. You happened to be in the area and here we all are.'

'He said he'd give me a hiding if I called the police,' Mrs Kennedy yelled, 'and I was scared. She's a moll, sergeant. Just have a look at the outfit she's got on if you don't believe me. Go on, take a look.' She pointed her witch's finger at Pepper.

'Ohhh shit,' I moaned.

The sergeant glanced at me, then turned to Pepper. 'Now what's she talking about, eh? C'mon, open up that coat,' he ordered.

Pepper stood there frozen but didn't look frightened, more embarrassed at the thought of what was underneath.

'No!' she said defiantly. 'I won't.'

'I said open that coat! Remove her coat,' he ordered one of the cops. The constable moved towards Pepper and she grabbed the lapels of her raincoat, pulling it tight around her like she was trying to keep out the cold.

'Come on, child,' Ma Harrigan said calmly. 'Do what Sergeant O'Malley asked, there's a good girl, come on.'

The woman seemed to have a golden tongue, because no sooner had she spoken than Pepper relaxed and threw the coat open.

'Jesus!' said the sergeant.

'Wow!' said the young copper.

'Oh my,' said Ma Harrigan.

Rrruuuufff! said my dick.

Pepper stood there holding her coat wide open. All she was wearing was her garter belt, white stockings and high heels. She stood there staring the sergeant down with a 'well are you having a good enough perve you dirty old bastard' look on her face . . . and he was.

'Cover yourself up, Pepper,' Ma Harrigan ordered. 'Cover yourself this minute.'

'You know this girl too?' asked the sergeant. 'Christ, what's going on here?'

'No need to blaspheme,' she scolded the sergeant.

'Oh sorry, Irene,' he replied timidly.

Irene? I thought. *Shit, this is getting better by the minute.*

'You know her too, Irene?' O'Malley repeated.

'Of course I do. This is Billy Thorpe, he works for me, and this is his fiancée, Pepper. They're good friends of mine and I know they're not doing what that old gaol bat is accusing them of.'

Fiancée! Pepper and I shot each other a look of disbelief. *You lying old sweetheart,* I thought . . . but 'gaol bat'?

'They're all in on it,' spat Mrs Kennedy. 'I tell ya she's a fuckin' moll. 'E's 'er fuckin' hoon, and . . . and . . . and 'e fuckin' bashed me in me eye! He bashed me, I fuckin' tell ya.' Nice old Mrs Kennedy had somehow just acquired the mouth of a street slut!

'What are you saying, Irene? What do you mean gaol bat? Do you know her too?' asked the sergeant, ignoring Mrs Kennedy, who was getting deeper in the shit by the minute.

'Take a good look, Brian,' she said.

Brian? Christ, I don't believe this!

'I think you know her as Jackie Marsh,' Ma Harrigan said to the bewildered sergeant. 'Forget about the blue hair and glasses. Picture her platinum blonde, lots of lipstick and make-up. She's got a record as long as your arm! Just call the station. When I came here the other day I knew I'd seen her before and she acted funny when I mentioned it. The name just came back to me this instant.'

Bless you, you old darling, I thought.

The sergeant took a long look at Mrs Kennedy.

'Oh Christ . . . er, sorry Irene, it is too. It's been bloody years. Jackie bloody Marsh. I've got a dozen warrants on you, old dear. What's with this get up, eh? You used to be such a good sort. Up to your old tricks again, are you, Jackie?' The sergeant turned to the constable who was fully conscious. 'Why don't you escort Miss Marsh out to the wagon while we get this matter sorted out.'

By this time the other two coppers were up and dusting themselves off, looking at me like, 'we can't wait to get you by yourself in a cell, you prick!'

Mrs Kennedy, or Marsh or whatever her name was, started verballing the sergeant again. 'All right, all right, but I tell you these two 'ave been working the joint all week and 'e fuckin' bashed me.'

'Sure, sure, take her outside,' the sergeant said to the

constable again and the young copper started to walk over to her.

'You're not gunna stitch me up with another fuckin' lag, yer fuckin' copper mug,' she snarled.

And with that kind, sweet, caring, motherly, old Mrs Kennedy, aka Jackie Marsh, took off out of the hotel door like Percy Cerutty in the last thirty yards of the Stawell Gift.

'Get her and put her in the wagon!' yelled the sergeant and all three young coppers took off after her like whippets after a rabbit.

'Now then, young fella,' the sergeant said sternly. 'Regardless of what did or didn't happen, you've just assaulted two of my officers and that's a serious offence. I'm afraid I have to charge you with assault on two police officers and place you in custody.'

He pulled out his cuffs and clipped them on my wrists.

Oh Jesus, I thought. *Two weeks in Sydney and straight in the nick. My parents* will *be proud!*

'Aw come on, sergeant,' I said, 'gimme a break. I was just about to get a hiding and nicked for something I didn't do. You know as well as I do it was self-defence.'

'I know no such thing,' O'Malley said authoritatively. 'And what about your moll's, er, humph, fiancée's outfit. What do you take me for, son, a mug or something? Is that how she gets around all the time, or what?'

'No sergeant, it isn't. We were just having a bit of fun, that's all,' I told him. 'Give us a break.'

'Come on, Brian, we were all young once, weren't we?' Ma chipped in. 'Give the kids a break, I'll vouch for them. I tell you what, are you still looking for a band for the police ball next month?'

'Yes Irene, I am. But what's that got to do with anything?' he asked, totally lost as to where she was going.

'Well, Billy is the singer in one of my bands,' Mrs Harrigan said, 'and I'm sure he'd be happy to do a free performance for the boys in blue, wouldn't you Billy?' She flashed me a 'for God's sake say yes' look.

'What, oh, er yes . . . I'd be happy to,' I replied. *Jesus, you should be Prime Minister,* I thought. *What a hustler!*

'Weeel,' the sergeant said, nervously scratching his temple, 'it's highly irregular. Do you have any priors, son?'

'Priors? Oh, you mean arrests,' I said nervously. 'Well yes, just one in Brisbane. I brown-eyed a bunch of schoolgirls from the bus and got fined. Does that count?'

'No, son,' he chuckled, 'not in my district. You sure that's all?'

'Yes sergeant, honest.'

'Well then, if Mrs Harrigan says she'll vouch for you that's good enough for me, but I don't want to ever have to come round here again, you understand?' he said gravely. ''Cause if I do you're straight inside, do you understand? And that goes for you too, young lady,' he said to Pepper. 'I don't ever want to see you on the street dressed like that again.'

'I wasn't dressed like this on the street! It was only in Billy's . . .' she started to argue.

I caught her attention mid-sentence and gestured to the handcuffs with my eyes. Pepper picked it up immediately.

'Oh, er yes. Of course, sergeant,' she said, smiling timidly. 'I understand. I promise I'll be good.'

Pepper's smile melted the big copper's heart.

'Oh, all right then,' he said, and click! Off came the cuffs. 'You're responsible for these two, Irene. I'm taking your word no more trouble, OK?'

'Now Brian,' Ma Harrigan said, sweet as syrup. 'They didn't really do anything you and I didn't do when we were young, did they?'

The sergeant went scarlet and tried to reply but all that came out was 'ahem, humph, well, mmm . . . er.' Just then the other three coppers came panting back into the lobby. Mrs Kennedy was nowhere in sight.

'Where's Jackie Marsh?' O'Malley shouted at them in disbelief.

'Um, she kind of, er, got away, Sarge,' mumbled Constable James.

'She *what*?' fumed the sergeant. 'Do you mean to stand there and tell me that three of Sydney's young finest were just outdistanced by a sixty-year-old con woman. Oh Mother of God give me strength.' He took off his cap and crossed himself. 'Come on, we'll have a quick look round. She can't have gone far.'

'What about them?' one of the other coppers said, pointing at Pepper and me.

'Oh they're free to go, constable, just a misunderstanding, that's all,' the sergeant calmly replied.

'Misunderstanding my arse!' the copper replied. 'He bloody near broke my neck.'

'Mine too,' his partner echoed.

'Watch your mouth son, there's ladies present,' O'Malley said to them, nodding and smiling at Ma Harrigan and Pepper.

The three young coppers just stood there with their eyes wide, not believing their ears.

'See you at Saint Pat's on Sunday, Irene?' O'Malley said.

'Yes, Brian. Love to Ginny and the kids,' she smiled back, and off out the door went Senior Sergeant Brian

O'Malley and his posse to hunt down big bad Jackie Marsh.

'Er, is ev-ev-erything OK now, er Ma—Mrs Harrigan,' stuttered Ivan. I had totally forgotten that he had come in with her.

'Yes, dear,' she said. 'Why don't you go back to work. I'll be along in a little while.'

'O-O-OK,' he said, ducking his head as he squeezed through the front door.

'Now you two,' said Mrs Harrigan. 'No more tomfoolery tonight! Billy's got a really big night tomorrow so why don't you two come over and have something to eat, then call it a night. He needs to be nice and fresh. Don't you?' She winked at me. 'And don't worry about that policemen's ball. I'll think of something.'

'Well I was wondering about that,' I said, giving her a peck on the cheek 'seeing as I don't have a band or anything. Thanks, Ma.'

Pepper went upstairs and got dressed and I sat quietly in the lobby with Mrs Harrigan, not saying a word until Pepper came down. As the three of us crossed Victoria Street I said, 'Ma, I don't know how we'll ever be able to thank you for this.'

'Oh shoosh,' she replied. 'I've known Brian O'Malley for donkeys' years. He's a really nice man. It really wasn't anything at all, son.'

Nothing at all, shit, nothing at all, I thought. From a hiding by the police, to a hooning charge, to a thirty-eight in the face, to a free concert for the coppers' ball. *Nothing at all, eh?*

'Ma Harrigan, you're a bloody genius and I love you.'

7
A Rude Awakening

MY career seemed to be following a distinct pattern of late. First I go to Surf City, then I get smacked in the mouth. My first visit had resulted in near death at the hands of Ivan the Ox. The latest with a backhander from a police sergeant, a fight with two coppers, a thirty-eight in the face, handcuffing and a near hooning charge. Is someone trying to tell me something here, or am I just lucky, or what?

After the rousting in the Canberra Oriental, Ma Harrigan, Pepper and I walked up to the Spaghetti Bar on Darlinghurst Road. Angelo, the owner, was pleased to see us as always and when he heard the story he joined us for a cup of coffee on the house. Ma Harrigan had some things to take care of so she excused herself, reminding me yet again to get some rest. Pepper and I quietly ate a bolognese together, hardly speaking, still a little in shock from the events of the last hour and a half. I told Pepper I was going to have an early one and asked her what she wanted to do.

'May as well go to work, mate,' she said. 'No point losing money over that bitch. I'm a bit late, but. Will you walk over wiv me and talk to Wayne?'

I walked Pepper to the Pussycat and we told Wayne about our little run-in with Jackie Marsh. He laughed so hard he could hardly stand up. When he got it together he offered Pepper the night off but she wanted to work. Mrs Kennedy, aka Jackie Marsh, was nowhere in sight and as I wandered back to the hotel I had the feeling she was long gone.

The dimly lit hotel lobby was quiet and deserted. As I entered the phone at the front desk rang loudly, scaring the shit out of me. Knowing that the night manager was last seen doing the hundred yard dash up Victoria Street, I thought I'd do the right thing and answer it. For all I knew it could have been for me. The phone system at the Canberra Oriental was very simple. No switchboard, patch cords or tie lines, it consisted of the one phone. I picked up the receiver, asked who it was and it went dead.

As I walked out from behind the front desk, my foot caught on something sticking out of the cupboard underneath. I half pulled whatever it was out onto the floor and it was quite heavy. On closer inspection I realised it was real bloody heavy! It was a large carry-all. The top of the bag was half-open and there inside, as pretty as you please, were a sawn-off 12-gauge shotgun, a couple of pistols of some sort, shotgun shells and several boxes of ammunition.

'Jesus Christ!' I said out loud as I heaved up the bag and walked up the stairs to my room.

Once inside I took a better look and found I'd missed a couple of switchblades and a knuckle-duster. What the hell was Jackie Marsh doing with this small arsenal under the counter of the hotel? More to the point, what was she *planning* to do with it? I knew I didn't want the bloody things, but after my earlier adventure with the coppers I didn't feel that inclined to go waltzing up to the Darlingston nick with a bag full of guns and hand them over at the lost and found like some concerned citizen.

'Oh by the way, sergeant, I just found these.' Yeah, right. Too many bloody questions to answer. It didn't take Einstein to work out they belonged to Jackie Marsh and I figured me and the whole world would be a little safer if she didn't have them!

They'll be safe enough in my room for the night, I thought. Tomorrow I'd work out the best way to get rid of the bloody things without having to go through the third degree. Even if she had the balls to come back and look for them, Jackie Marsh'd probably think the coppers took them and there'd be no way she'd connect me to her missing ordnance. I was really tired, so I stuck the bag in the corner behind the dresser, took a shower and started racking zeds.

I was in that tunnel again! A strange scent filled my senses and I couldn't breathe. Someone was choking me. 'Get off me, get off!' I screamed through my dream. I woke up gasping for breath. A huge hand was clamped tightly over my mouth, its fingers pinching my nose closed so I couldn't get any air!

'Where's me fuckin' swag, ya bludger?' a voice said.

My brain shot awake as it recognised Jackie Marsh's voice. I couldn't make out the thug behind the bed with the death grip on my face. I just knew he had wrenched me from a tranquillisingly deep sleep and now had me in some terrifyingly deep shit! The neon sign outside my window pulsed its electric message to the walls of my room and in its eerie glow I saw that Mrs Kennedy had metamorphosed from a sweet, caring old auntie into something out of a cheap Hollywood flick. Gone was the blue-rinsed hairdo and gentle countenance. In its place, a gutter-mouthed, platinum blonde wearing bright red lipstick and garish make-up. Dear old Mrs Kennedy now looked like an ageing Mamie Van Doren. The stink of her stale liquor breath and cheap perfume filled the room.

'I said where's me stuff, ya little prick?'

'Mmnnn, imm glerrr buuuug . . . mmm glerrr buuug,' I tried to say, gasping for air.

'What?' she snapped.

'Candbreef! cand fggn breeeeefe!' I screamed through the hand.

'Let 'im go,' she ordered and the thug took his clammy, tobacco-reeking hands off my face.

I took a huge gasp of air and the sweet taste of life filled my bursting lungs.

'Aahh shit! What the fuck are you trying to . . .'

Slap! Right in the mouth.

'What are you doing here?' I said. 'I don't want any trouble with you. I'm just a fucking singer.'

'Shut ya mug mouth or I'll do ya,' spat Jackie. 'Where's me fuckin' goods? I know you got 'em.'

'They're behind the dresser. Still in the bag,' I said, shitting myself. 'Take the fucking things, I don't want them.'

I could see Jackie Marsh clearly now and she looked grotesque in her pathetic attempt to relive some former era of her long-forgotten beauty. Her heavily made-up eyes and false lashes adding a demented quality to her pathetic idea of glamour.

This bitch is mad, I thought. *I've got to keep cool or I'm gonna wind up dead before I'm a legend, and there's no future in that.*

'You find 'em?' she asked the thug as he stumbled around in the dark, looking for the all-important bag.

'Behind the dresser,' I repeated. 'It's right by the fucking door.'

Slap! 'Watch yer mug mouth,' Jackie snarled. 'For Christ sakes, 'aven't you found it yet?' she asked her bumble-footed accomplice.

'Yeah . . . I've got 'em,' the thug replied.

'Check and see it's all there, will ya?'

''Ang on, let's see . . . Yeah, sweet Jack. It's all 'ere.'

I lay there, motionless except for the thumping in my chest. Jackie Marsh leant over me, her leering face just a few inches from mine, her breath stinking of cheap liquor. I wanted to turn away but my instincts told me that she would take it as an insult and I didn't want to piss her off any more than I already had.

'Fuckin' good for you, me young William,' she said, her spittle splashing my face. 'Otherwise you'd be singing through the back of yer fuckin' neck from now on.'

I had no doubt she meant it.

'I didn't mean to interrupt yer little fuck fest last night,' she said. 'I shit when that copper come in. I 'ad me swag under the counter and I wanted to get 'im the fuck outta here quick. I never thought the young mug'd bring the fuckin' cavalry in.' She laughed. 'I thought 'e'd just go up an' bust yer young moll and split. If that old bitch 'adn't picked me, I'd've been sweet too. You've been enjoying yerself fer the last few days, 'aven't ya? Ya dirty little mug.' She leered. 'With all the screwin' you and yer moll've been doin' lately ya must be quite a little stud, eh? Come on, give us a feel.' She grabbed my goods through the sheets.

'Jeez she looked good in that get-up, eh? I'd like to do her meself. I bet I could make her scream.' She laughed. 'Maybe youse both should try it with a real woman fer a change, son,' she said, rubbing me. 'My, yer do 'ave a nice little package don't yer? Come on give yer Auntie Jackie a big goodnight kiss, darl.' Then she kissed me, forcing her tongue into my mouth.

You sick bitch! I thought, nearly gagging from the kiss and the stink of booze and perfume.

'Now, one fuckin' inch of grass 'bout this an' I'll do ya and yer fuckin' moll girlfriend. Unerstand?'

'OK! Sure! I won't say . . .'

Whaaack!

When I came to it was 5 a.m. by the bedside clock. So many bells were ringing inside my head I thought it must be Christmas. First Ivan, then O'Malley, and now a Jackie Marsh egg on my head the size of a bull's ball. *How the hell did I get into this Mickey Spillane movie? This shit can't be happening to me.* The lump on top of my head told me it was happening all right.

The first thing I did was pack a bag, then slipped down the back stairs of the hotel and out into the early morning light of Kings Cross. At five-thirty, Victoria Street was deserted and quiet. Apart from a lone moggie picking at a garbage can and a crisp, whistling breeze blowing up from the docks, I seemed to be a lone soul in the daybreak netherworld of a red-light district. As I stepped onto the street a mobile street-sweeper came out of nowhere, nearly taking my legs off at the knees, spraying my feet with water as it drove ominously past.

'Move ya fuckin feet, ya mug!' came the haunted, face-less voice from inside the cab.

Struggling with a suitcase, it took me a few minutes to cover the distance down Bayswater Road to the Golden Pagoda. I took the elevator to the fifth floor, then spent two or three more minutes knocking on Pepper's door, cursing the fates, before her sleepy voice asked innocently 'Who is it, please? . . . Who's there?'

Like Alf the axe murderer is going to answer, 'It is I, Alf the axe murderer. Let me in, dear'!

'It's me, Pepper. For Christ's sake let me in.'

Pepper opened the door rubbing the sleep from her eyes. 'What's the matter? Shit, you look awful. Are you OK?'

'Well, I'm still alive,' I said as I fell into the room, 'and that's a start.'

I dropped my bag on the floor, went straight into the bedroom and lay down. Then I told Pepper about my late-night soirée.

'Shit, mate,' she said. 'What's going on?'

I shook my head. 'You tell me.'

'Are you going to the cops or what?'

'Mate, I don't know. What do you think?'

'Well, Ma Harrigan seemed to know that sergeant really well,' she said calmly. 'Maybe we should give her a call later and ask her what to do.' That was another great thing about Pepper. Nothing ever seemed to faze her.

'Good idea, mate,' I told her. 'Now let's get some sleep and deal with it when we wake up.'

'Let me see your head first.'

'No, I'm fine,' I lied.

'I said show me your . . . Oh shit! There's a huge lump here. I better get somefing and baive it before it gets infected. Why don't you get into bed and I'll be right back.'

It was noon when I woke up for the third time that day. This time the smell of coffee and bacon drifted invitingly down the passage from the kitchen, penetrating my daze. For a long minute I forgot what had happened the night before. Then it all came screaming back. After a restful sleep, the reality of those bizarre events was even more scary. This was no longer the continuing adventures of Nurse Pepper and her patient. This was the goods and we had to be careful or we could both end up in deep shit, or even worse in deep water in Sydney Harbour. Pepper came into the bedroom.

'Oh you're awake, mate,' she said. 'How's your head? You went out cold and I washed it with some warm salt water. It doesn't seem to be cut or anyfing, only bruised. How's it feel?'

I felt the top of my head and the bump seemed to have gone right down. It still hurt to touch, but I could tell it wasn't that serious. 'It's OK now. Whatever you did, Nurse Pepper, you've cured me again.'

'Enough of the Nurse Pepper crap,' she said. 'That's what got us into this shit in the first place. Let's eat, then call Mrs Harrigan.'

We sat in silence, looking at one another as we ate, then took a shower together and let our bodies do the talking. The sex eased all the tension and for a while I put the whole thing away, but we still had to deal with the real world. I got dressed and called Ma Harrigan. As soon as I told her what had happened she took down the address and said she would call Sergeant O'Malley. It took about ten minutes for the Jacks to arrive, inconspicuously announcing themselves with a thump! thump! thump! on Pepper's door. I opened it and there was O'Malley looking distinguished in a sharp black suit, white shirt, spit-polished shoes and a red and black silk tie. He had two uniformed constables with him, but when I asked him in he told them to stay outside.

The first thing Sergeant O'Malley did was ask how I was feeling. When I said I was fine, the second was, 'Why the bloody hell didn't you call me when you found the guns, you bloody young mug? She wouldn't still have the bloody things if you had.'

'Well, sergeant, when you left last night I wasn't exactly one of the most popular people in your life. I was so tired I thought I'd sleep on it and sort it out this morning. I'm a singer, sarge. I've knocked about a little, but guns are way out of my line, they scare the shit out of me. I wasn't going to keep the bloody things, honest.'

'Don't worry, son,' he replied. 'I believe you, but I'd like to try and get to the bottom of this. If Jackie Marsh is back and carrying, then I want to know what she's up to. Pepper, love,' he said, as sweet as you like. 'Could I please have a cup of coffee or something while I talk to young Bill here? How old are you, son?'

'I'll be eighteen next March, if I live that long.' I was only half-joking. 'Is she very dangerous?'

'Dangerous! Well, she shot her old boyfriend in the balls just for talking to another moll on the street. Jackie Marsh has seen as much time as the Sydney Town Hall clock, son. She's as dangerous as a black snake and shiftier than a shit-house rat. I want her off the bloody streets before somebody else gets hurt. Now enough of *your* questions, tell me exactly what happened, from the beginning.'

I went through every detail of what I could remember,

including the bit where she grabbed my package and kissed me. 'She's a sick, dirty old moll all right,' O'Malley said. Pepper brought us both some coffee and toast and for the next half-hour he checked and double-checked my story. 'Now look, son,' he said, 'have you checked out of the hotel yet or what?'

'Well I packed some of my stuff and brought it here,' I replied, 'but I've still got some things over there, and I haven't paid my bill. Why?'

'Well I don't think you're in any real danger. If she wanted to she could have done you last night, but I don't think even she's that stupid. She probably thinks her little performance scared you too much to grass. Listen, just stay here a couple of nights before you go back to the hotel. I'll give you my direct line and home number. Call me any time, day or night, OK? Don't speak to anyone about this but me, you understand. Nobody but me.'

'OK,' I said, 'I'll be all right, don't worry. I may look like a kid, but I can take care of myself a bit, you know, but only Superman can catch bullets in his fucking teeth.'

That made him laugh and he shook his head as if to say, 'oh dear me.'

'I know you can handle yourself, I saw you last night. Where'd you learn that stuff?'

'Oh, up in Brisbane. I've been learning since I was a kid, had to. Because I was little I was always getting my arse kicked by bullies and I just had enough, that's all.'

'Good on ya,' he said. 'Bloody good on ya.'

This was not the same man who'd backhanded me over a table the previous night. He was still a copper, but acted with compassion, not power. He was genuinely concerned and I felt it. I also knew right then that Sergeant Brian

O'Malley was someone I could trust, and once again I was indebted to Ma Harrigan.

'Well, son, that will do it for now. Mrs Harrigan tells me you're singing tonight at Surf City. Are you up to it or what?'

'The show must go on and all that shit, sarge.'

'Then I might stick my head in and take a look. Keep your eyes open, eh?' he added. 'I'll be off now. Here's my card. Don't forget to call if you need me, but don't talk to anyone else, all right? No-one else but me.' He slapped me on the shoulder. 'Don't bother to get up. I'll see myself out.'

'Why no one else?' I asked.

'Never mind, son. I've got my reasons. Just do as I ask, eh? See you tonight, young Will.'

'OK, bye sergeant. And thanks.'

'Yeah, thanks a lot Sergeant O'Malley,' I heard Pepper say as she let him out.

'My pleasure, young lady,' he replied politely as he left.

'God, I can't believe that's the same copper that hit you last night, can you?' Pepper asked. 'He's so nice. I really like him.'

I nodded. 'Me too. I'm glad we called him.'

8
Meeting the Aztecs

IT was right on six-thirty when Pepper woke me with a cup of coffee and some sandwiches. I sat up in bed and ate, mulling over the Jackie Marsh incident.

'Jesus, Pepper, was that some weird shit or what last night?'

'Forget about it, mate,' she said. 'Why don't you pick out what you're going to wear tonight and I'll give it an iron?'

'Oh shit, I forgot all about it!' I said and leapt out of bed.

'Mmnn, you should go just like that. You'll definitely get their attention.' She giggled, looking at my naked winkie. 'Maybe I should just tie a ribbon on it or somefing. What colour do you fink, Elvis Presley purple or what? He looks so sad when he's not happy, doesn't he?' she laughed and flicked the end of it with her finger.

'Ow that hurt!' I yelled and she took off with me chasing her.

'If you catch me you'll never get to Surf City,' she called out as she ran. 'Now jump in the shower or you'll be late.'

The shower made me feel new again. I had decided to wear a light grey Thai silk suit that I'd had made by Pineapple Joe on George Street the last time I was in Sydney. Joe is a great tailor, fast and cheap. I had described what I wanted, picked out the material, and he had it finished in two days. Cost me twenty quid and it looked like two hundred and fifty. A lot of Sydney musicians including Johnny O'Keefe had their clothes made by Joe and I'd found out about him from one of the Allen brothers, I think it was Peter, who'd done a 'Saturday Date' TV show with me some months before. I opted for a black shirt, black silk tie and a brand new pair of Edward Mellor triple-D point, black patent leather boots. Pepper gave my things a quick iron and I tried on the outfit to see what she thought.

As I walked out into the living room she wolf-whistled. 'Ooh what a young spunk you are, young William. I better brush up good tonight myself or I'll lose you to the first bird that sees you.'

'I'm not available at the moment,' I said.

'Good.' She smiled. ''Cause I'll flatten the first bitch that tries to race you off.'

I took off my stage gear and put on some jeans—a T-shirt and sneakers, then waited for Pepper to get herself together. When she came out of the bedroom my heart nearly stopped. She had on the shortest black suede skirt I'd ever seen. It must have come to about an inch and a half below her bum, but what there was of it was beautifully tailored. Her top was a tight, plain black T-shirt with the sleeves rolled up and she was wearing a pair of medium-heeled, over the knee boots, also black suede, with no stockings. To finish off her outfit she wore a matching four-inch-wide black suede belt with a big square silver buckle. She looked gorgeous.

'Christ, where's the rest of your skirt?' I asked in all seriousness.

'This is the new rage in Europe, mate,' she replied. 'It's called a mini. I saw it in a magazine Jean-Pierre gave me. Jane Fonda had it on. She wore one like it in a film or something. I saved up and got Jean-Pierre to get a friend of his in France to buy it for me. What about the boots, aren't they great? Jean-Pierre's friend got me these as well. Do you like it?' she asked, slowly turning like a fashion model at a parade.

'Haaate it!' I replied, ogling the beautiful creature standing in front of me. 'Who's Jean-Pierre?'

'You've met him, Bill,' she said. 'You know the Frenchman who works on the door of the Hasty Tasty? He's a real nice bloke. Walks some of the girls home if they finish late. Never comes on or anyfing. He's been a good mate since I started at the Pussycat. I introduced you to him the uvver night, remember?'

I'd met so many new people lately that it was hard to put names to the faces, but I remembered him now. He was extremely gentle and polite for a bouncer.

In her black mini skirt and suede knee-high boots, bare thighs, big green eyes and bright red hair, Pepper was like nothing I'd ever seen.

'You should be a model,' I said, still gawking at her.

'I don't like photographs,' she said, 'but I'll let you take some of me if you like.'

'What kind?' I asked.

'You're the photographer, it's up to you. You'll have to

use your imagination,' she said, smiling. 'Can you see my bum in this? Do you fink it's too much or what?'

'Only if you cough. But I can't wait till Sergeant O'Malley gets a squiz of you in it. He'll probably lock us both up.'

'Well, I've got the original photo in my bag. If he hassles me I'll bloody show him where it came from,' she said, full of piss and fire.

'Have you got any knickers on under there?' I asked.

'Ooh, why? Don't you want me to wear any, you dirty old man?' she said in a teasing voice. 'Maybe I can sit backstage where you can see me and I'll flash you and give you some perspiration . . . er, inspiration, I mean.' She turned around and lifted her skirt just slightly with the tips of her fingers, revealing her black silk undies.

'Will this help you get up to the high notes or what?' she asked, looking over her shoulder as she kicked up her heel.

'Pepper, you're gorgeous, you really are,' I told her.

'Am I?' she asked innocently. 'Do you really fink so?'

'Yes, mate, I do,' I said and stood up and gave her a big hug. Pepper put on one of my black suit jackets and rolled up the sleeves. It came down to just above her knees, giving no hint of what was underneath.

'Why bother wearing that skirt if you're going to cover it with a jacket?'

'Just in case it freaks people out,' she replied. 'Specially Sergeant O'Malley. Anyhow, you know what's underneaf, don't you?' She smiled.

'No idea, mate,' I laughed. 'Come on, we better get going, I've gotta be there in ten minutes. You got everything?'

'Yep, let's go.' She paused. 'But before we leave I want to wish you all the luck in the world. I hope you knock 'em dead tonight. I want to give you a good-luck kiss.' She planted a big one right on my mouth. 'I have to be at work at nine, but Wayne said he'll bring me over to see you sing. I fink Sammy and some of the girls want to come too. Do you know what time you're on?'

'No, I won't find that out until I sort it out with the Aztecs.'

'The Aztecs?' Pepper laughed. 'What are they, a Mexican band or somefing?'

'Fucked if I know.'

We arrived at Surf City at one minute to eight and Big Ivan was standing at the door, waiting.

Groups of teenagers stood around on the footpath outside, waiting to get in, and I could hear 'Surfin' Safari' blaring from inside. Pepper and I made our way through the crowd of young surfies and Eastern Suburbs kids and every male head did a double-take as she passed. The girls couldn't believe their eyes when they saw her boots and some of them went into little huddles, pointing at them admiringly.

'Hello, B-B-Billy and, er, hello, erma-ma-miss,' Big Ivan said as he walked up. 'Can I t-t-take y-your clothes?' he said as he took my suit carrier from my shoulder.

'Thanks, Ivan, I know you've met Pepper before but I'm not sure you've been formally introduced,' I said, gesturing to her. 'Pepper . . . Ivan.'

Big Ivan the Ox went red as a beetroot, bowed his head a little, put out his massive hand and said, 'I, er . . . um, I'm pleased to, um, m-meet you, Miss P-P-Pepper. Er, y-y-you're beautiful.' He gently shook her hand, swallowing it in his.

'Pleased to meet you too, Ivan . . . and so are you.' Ivan went even redder.

'Th-thanks,' he said. 'Er, B-Billy, Mrs Harrigan said I

sh-sh-should take you backstage and, er, if you h-had a l-l-lady with you she c-could go upstairs and wait in h-her office.'

'Great, Ivan, let's go,' I said eagerly. I explained where Ma's office was and told Pepper I'd see her later, after the gig.

'Good luck, mate. See you.' And she took off like a happy kid.

Ivan and I headed through the curtains into the old theatre. To my surprise, the place was already jumping big time even though it was only 8 p.m. There must have been about a thousand kids already inside. The dance floor was full of tanned, stomping, surfie couples and groups of pretty young surfie girls dancing without guys. Altogether there must have been 500 of them leaping frantically around to the screaming music, all looking like they were trying to stamp out the same cigarette with their bare feet. Along the left-hand wall were large groups of Eastern Suburbs girls in their familiar beehive hairdos and outfits, all doing the Wellington in lines about twenty girls long and four deep. The purple-black light gave the place an almost mystical feel, making all the tanned young bodies and sun-bleached blonde hair stand out in the dark like huge bobbing dayglow ghosts. Groups of young guys stood all round the room ogling the single young spunks on the dance floor. Plotting their next move, which one they'd take a crack at for a dance and whatever else the night might offer.

The huge velvet curtains on the main stage were drawn and I figured that must be where the Atlantics would be performing later in the night. On the smaller stage I could see some amps and gear and I figured it must be for my Mariachi band of Aztecs. 'Pappa-Oom-Mow-Mow' came on the sound system and as if by magic all the surfies left the dance floor and started stomping around the sides of the room and all the Eastern Suburbs girls and their partners replaced them in an instant. Some continued the Wellington in large groups while couples did a really cool version of the jive I'd never seen before. The change-over was magic to watch. The surfies and those from the Eastern Suburbs were two distinct groups and when a surf song came on the sound system, the surfies took the dance floor. When one of the Eastern Suburbs favourites came on they got the floor.

I'd never seen it before. It was really cool and for some reason it made me feel good to be a part of this unspoken mutual cooperation. I'd never felt electricity like this at any gig and if ever I'd felt the right vibe, this was it. It gave me goosebumps just being there. As Ivan and I walked down to the edge of the smaller stage, I thought to myself, *If this band is any good, with a bit of luck, people, I'm gonna rip your heads off tonight.*

Ivan shouted at me: 'It's OK to go up on the stage if you want.'

I couldn't believe my ears. When he shouted, Ivan could speak normally.

'You sure?' I asked, ribbing him about the last time he'd launched me from the top.

'Yeah, it's OK, just go up and I'll take your stuff backstage,' he shouted as he loped up the stairs in front of me. 'Go down to the dressing-room whenever you feel like it.'

I climbed the stairs and stood at the top, looking down at the crowd fifteen feet below. At the back of the theatre, about twenty-five feet above the floor, was the balcony. To my surprise, it was already about half full with people sitting in the old movie seats, laughing, talking and watching the dance action on the floor below.

'What a fucking groove!' I said out loud.

'It's not bloody bad is it,' a voice behind me said.

I turned around to see a bloke about my size, with black hair, smiling eyes and a pair of big lips that made me think of the old comedian Joe E. Brown.

'Ow ya goin', mate?' the smiler said. 'I'm Colin Baigent, the Aztecs' drummer. Call me Col. Are you the bloke who's gonna get up with us later? It's Billy, isn't it?' he asked, putting out his hand.

'Yeah Col, that's right, it's Billy . . . Billy Thorpe.' He had a strong firm handshake and an instantly likeable 'ya wanna come and have a beer, mate' personality. His natural good-bloke attitude made me feel very comfortable.

'Come an' 'ave a beer, mate, and meet the rest of the boys. They're downstairs gettin' changed.' I followed him down to the dressing-room.

'I 'ear yer from Brisbane, Bill,' Col said. 'Is that right? I like it up there. Used ta run a rig up and down the coast a bit, always loved the Brissy sheilas, mate. They know how to 'ave a good time, eh?' He laughed. 'What kinda music do ya like to sing? Ya think we might know some of yer songs? Anyway let's meet the boys and we'll sort yer out, c'mon. If we get stuck we can always do a bloody tap dance, eh?' He laughed.

Col had a big, deep, friendly voice and it was hard to pick his age. Early twenties, I guessed, and the more he talked the more I liked him. Col was as friendly as a big old sheepdog. A real Aussie good bloke who'd drink with anybody and call 'em mate and mean it. He walked ahead of me into the dressing-room, announcing me to the rest of the band like an emcee at a bucks' turn.

'Fellas, eh fellas!' he yelled over the talking. 'Let's 'ave a bit of bloody quiet, eh? I've got a young bloke 'ere I want ya to meet. Everybody, this is Billy Thorpe. 'E's down 'ere from Brissy an' 'e's gonna have a sing with us later. Mrs Harrigan reckons 'e's real good so come over 'ere and shake 'is bloody hand, will ya.'

There were four guys in the room in various stages of undress. They all yelled out in unison 'G'day, Billy.'

'G'day,' I replied, nodding hello to the smiling strangers.

One by one they came over and said hello and shook my hand. The first was a red-headed bloke about my height and age.

'Brisbane, eh?' he said. 'Cunt of a place. Worst beer on the bloody planet. Can't drink the bloody stuff, but the sheilas're all right! Ger' day, Billy. Bluey . . . Bluey Watson. I'm the bass player. Pleased to meet ya.' There was no doubt in my mind Bluey was the character in the band. Every band has got one and he was it.

'Great thanks, mate. How are you?'

'Bloody beaudy, mate.'

'Don't take any notice of 'im,' said Col. 'He's just the drongo bloody bass player.'

'Ahh get fucked,' said Bluey.

'You get fucked,' said Col.

'No you get fucked,' said Bluey again. 'Get fucked, get fucked, get fucked' they shouted over one another, bursting into laughter.

'Don't take any notice of them,' a quiet voice said from behind me.

'Billy, this is Vince Maloney,' Col said. 'He's the lead guitarist and 'e's bloody good too.'

'Hello, Billy,' Vince said in that soft gentle voice. 'I'm really pleased to meet you. Would you like a beer or something? Please help yourself.'

'Yeah, 'elp yerself, mate,' said Bluey.

'Pleased to meet you too, Vince,' I said and shook his hand. He had a soft gentle handshake like a woman and for a second I thought he might be a swisher, but I couldn't have been more wrong.

'I've had a couple of rough days and I don't usually drink grog when I'm performing,' I told him. 'I better stick to Coke.'

'Aw shit,' I heard Bluey mumble under his breath.

Vince was a good-looking guy about the same age and size as me, with shining, smiling eyes and auburn brown hair. He had a sort of film star quality about him and was immaculately dressed in tailored black slacks, spit-shined shoes, a creaseless white shirt and black tie. 'If you'd like a Coke they're over there in the esky. Please help yourself.'

''Ere y'are, mate,' said Col, handing me a bottle.

'Thanks, Col, much appreciated.' I took a big swig.

'Billy, have you met Johnny and Valentine yet?' asked Vince. 'This is Johnny Noble our lead singer and this is Valentine Jones our rhythm guitar player.'

'G'day, Billy,' 'G'day, mate,' they said. 'Pleased to meet you.'

'G'day,' I said to them both, 'pleased to meet you too.' *Valentine Jones?* I thought. *Valentine Jones? How does a guy from Hornsby come up with a name like Valentine? Must've seen too many Elvis movies or something.*

Johnny was about my age and nearly six feet tall. Valentine looked closer to thirty and overweight. They both seemed like nice blokes, but out of place against the other three. Particularly Valentine, who looked more like a cabaret emcee than a guitar player in a young rock band.

'Listen, thanks for giving me a chance to get up with you tonight,' I told them. 'I won't make an arse of myself, so don't worry.'

'Mrs Harrigan said you were really good,' said Vince. 'Have you got anything in particular you want to do?'

'Well, do you fellas know the Isley Brothers' "Shout"? And how about "High Heeled Sneakers" or "Great Balls of Fire" or "Jenny Jenny"? How many songs can I do?'

'As many as you want, Mrs Harrigan said,' Vince replied.

'OK then, how about those songs? Any problems there? I'll have a think about a ballad. OK?'

They all answered at once, talking over the top of one another. 'I know "High Heeled Sneakers".' 'I don't know "Shout".' 'I do.' 'I don't.' Yatta yatta yatta.

After about five minutes of going around with this routine it was decided most of them knew 'Shout', 'High Heeled Sneakers' and 'Jenny Jenny'. At least Col, Vince and Bluey did and that was the rhythm section, which was all that mattered to me.

'I'll tell you what,' I said. 'If it goes well and I need some other songs, if Val will lend me his guitar I'll start some on my own and when you get the arrangement you come in, how's that?'

'You play guitar as well?' Val asked.

'I can play a little.'

'Fine with me, Bill,' said Col.

'Fuckin' oath,' Bluey added.

'That will be all right,' said Vince.

'Does that mean I'll have to sit them out?' Val asked.

'I don't know any of them,' Johnny said, 'so I'll just sit the whole thing out. OK, Vince?'

'OK Johnny.'

'But it's our show,' said Valentine. 'What about the band? I don't really want anybody playing my guitar, either.'

Ah fuck, there's one in every band, I thought. *A Prima Fucking Donna!*

'Well, if it's a problem then I'll . . .'

'No problem,' Vince assured me. 'You can use my spare guitar through Val's Twin. That all right, Val? John Harrigan said he wants Billy on stage with us tonight, so that's the way it is. Let's not make it a shit fight for him, eh Val?'

Val nodded his head reluctantly.

'OK, Billy,' said Vince, 'our second set starts around ten forty-five. Why don't you let us do, say, twenty minutes on our own, then we'll introduce you and bring you on. If you write out a list of the songs and keys, we'll do them in whatever order you want. We've got to go on now so we'll see you in the break before the second set.'

'Fair enough,' I said. 'And thanks a lot, fellas. I'll see you in an hour or so.'

I shook all their hands and left them to finish changing for their first set. In the short time I'd been backstage the crowd had almost doubled. As I walked through the crowd I felt perfectly at home, as if I'd been there all my life. Like I said, some old places just have that magic feel, and Surf City was one of them. I made my way upstairs and told Ma Harrigan that everything had gone just fine, told Pepper what was happening, then walked her over to the Pussycat.

The Aztecs were in the middle of some instrumental by the time I got back and their sound instantly reminded me of the Shadows. Every young Australian guitar player in those days was into Hank Marvin and it was rare to find a good band without a Fender Stratocaster-playing guitarist with a Klempt echolette and a Fender Twin or Bassman amp. Vince was using a Strat and Twin and he played and sounded great. He stood at the front of the band in a white spotlight, playing what was obviously one of his featured numbers in the set.

Col had a set of grey Pearl Ludwig drums with a big twenty-six-inch bass drum and laid down the feel like his life depended on it, his smile as big and friendly as the room. Bluey stood stage left, playing a red Fender bass through a cream Fender Bassman amp. He was a good player too, hanging in the groove with Col like they were joined at the hip. Val stood stage right, half in Vince's spotlight, playing a sunburst Gibson 335. He played good solid rhythm over Bluey and Col's feel, but my first impression of him had been right. He was a fine player, but looked totally out of place in front of this band. He seemed to be from another era and the image was all wrong. Johnny was nowhere in sight and I figured he was sitting the instrumental out. All the Aztecs were dressed the same and, although immaculate in their pressed white shirts, black ties, black slacks and shoes, together they reminded me of a bunch of off-duty St John's Ambulance drivers. It was square.

The crowd was dancing its arse off and when the number ended they gave the band a great round of applause. I was knocked out. This band rocked and I couldn't wait to get up with them later and do my stuff. Someone in the crowd yelled out '"Jet Black". Play "Jet Black".' A big grin came over Bluey's face. He looked at Vince, Vince nodded, counted the four and the Aztecs took off into another instrumental. 'Jet Black' had been a hard rocking instrumental hit for the English bass player Jet Harris and the bass shared much of the lead melody work with the guitar. Several times the band stopped and yelled 'Jet Black' into the microphones and the crowd answered in time. Every time the crowd answered with 'Jet Black', Blue yelled 'Get fucked' into his mike and the crowd loved it. I was right, he was the clown. The number got another big response and Johnny Noble walked on stage for the next song. I couldn't believe it, he had the same outfit as the rest of the band. *Jesus, Johnny*, I thought. *When you're the lead singer you got to flaunt it, boy . . . flaunt it!*

Maybe they all had gigs as waiters at a coffee shop or something. Whatever it was, it needed some flash. Valentine counted in the next song and the band went into a dreamy ballad. Johnny took the microphone and started crooning and the crowd on the dance floor scattered, leaving it almost empty. *Wrong!* I thought. *This crowd is here to rock*. Ballads are fine, but the spot you pick for them is crucial, especially for a dance crowd. I'd learnt that watching Johnny O'Keefe, who was a master of stage dynamics and crowd manipulation. He knew instinctively when to drop the crowd down or bring them up for the most effective response. The many times I'd stood backstage and watched him perform he rarely put his ballads in the same place in his set, keeping them for just the right moment for maximum effect. This was definitely the wrong spot in the Aztecs' set for a ballad. Johnny had a good voice, it reminded me a bit of Bobby Vinton . . . you know, 'Blue Velvet'.

Johnny sang really well and the band played great, but from where I stood in the middle of the room, the babble and banter from the crowd was drowning them out. The song ended to polite applause and the band went straight into another up-tempo song. The crowd immediately shot back on the dance floor and the vibe was back. They played for about another half an hour and got a big clapping and whistling response to their last song. Valentine stepped up to the mike and announced, 'We're going to take a break now and it won't be long before the Atlantics hit the stage.' A big cheer went up. 'We want you to stick around after the Atlantics because we'll be back to play another couple of sets. We've also got a special guest joining us later. His name is Billy Thorpe, so stick around, folks.'

'Who the fuck is Billy Thorpe?' I heard some guy next to me ask. 'Dunno,' his girlfriend replied.

'The Locomotion' hit the sound system and the crowd went right back Wellingtoning and stomping. I headed backstage and as I got to the bottom of the stairs I heard the usual between-set rave going on.

'I wish you'd stick that ballad in your arse, Johnny,' said Bluey. 'It's a bloody poofter's song!'

'It's my big number,' Johnny shot back. 'You gotta give it a chance, let the crowds get used to it, you know.'

'Bullshit! It dies every time you do it. If ya wanna do a fuckin' ballad, why not pick something that they're gonna like?'

'I don't tell you what to play, so don't tell me what to sing, OK?'

'Ah, get fucked!'

'That was great, guys,' I said as I walked into the dressing-room. 'You really rock. Great guitar sound, Vince, Val. Great drums and bass too. Everything was great.'

''Cept fer that poofter fuckin' ballad,' mumbled Bluey.

'Naw, the ballad was good. Just the wrong place in the set, that's all,' I commented, wishing I'd kept my mouth shut even as I said it.

'See!' said Johnny.

'Ah, get fucked!' Bluey snarled and the whole thing started again.

'OK, OK,' Vince cut in. 'There's always the next gig, eh? So you liked it, did you?' he asked me.

'Yeah, I thought it was bloody great. The band sounded real good. Can't wait to get up with you later. I've written down the songs, keys and a rough order. Don't think I'll bother with a ballad.'

'Fuckin' oath,' mumbled Bluey.

From upstairs I heard an announcer saying: 'And now, ladies and gentlemen, the band you've been waiting for. C'mon, give a big round of applause for the Atlantics.' I saw some Greek-looking guys in white suits run by the dressing-room door and up the stairs to the stage.

'Ah the surfing wogs,' laughed Bluey. 'You know why wogs make such great surfers?' he asked the room. ''Cause they can't drown. All the fuckin' grease keeps 'em floating. Ha, ha, ha, ha.' He laughed uproariously at his own corny gag.

'Knock it off, Bluey,' Vince told him.

'Yeah, Bluey, give it a rest,' said Col. 'They're bloody great blokes and a great band.'

'Ah, get fucked!'

'You get fucked,' said Col.

'No, you get fucked,' said Bluey.

'Get fucked, get fucked, get fucked.' They both said together and we all cracked up.

'Well, that's lovely language from a bunch of young gentlemen,' said Ma Harrigan as she walked in the door.

'Oh sorry . . . Yeah, sorry Mrs Harrigan . . . Sorry,' they all chorused, going as quiet as embarrassed schoolboys.

'Well, I should expect you are,' she said, looking at me and winking. 'I've just come down to see if everything's all right and that you've got Billy sorted out. John will be in later. He'll probably come and see you after the show, all right?'

'Fine . . . yep . . . OK . . . that's fine . . . beaudy,' they chorused again.

'Break a leg, Billy,' she said to me, smiling as she left.

'OK, Ma, thanks.'

When she'd had enough time to climb the stairs out of earshot, Bluey said, 'Ma? Mrs Harrigan is your mother?'

'No, mate, that's just what she likes me to call her. Either that or Mum.'

'*Get fuuuucked?*' said Bluey.

'No, you get fucked,' said Col. 'No, you get fucked,' said Bluey. 'Get fucked, get fucked, get fucked,' I heard as I climbed the stairs to the stage to take a look at the Atlantics.

I stood in the wings and watched them play their set. They were a good strong instrumental band with a style somewhere between the Surfaris, the Ventures and a Greek folk band. The surfing crowd in particular loved them and when they played their big hit, 'Bombora', the whole joint went berserk. Although they were great, they weren't exactly my cup of tea. Instrumental bands are OK, but unless they're the Shadows, the Ventures or the Sputniks they all start to sound the same after a while and it was like that with the Atlantics.

Dressed in their white suits and boots, they had all the Shadows-type unison steps down and played really well, but it seemed dated and tired to me and so did the music. *It's time for something new,* I thought as I stood there watching them and the crowd. *Surfing music is over.*

9
The First Gig

THE dressing-room was empty when I went back to change into my stage clobber. I'd just finished dressing when I heard the Aztecs coming back down the stairs. 'Ah get fucked,' said Bluey, followed by lots of laughter.

Vince was the first into the room. 'Maaate, that's a great suit.' He walked straight over to me and felt the lapel like an old Jewish tailor admiring the cloth. 'Where'd you get it?' he asked, then whistled. 'It must have cost a fortune.'

'I had it made. You like it or what?'

'Like it,' he said. 'It's mighty! My dad's a tailor, has a shop over in Hornsby. He made all the band's gear. I know a good suit when I see one and this is great, mate, honest.' His reaction was open and real. There was no sign of envy. He really admired it and was gracious with his comments.

Col thought it looked great too. He reckoned it made me look like a young O'Keefe.

'Poofter!' yelled Bluey as he saw me. 'Aw, just kidding, mate. I fancy one like that meself. What's it worth?'

'Mind your own bloody business, Bluey,' said Col.

'Ah get fucked,' he shot back and they started up again. 'No, you get fucked. No you get fucked, get fucked, get fucked.' Bluey and Colin were like two-thirds of the Three Stooges and I was beginning to like them a whole lot.

You've got to have a sense of humour in a band, and be able to take the piss out of one another, it's essential to your sanity. I'd known quite a few bands that didn't. They took the whole deal and themselves very seriously and it's a bloody pain in the arse to be around. Most of the truly great bands I'd seen were made up of lunatics and, along with their music, the lunacy was always a big part of their attraction . . . part of what made them so popular with the fans. That lunacy doesn't just stay in the dressing-room, it comes through in the music, and from what I'd seen of Bluey and Col on stage this was obviously the case with them. The opposite seemed to apply to Valentine and Johnny. Val's big comment on my threads was 'Mmm' and Johnny didn't say that much, just sat there suspecting his job was about to fly out the window.

I caught his look. *Johnny,* I thought, *you've never been more right in your life.*

'That suit eesa sharper than shark shit, my son!' came Sammy's voice from the corridor as he walked into the dressing-room. 'You look a beeyutiful Sir Gil my son, forrr shure. I'm fattening up just a watching your little bum in those tighta trousers.'

The band just sat there with their mouths open, wondering who the hell this madman was. 'That's the nacktie, nacktie with the whole fuckin' whoopie crrash malik and crrraaap handle pal,' he said and cut into one of his outrageous laughing fits that took about five seconds to infect the room. When the laughter died down I introduced Sammy around and they all said g'day as they wiped the tears from their eyes. It wasn't until Vince asked, 'Would you like a drink, Father?' that I realised Sammy had his bloody priest outfit on again.

'Father, my arse,' I said. 'Take that bloody thing off, Sammy. Save the last rites for me in case I die up there.'

'Pig's arse!' laughed Sammy. 'The bloody sheilas love it, my son. I pull nearly every time when I've got it on, honest. When Father Sammuel gets 'em, they think they're having a religious fucking experience.'

More laughter.

'Ah get fucked,' said Bluey.

'After you, my son,' Sammy replied in a heartbeat.

'Eh, father,' said Bluey.

'Yes, my son?' Sammy answered reverently.

'Have you ever seen a Baltic?'

'No, my son, I haven't.'

'Hang on,' said Bluey, turning around and fumbling with something. Suddenly he spun around holding his arms out, palms up, like a great magician at the crucial point of an illusion. 'Ta taaahhh!' he yelled ceremoniously.

When I looked down, I saw Bluey had his dick and balls sticking out through his fly with a watch strapped around them.

'You have now,' he said and the whole room cracked up again.

Sammy laughed so hard he fell on the floor holding his gut, and the harder he laughed the more it got the rest of us going. We just rolled around pissing ourselves. It was total lunacy.

'Well, it's great to see everyone having such a great time,' said John Harrigan as he walked into the room.

Once again a chorus of g'days came from the band.

'And how are you, Billy?' he asked. 'My mother tells me you had quite a week. Is everything OK now?'

'Yes, I'm fine thanks,' I said, tears still in my eyes. 'I've talked through my songs with the boys and everything's fine.'

'Good, good.' He nodded. 'I'm looking forward to seeing how this all works out. I caught most of your last set, boys, and I thought some of it was really good. The crowd enjoyed it too.'

Another chorus of 'Thanks, Mr Harrigan . . . thanks . . . beaudy . . . great.'

'But I'm not sure about that ballad, Johnny,' he added. 'It's just not going over. I mentioned it the last time I saw you play.'

'Fuckin' oath,' Bluey mumbled under his breath.

'Oh, you agree,' John said, looking at him.

'Fuckin' oath! Piece of shit if you ask me. Dies every bloody time, but he keeps wanting to do the bloody thing.'

'Why do you keep doing it then?' John asked.

'Well, it's my big number,' Johnny replied. 'It always goes over great when we play it at the Hornsby Police Boys Club.'

'That's because your girlfriend and all her screaming bloody mates are standing in the front of the stage, swooning,' said Colin.

'It's a cunt of a song if you ask me,' added Bluey, ever the diplomat.

'Er, yes, well,' said John. 'Maybe you should look at replacing it, Johnny. Find something that's better for the set. Why don't you give it some thought, eh?'

Johnny sat there and made no reply. I had been watching this little drama and the band seemed to be in awe of John Harrigan. It hadn't occurred to me until then that this was also their big shot.

Surf City was the biggest regular venue anywhere in Australia and a young, new band like the Aztecs could have a serious change of fortune if they became one of the regular weekend drawcards. John Harrigan obviously liked them and thought they were talented enough to give them a go, but I had the feeling that he thought there was something missing and that we both knew what that was. The other thing I'd noticed watching the conversation was that Valentine had not said a word. He sat quietly in the corner sipping a drink, letting the others do the talking. Vince had listened intently to what John had to say, nodding his head from time to time in agreement. I got the impression that Vince wasn't a particularly vocal or aggressive person, but definitely the most intelligent and best educated of the group. It's funny how you can suss out the pecking order in bands. It becomes real obvious who wears the pants as opposed to who thinks they've got them on. There was no doubt that Vince, Col and Bluey were the serious core of the Aztecs.

The other two were both very talented but their personalities, style and talent clashed with the other three. Sooner or later they were destined to spin off into other things. The Aztecs didn't know it then, but anyone who knew bands would pick it up in a heartbeat. This line-up would have to change in order to succeed. The Aztecs' break-up was inevitable.

When John started talking about songs, Sammy and I politely manoeuvred our way over to a quiet corner, so as not to get drawn into a band hassle where we didn't belong. 'Have you seen Pepper?' I asked. He told me she was out the front with Wayne and some girls from the Pussycat. Evidently, she was much too nervous for me to come backstage.

'She said she'll see you after the show,' Sammy said. 'Are you nervous, my son? That's a bloody big crowd out there, you know.'

'Not unless some arsehole says something to make me nervous, you dick.'

'Oh shit, sorry mate. I didn't mean . . .'

'That's all right, Father,' I laughed.

'OK boys, time to go on,' John announced. 'Let's kill 'em with this one, eh?'

We all went up the stairs together and the band went back on stage to the applause of the crowd. To my surprise, not that many people had left even though the headliner had been on. The place was still pretty packed. The Aztecs played another five or six tunes and most of them went over well, getting the same strong response from the crowd as the first set.

Johnny sang great and a couple of times knocked me out. Once or twice I caught him checking me out to see if I was watching. At the end of their last number Valentine took the microphone, saying 'Thanks, thank you everybody' to the applauding crowd.

'Now,' he said, 'I want you to put your hands together for a young guy who's come all the way from Brisbane to be with us tonight. He's a bit nervous, so why don't you give him some help with a big hand. Come on, let's hear it for Billy Thorpe.'

I stood behind the curtain listening to my introduction

and felt the butterflies in my stomach playing basketball against my ribs. Butterflies are not being nervous, they're the adrenalin build-up, the anticipation of what's about to happen, and I always enjoyed the feeling. It psychs me up. I didn't get nervous any more, that stopped when I was a little kid. Years of performing every conceivable kind of gig from circus sideshows to television had given me steel balls as far as performing in front of people was concerned. I loved it.

As I heard my name I stepped out from behind the curtain, walked to the front of the stage and took the microphone out of the mike stand. The crowd gave me a warm polite applause as I walked on and a voice yelled, 'Sharper than shark shit, son. Kill 'em.'

Good on ya, Sammy, I thought. The crowd had no bloody idea who I was and I knew I only had a few seconds to get their attention before the talking started and it would be a shit fight to get them back once their minds wandered from the stage. I turned to the band and said, 'Let's do "Shout".'

'OK,' Vince said. 'You start it.'

I turned to the crowd and said, 'I'd like to start with a great Isley Brothers' song.'

''Oo the fuck are the Isley Brothers?' some yahoo yelled from the crowd.

'Yeah, get on with it, dick'ead!' another yobbo called out.

'OK,' I said to the crowd. 'I'm going to need a little help with it . . . OK?'

'Get on with it, ya mug!' the yahoo yelled again and some people laughed.

I stepped back, took a deep breath and yelled, 'OK everybody, repeat after me . . .

'Oh . . . oh . . . oh,' I belted into the mike, wanting the crowd to respond.

Nothing! Not a bloody peep!

Two thousand people just stood there, staring at me in silence.

Oh shit, I thought. *Don't panic! Try it again, come on . . . try again.*

'Oh . . . oh . . . oh,' I belted as hard as I could.

Still no response. I looked around at the band and they were all doing the embarrassment shuffle.

'Come on,' I yelled at the crowd. 'This is my one and only shot up here with this band. There are only so many chances in your life and this is definitely one of mine. Do you like the Aztecs or what?'

'Yeah,' went the crowd.

'What? I can't hear you,' I sang out at the top of my lungs.

'Yeah,' yelled the crowd, a little louder the second time.

'Do you like rock 'n' roll?' I screamed.

'Yeah,' went the crowd, even louder.

'See, you *can* sing. Come on, try it again with me. I want you to feel it.'

'I'd like to feel what's in those tight pants,' a lone girl's voice yelled out. It was Pepper.

'If you can find it, it's yours,' I called back and the audience cracked up. The ice was broken!

This is it! It's now or never. No more chances. I took a deep breath and sang the strongest three notes of my life.

'Oh . . . oh . . . oh,' I belted. 'Oh . . . oh . . . oh,' sang the crowd.

'Thank you, God,' I whispered.

'Oh . . . oh . . . oh,' I sang again. 'Oh . . . oh . . . oh,' went the crowd.

'That's it! You sound great,' I yelled. 'Can you feel it now?'

'Yeah!' they replied.

'I said can you feel it?'

'Yeah!' Louder this time.

'Oh . . . oh . . . yeah a—a—a—yeah,' I sang. 'Oh yeah a a a yeah,' they responded loudly.

I let their voices die and silence filled the room. You could hear a pin drop.

You've got 'em! You've fucking got 'em! said the voice in my head, then at the very last second of silence, I belted, 'You know you make me wanna shout!'

The band came screaming in right on cue, playing like demons and singing 'Shout' in exactly the right spots. The place went berserk.

It's amazing what goes through your head on stage, particularly at moments like this. Everything seems to be in slow motion and your brain takes in every look, gesture, nod and wink. I looked around the stage and the whole band was jamming, grinning from ear to ear. Colin gave me a wink and Bluey mouthed 'Get fucked'. Vince smiled as he pumped out the guitar rhythm and Valentine was playing solid and smiling as he pumped along with him.

It was magic! I took the microphone over to Vince and held it for him to sing his 'Shout", then moved around the stage from player to player, giving them all a share of the spotlight as I belted out the lead vocal. When I got back to Col on the drums he looked at me like a big friendly dog and his eyes filled with tears. I'll never forget that look. What was happening on stage was one of those magic moments that all performers strive for and dream about. I'd never felt anything like it. It was as if a giant hand had reached down and connected us to some cosmic generator that was pumping the energy straight into the microphones and amplifiers. That stage was definitely in someone else's hands.

'Hey hey hey hey,' I sang.

'Hey hey hey hey,' sang the crowd and the band, following me.

'Hey hey hey hey' . . . 'Hey hey hey hey,' and on and on and on.

I hoped the song would never end. It may sound corny to someone who has never had the privilege of experiencing it, but you know deep in your heart when the muse has blessed you with her presence and there was no doubt she was standing next to me on that stage. It was pure magic, sublime, and I knew this was something very, very special.

I knew it. The band knew it. And more importantly, two thousand dancing, cheering, singing kids knew it. This was a very different sound. One that nobody, including me, had ever heard before. I'd heard this song sung by O'Keefe dozens of times, I'd played my Isley Brothers single until it melted and I'd had great reactions to it when I'd performed it a number of times with Peter James back in Brisbane. Right here, right now, I knew this was as good as it had ever been done anywhere. It was real. No rehearsal, special arrangements, or fancy moves. Just kick-arse spontaneous energy by the megaton.

The song ended to a tremendous ovation from the crowd and a cheer of 'More! More! More! More!' went up. It was deafening. I stood there looking around the room at all the cheering, smiling faces, trying to take it all in, store it away for the colder times. I looked over at Ma and John Harrigan standing on the side of the stage and they were both applauding and cheering wildly. I looked around the band and they were all beaming, wallowing in their well-deserved share of the applause. The noise from the crowd was still as loud and spontaneous as when we'd finished playing a minute before and it started to grow even louder as all two thousand of them started to chant in unison, 'More! More! More! More!'

'Do another one, mate,' I heard Vince yell from behind me. 'Do another one quick.'

'Where's your spare guitar?' I yelled back.

'Behind my amp,' he said and went back, reached over and handed it to me.

I went straight over to Valentine. 'Sorry mate,' I said as I unplugged his guitar and plugged mine into his amp. I wasn't being an arsehole. There simply wasn't another amp, and right then and there I owned the stage and he knew it.

'Knock 'em dead, mate,' he said, smiling.

As he left the stage I said into his microphone. 'C'monnn, what about a big round of applause for Valentine Jones,' and the crowd cheered. Valentine took a long bow and went off happy, without losing face. I went back to his amp, turned the treble and bass controls to half and the volume to ten, walked over to the microphone and said, 'You sure you want another one?'

'Yeah,' the crowd roared.

'You sure?'

'Yeah,' they roared.

'What about a big round of applause for the Aztecs,' I said.

'Yeah!' the crowd cheered.

I turned to the band and yelled 'E!' then walked back to

the microphone and just stood there. The crowd went silent and once again you could hear a pin drop. I let the silence get loud, then hit with . . .

'You shake my nerves and you rattle my brain . . . too much a love drives a man insane.'

The band came in on the B chord as I sang 'you broke my will,' then hit the A as I sang 'ooh what a thrill.' I raced over to Vince's mike and he sang the harmony with me as we all hit the E chord, and I sang 'Goodness gracious, great balls of fire.'

The band started rocking and we took off like a freight train. The crowd let out an enormous cheer and the whole place started dancing flat-out. I don't remember too much after that, other than doing a spontaneous version of Gene Vincent's 'Be-Bop-A-Lula', then straight into Jerry Lee's 'High School Confidential'. The band's momentum never let up for a second and I had the audience in the palm of my hand for the twenty-five minutes it took to play the songs.

At the end of the last number I took a bow and said, 'Thank you, thank you so much. Won't you please thank the Aztecs. We had no rehearsal for this.' To a thunderous ovation I took the biggest bow of my life, left the stage and went and stood behind the main curtain. I was in tears, not knowing how to accept the response I'd just received. I had hoped to go over well. But this? I'd never expected anything like this in my wildest dreams. Even my ego wasn't that big. John and Ma Harrigan came running backstage and Ma had tears in her eyes.

'Mate, mate,' John said, 'you've bloody killed them. Just listen to that. Nobody has ever got a reaction like this here. You've got to go back on. You've got to do an encore.'

I was in shock, numb. The crowd was at a fever pitch, yelling 'More, more, more, more', and I said to John, 'If I do anything else, I think it'll kill it.'

'Bullshit!' he said. 'Get back on there before they wreck the bloody place. It's your night, son. You can do whatever you like.'

'You think so?' I asked nervously.

'Billy, get out there and finish them off,' yelled Ma Harrigan. 'Go on, son, they're yours.'

I walked out from behind the curtain to a massive cheer from the crowd. *What the fuck am I going to do to top that?* I walked over to the microphone and just stood there. The emotion of the moment was so intense that for one of the few times in my life I was lost for words. Usually you can't shut me up. The cheering continued until I put my hands up in the air to quiet them so I could say something. *Don't say a word*, the voice in my head told me. *Let it die and hit them with 'Shout' again. Do 'Shout' again. Do 'Shout' again!*

Once again I let the crowd fade to silence. Then I waved Valentine back on from the side of the stage and he plugged back in. Bluey, Col and Vince all stage-whispered to me at the same time, 'Do "Shout" again. Do "Shout" again!'

'Oh . . . oh . . . oh,' I sang, fighting back tears, and that was it!

The next seven or eight minutes were a blur. The reaction from the crowd far surpassed anything they'd given us before and the place broke into pandemonium. One young blonde surfie girl dashed up the stairs onto the stage and kissed me, then two . . . three. Within seconds the stage was crammed with hysterical screaming girls. I had a couple hanging off me and so did the other guys. None of us knew what to do so we just kept playing and the crowd went crazy. Ivan jumped up and carried some of them off, but as soon as he got them off the stage, more ran up. Finally it just all fell apart. The drums got knocked over, the amps went down and we all ran off the stage followed by a gang of hysterical screaming teenage girls. As I got to the bottom of the stairs I heard John Harrigan yelling into the microphone.

'Billy Thorpe and the Aztecs, ladies and gentlemen,' he told the still-screaming crowd. 'Billy Thorpe and the Aztecs. They'll be back next Saturday night. Come oonnn! Billy Thorpe and the Aztecs!'

A tremendous roar went up. We all raced into the dressing-room and so did about a dozen of the girls. They were kissing and grabbing us and through the hysteria I saw Vince across the room not trying real hard to fight off a couple of spunkies that were hanging off him.

He saw me looking and we both stared at each other, laughing. Through the squealing he yelled to me, 'Billy! Billy! You want to join the band?'

'Fuckin' oath!' I yelled back and a new band was born.

10
The roll is on

THE most important event of my life had taken place at Surf City that Saturday night, and all involved were still trying to work out exactly what had happened. Time just seemed to fly by, caught up in the unstoppable rolling excitement of something new. Yes, my first ever performance with the Aztecs had been a personal triumph in every respect and the crowd had told us there was no doubt we had the potential to go somewhere. But it was much more than that. The sound of the band that night and the crowd's spontaneous reaction to it were unique in all our experiences. The Aztecs still had their surf-based, Shadows-influenced sound, but playing my kind of material with me as the lead singer, something else had emerged. There had been a definite change in the Aztecs' musical personality. It was fresh, original, exciting and an indefinable new sound had emerged.

After the show John and Ma Harrigan came down with

Ivan and a couple of the other bouncers and cleared the screaming fans out of the dressing-room. We were all completely shellshocked by the experience and chattered away excitedly like bridesmaids. Outside the back door in Victoria Street about a hundred young girls, some with their boyfriends, waited for nearly an hour until we finally came out and signed autographs. Back in Brisbane I'd signed a few from time to time, but for the Aztecs it was a brand new experience and they revelled in it. Even for me this was new. None of the fans in Brisbane had ever been this frantic to get my autograph and the way these new ones reacted was completely foreign to me. When we all appeared at the back door a huge scream hit the night air and the crowd mobbed us. It took half an hour or more to satisfy their frantic demands for signatures. John Harrigan called the newspapers, but nobody gave a shit and the first ever mobbing of one of Australia's first new 'sixties bands went unnoticed and unrecorded, except by those of us who were there.

When we finally got back inside John had organised drinks and food and we celebrated like it was New Year's Eve. I'd made up my mind that, two singers or not, I wanted to join the Aztecs and we decided to meet at Surf City the coming Monday at 11 a.m.

Sunday I did absolutely nothing. I was drained and I spent the day and night with Pepper at the Golden Pagoda. Monday morning I took my bag back to the hotel and at eleven I wandered over to Surf City.

When I walked into the lobby the Aztecs were already there, talking to John Harrigan. As soon as they saw me they all came up, shaking my hand with a chorus of 'G'day mates'. At first I thought everybody was present, then I noticed Johnny Noble was missing. Before I'd said a word, Vince said to me, 'Johnny's left the band.'

Thank you, God, I thought. No offence to John, but two lead singers in this band was one too many and dealing with that situation would have been nothing but an emotional shit fight, guaranteed to generate bad vibes and animosity.

'What happened?' I asked.

'Well,' Col said, 'he called me last night and said he really couldn't commit the kind of time to the band that we'd talked about on the way home. So he quit. No aggro, mate, he's not pissed off at you or anything. In fact he asked me to wish you good luck.'

'So you still want to join the band or what?' Vince asked.

'What do you think,' I laughed. 'Just try and keep me out.' They all rallied around, shaking my hand, and I knew I'd found a group of great new mates.

'All right,' John said, 'we need to talk about this whole thing. I want to manage the group and get a recording contract as soon as the time is right. Does anybody have any problems with that?'

'Not me!' 'Great!' 'Fuckin' oath!' 'Fantastic!' we all agreed excitedly.

'Great,' he said. 'Now, Valentine, I know you expressed some concern about changing the band's name and calling it Billy Thorpe and the Aztecs, but after what happened here the other night there's no doubt in my mind that's the right name.'

One of those oh-oh silences hit the room and the Aztecs looked everywhere except at me.

'Well, I started the band with Col, Bluey and Johnny,'

Valentine replied. 'Then Vince joined. This isn't a new band. We've worked hard for a year to get to this point and I think it's bloody unfair to get a new singer and the same day change the name to make it sound like it's his band.'

'Well, you can always get Johnny back, mate,' I said. They all looked at one another, astonished.

'Well, er . . . that's not what I mean,' he said.

'I know, but that's what I mean,' I shot back, calling his bluff. 'I've been performing professionally since I was ten and I've worked a lot longer to get where I am at this point. Now I don't have a big head or anything, but last Saturday told me that, one way or the other, I've got a shot in Sydney as a singer. I'd love to do this with you blokes, but if I do it in a band, then I want my name in its title.'

'But that's just not fair,' said Valentine. 'You're acting like you're a big bloody star or . . .'

'Hold on,' John cut in. 'I don't think that's what he's doing at all. Let me try and make this very simple. If I'm going to manage this band and make it a regular attraction at Surf City, which I very much want to do, then I want Billy in it. Otherwise I'm not interested, OK?'

'OK,' they all agreed, looking at one another.

'Now if Billy wants his name in the band, which is something I happen to agree with, it's Billy Thorpe and the Aztecs and that's all there is to it.'

There was stone cold silence. I'd never been through this experience before, but something told me they had. The Aztecs or Billy Thorpe and the Aztecs didn't change the sound I'd heard on Saturday, but like my Dad always said, 'You don't ask, you don't get.' I knew full well what had happened the other night. Although it all came off making me look like a hero, I had no doubt in my mind that I was the catalyst, not the cause. My voice and personality had been all the Aztecs had needed to ignite the talent that was already there. They just hadn't had the chance to show it. My style had changed theirs and I knew they knew it. They became ten times the band they had been only two days ago.

'What do you think, Col?' Vince asked. 'What about you, Bluey?'

'I don't give a fuck what it's called,' said Bluey. 'All I know is that we're being offered a bloody great chance. Billy Thorpe and the Aztecs or Billy Thorpe and the fuckin' shitbags, I don't care what it's fuckin' called as long as I'm the bloody bass player.'

'Great, mate,' said Col, ''cause I don't care either as long as I'm the bloody drummer.'

'Well, I'm perfectly happy with it,' said Vince. 'It's still the Aztecs the same as before and I think it's a great name. Welcome to the band, Billy.'

Valentine's face dropped. He knew he was outvoted and there was no point in arguing. It was a done deal.

'OK,' he said. 'Billy Thorpe and the Aztecs it is.'

'Fine,' said John. Everybody shook hands and that was that. 'Now let's talk about the future. Billy, what do you think of the band as it is?'

John's question put me right on the spot but I had nothing to lose. I knew I'd have to say it sooner or later so here we go.

'Well, I only have three comments,' I started. 'One, I think the band plays great. Two, I think that some of the material needs updating and some needs scrapping altogether. And threeee . . . I think you need to change your look. It's too square.'

I think it was the last comment that did it, because Valentine, Vince and Col blew up at the same time.

'What do you mean square?' Vince demanded.

Valentine said, 'Well if you think you're going to get me into one of those rock 'n' roll suits like you had on the other night, you've got another think coming, mate.'

'It's not square,' Col added, 'it's just practical. Plenty of other bands dress like that, so what's wrong with it?'

'Well, that's the whole point. You're not just another band from now on,' John told them. 'From now on you're going to be the best and I happen to agree wholeheartedly with Billy.'

I knew he'd agree with me on this because he'd already asked me the other night and knew what I thought.

'I'd love to wear clothes like Billy's,' Vince said, 'but I honestly can't afford it. Not on what I make.'

'Yes you can, Vince,' I butted in. 'That suit cost me twenty quid, tailor-made at Pineapple Joe's.'

'But I thought you said it cost a . . .'

'No, mate, that's what you said, remember?'

'You bastard!'

'When can I get one?' asked Bluey. 'The fuckin' sheilas loved 'is.'

'Well,' said Col. 'I suppose it's important that we look good.'

'Not me!' Valentine countered, determined to stand his ground on this one. 'I've dressed like this on stage for years and I'm not about to change now.'

'Well, all right,' said John. 'We can talk about clothes later. What about music?'

'John, does anything much happen here during the day?' I asked.

'Only cleaning and maintenance.'

'OK then, I think we should start rehearsing every day, starting tomorrow. If we're going to be good we have to work on new and old material. It's the most important thing we can do at this stage.'

'Oh yeah? And who's going to decide what that material is?' snapped Valentine.

'The audience,' I shot back.

'What do you mean?' Vince asked.

'Well, I think we should all have a say in what we rehearse,' I explained, 'but when we play the songs to the crowds, let their reaction decide what's in and what's out. You get what I mean?'

'Fuckin' oath,' said Bluey.

'John, how many times a week do you want us to play here?' I asked.

'Five nights a week and Saturday and Sunday afternoons,' he replied.

'Fuck me!' 'Shit!' 'Jesus!' 'Wow!' they all reacted.

'But what about our day jobs?' Vince asked.

'I'll get to that in a minute. Let's keep talking about the music,' John told him.

Now I had everybody's attention, including Valentine's. John already knew where I was going in all this because the first thing he'd said to me in the dressing-room after the show was that he wanted us to play seven gigs a week. I'd told him what I thought was necessary to build up a following and he'd agreed. I kept my pitch going.

'Look, there's no young bands out there doing what we did the other night. All of the big names are mostly 'fifties rockers and surf bands and I think they're all on the way out. The Atlantics were great the other night but they were all a lot older than the crowd. Most of the audience were our age. Part of the reaction we got was because they're not used to seeing kids their own age like us put on a show and that's what we have to do. Look, I'm not saying I have all the answers, but the style of some of the songs I did will work and some of your material is great. I think I can make them all kick much harder if we rehearse hard and get tight as a crab's arse. And that's watertight.'

'Fuckin' oath,' said Bluey, shot full of enthusiasm.

'Shit, that's going to take a lot of time,' Col said. 'How are we going to work our day jobs and do all this? It'll kill us.'

'I think John has the answer to that question,' I replied.

'Well, here's what I propose,' he said. 'I'm prepared to draw up a management agreement between us immediately, making me your exclusive manager. I'll put you each on a salary of fifty pounds a week. For the moment you will play exclusively at Surf City and another club I'm opening in the city called the Beach House. Once you've built up a following, I'll raise it to a hundred. If you really start to draw here, I'll raise it to two hundred pounds a week. There are going to be other expenses such as equipment and clothes and you'll probably need some sort of person to help you. I'll cover all those costs on an as-needs basis. But for the next few months I want you playing exclusively at these venues. They will be your gigs. They're the best in the country and when word gets around that you only play here, anyone who wants to see you will have to come here. We're already getting great crowds on the weekends no matter who's playing. That exposure alone is guaranteed to pick up some fans. It's a foolproof way to build up a following. Hopefully at some stage when the time is right, you'll start going out and doing other shows. At that time I will get 50 per cent of everything you earn. Once the band starts to make money and you've paid me back half of what I've advanced you, I'll reduce my percentage to thirty-five and you get the rest. How's that?'

To me and the others this was an incredible deal. John was offering us an airtight way to get the band happening in a way that guaranteed us exposure. He was also promising up to two hundred quid a week each, which was a small bloody fortune in those days, plus costs. Sure, he would make plenty off the gigs, but that didn't alter the fact that he was committing to a substantial outlay with no guarantees other than his belief in us.

'Fuck!' 'Shit!' 'Jesus Chariist' we all responded.

'Well, I'm not quitting my job,' said Valentine, not missing a beat. 'I've been there five years and what's the guarantee that this band is going to make it, eh?'

Nobody answered.

'That's right, none!' he said. 'Look, this is all very well and good and I'm excited about the possibilities too. But it's too sudden. I've got to think of my future.'

'So 'ave I,' said Col, 'and I'll quit my bloody day job as soon as the bloody contract's signed.'

'Me too!' . . . 'Fuckin' oath!' Vince and Bluey agreed, nodding their heads excitedly.

John beamed at the enthusiastic response and looked at Val, saying, 'OK, that's my offer. Why don't you think it over for a couple of days, Valentine, and let me know what you want to do. If you boys decide you want to rehearse here this week let me know. I'll organise someone to be here to give you a hand. I've got to shoot off to a meeting now, boys, so use the place for as long as you like. It's your home now if you want it. See you all later. Once again, it was sensational last Saturday night.'

With that he shook all our hands and departed, leaving five young musicians in a state of shock.

Valentine ummed and aahed about signing a contract for the next two weeks. In the meantime we rehearsed as much as we could. The following Saturday night we played a one-hour show to nearly 2000 screaming kids, most of whom had been there the previous week. It went over as big as our first performance and the roll was on. Nearly a month later Valentine of course opted for the security of his twenty quid a week job, left the band and nobody blamed him.

And Billy Thorpe and three Aztecs started rehearsing our arses off.

11
Natalie

NATALIE sat quietly looking out the window of her tiny room on the third floor of the Hampton Court Hotel on Bayswater Road. Another night in the Cross was waking from a sleepy Saturday in late July and the festivities on the streets below were already well under way. That week Sydney was experiencing one of those unseasonably hot weather spells that came from time to time in winter and the whole city fell right back into the summer groove like it was still January. The usual crowd of punters, hustlers, Moreton Bays, footballers, cricket players and locals spilled out onto the footpath in front of the old Mansions Hotel on the corner of Kellet Street and Bayswater Road, directly across from Natalie's window.

The Mansions sat on the site once occupied by historic Kellet House and for years had been a favourite watering hole for locals, some of whom had been Australian legends. In the late forties it had been a favourite haunt of the actor

Chips Rafferty and on many an arvo he could be found holding court in the main bar, reciting Lawson and other Aussie favourites at the top of his lungs to anyone who'd listen. In real life Chips was the same quintessentially good Aussie bloke he was famous for portraying in his movie roles. He was always approachable in the Mansions, just as long as you were accompanied by a beer for the bard, which ensured the tales and anecdotes got more bawdy and rowdy as the recitals and drinking continued until late in the day.

The laughter and babble from the well-lit Mansions' patrons that Saturday evening comforted Natalie as she sat at her window. It sounded like summer. Like happy people having a beer with mates and friends. Finishing off another top day doing whatever they'd been doing, having a couple or three cool ones before hitting home, the shower, putting on the threads, and killing another couple of million brain cells in their favourite haunts until early in the Sunday a.m. In the half hour she'd been sitting there secretly spying on the street like a kid in her treehouse, two drunks had come sailing head-first through the front doors of the old pub, parting the crowd and landing flat on their arses in the road out the front. Although seeming to fly unassisted on their journey, Natalie knew Jean-Pierre had been their navigator.

Jean-Pierre usually worked Saturday arvos at the Mansions, then took on the late shift downstairs from the Pussycat at the Hasty Tasty, finishing at around 4.30 a.m. I found out that he'd been a boxing champion and Mr France finalist back in his homeland and sometimes taught the French Indo-Chinese street fighting art of savate to some of the Cross locals and bouncers to help make ends meet. Pepper had introduced me to him the first month I was in the

Cross. Jean-Pierre and I hit it off straight away and once a week I went around to his little flat behind the Darlinghurst fire station to get private savate lessons.

Savate is an amazing combination of martial arts kicking, punching, street fighting, weapon techniques with knives, machetes and objects such as nail files, all combined with graceful ballet-like jumps and leaps. It always amazed me the way Jean-Pierre could be standing in front of me sparring one second and either on the other side of the room, or standing behind me, the next. He would leap right over the top of me in one graceful motion that was both amazing and beautiful to watch. Standing in front of me he would begin throwing fast high kicks to the sides of my head, alternating with left and right feet without stopping, like a can-can dancer at double speed. He could maintain this for as long as he wished, his toes just clipping my ear lobes, his strength and accuracy deadly.

Having grown up in French Indo-China where savate originated, Jean-Pierre had become an expert at a young age and when I told him I had started doing jujitsu and judo when I was ten years old, martial arts became the common ground between us. It had nothing to do with the reality of life, or the Cross, and became the meeting place in our very different lives. The only method of payment he would accept from me for my private lessons was for me to bring him French rock 'n' roll records whenever I found them. His favourite French rocker was Johnny Halliday and after our sessions we would crack a couple of beers and listen to hours of French rock while he told me stories about Indo-China or Paris, and about meeting people like Brigitte Bardot and Edith Piaf.

Jean-Pierre was not a big man, at least not in stature,

standing a mere five feet nine inches tall. Apart from his obvious athletic build and big arms, there was nothing about him to give you the slightest hint of how tough he really was. Speaking in his soft, broken French-English accent, he was one of the politest and gentlest men I have ever met, but anyone who fucked with Jean-Pierre came in for a big surprise. Five or six to one suited him just fine. With lightning-fast hands and feet he was guaranteed to dispatch his opponents in a matter of seconds.

One night I saw him take on six big sailors on the street outside the Hasty Tasty. They were arse-grabbing young girls and one of them ran into the restaurant for help. I was having a coffee with Jean-Pierre when she came in screaming, 'Help me, please, somebody help me. That big sailor grabbed my boobs and took my purse, and he won't give it back. He's got my money and train ticket and he won't give it back.'

Jean-Pierre leapt up, went out the front and confronted them. 'C'mon fellas, I know zat ju jerst 'ave a leetle furn, but ze furn it overe now. Geev see gurrl 'er purse, eh?' he said politely to the biggest sailor who was rifling through the girl's purse and throwing her stuff in the air while his mates laughed and egged him on. As soon as Jean-Pierre spoke the big red-headed sailor threw the purse over his head into the middle of the heavy, late-night traffic on Darlinghurst Road, then turned on Jean-Pierre.

'And what've we got 'ere, eh boys,' he shouted, 'a fuckin' midget Froggy Mister fuckin' Universe or what? Piss orf, Froggy or I'll kick yer fuckin' 'ead in.'

The other sailors revved him on and it soon became six big, brave, drunken Aussie sailors against one little Frenchman. The one doing all the talking was about six foot three and 280 pounds and the other five stood a good head and shoulders taller than Jean-Pierre.

The six of them formed a menacing circle around Jean-Pierre on the footpath, jeering and yelling things like 'C'mon, Froggy muscle man, let's see if you've got any guts under yer fuckin' muscles!'

'C'mon Curly,' one of them said to the big sailor, 'kick his fuckin' 'ead in. Send the Froggy prick back to Frogland in a box.'

Big Curly started putting on a show, trying to humiliate the little Frenchman, not hitting him, but ring dancing, throwing combinations that stopped inches from his face, lairing for his mates and the crowd on the footpath. From his movements he'd obviously done some ring time and knew what he was about. As he danced and shadow boxed, he imitated Cassius Clay, skipping backwards and yelling 'Fly like a butterfly, sting like a fuckin' bee, no Froggy prick's gonna beat Curleeeey . . . I am theee greatest.'

Jean-Pierre just stood calmly with his arms by his sides, looking up at the big man towering over him. He slowly rotated, following Curly with his eyes as he danced around, so that he was always in front of him. After about a minute of showing off his shadow boxing skills to his adoring mug mates, Curly decided it was time to get serious. Voom! He leapt at Jean-Pierre, throwing a massive right hook at his jaw, going for the big king hit.

Jean-Pierre's body bent slightly back at the waist and the punch went rocketing through the air a quarter of an inch from his face, nearly knocking Curly off his feet with his own momentum. Curly couldn't believe he'd missed. Like all big bruisers, he was heavy and slow and before he could recover his balance and get back into a fighting stance,

Jean-Pierre hit him with a lightning-fast foot to the face that came straight up from the footpath in front of him like a meteor on the end of a chorus girl's high kick. One movement.

It hit with a sound like somebody hitting a side of beef with a sledge hammer. Ba-blaaat! Jean-Pierre's right foot had smashed upward into Curly's throat, chin and jaw like a massive uppercut. Curly's jaw snapped and he bit the tip off his tongue which flew out of his mouth in a spray of blood, shattered teeth and splintered bone. All 280 pounds of Cassius Curly was out cold on his feet and he toppled straight back like a giant oak, his skull cracking as it hit the edge of the gutter.

By the look on what was left of Curly's face, the silly big mug must have thought a bus had run up the kerb and hit him smack between the eyes. His sailor mates stood there with their mouths hanging open and Jean-Pierre spun around the circle throwing a blinding combination of hooks, rips, kicks, backhands and head butts and the other five went down in all directions like pins in a bowling alley. His combinations came so hard and fast the sailors must have thought they were surrounded by a baseball team on speed at a batting practice. They never knew what hit them. Jean-Pierre calmly walked out into Darlinghurst Road, picked up the young girl's battered purse, walked back, dusted it off and handed it to her saying, 'I yam zorry for ze trouble, mademoiselle, but 'ere eez your bag.' He hadn't even cracked a sweat.

The locals at the Mansions knew his skills only too well and liked to drink there because it was always secure from invading yahoos. If some poor unsuspecting mug new-comer started slinging off, causing trouble, the regulars would chuckle quietly to themselves, knowing it was only a matter of minutes until another astronaut would be launched into orbit.

The sky above the old pub and the buildings along the north side of Bayswater Road were now bathed in an amber glow as the sunset slowly disappeared into a warm evening. Although she couldn't see them, Natalie imagined the beauty of the billowing white sails dotting the harbour behind the buildings as the boats tacked gracefully home to their moorings. Most of them would be under the helm of some weekend sailor who would be well plastered by now from the afternoon's champers and grog-salted lunacy they called boating . . . so pissed they didn't know how to find their arses, let alone the mooring. For Natalie and anyone who knew and loved Sydney, the magnificent harbour was the heart, soul and pulse of the city, its beauty surpassed by none anywhere on this earth.

Natalie was born in Sydney's Eastern Suburbs a month after her parents came from Russia just after World War II. Apart from her Aussie accent, she was every inch a Rusky with jet-black shoulder-length hair, the fringe cut straight across her forehead just above her eyebrows, black eyes, and full, luscious lips framed by broad cheekbones. About five feet nine and model thin with long legs and huge boobs, Natalie always dressed in black, day or night. Usually long black dresses, looking like the prototype for Natasha, Boris's offsider in the 'Rocky and Bullwinkle' cartoons. Born Natasha Reminoff, when she left home she had quickly changed her name to Natalie, after the film star Natalie Wood.

Pepper told me Natalie had been a waitress at the Pussycat when she first started working there and she'd really done the right thing by Pepper in clueing her up to the rorts and rorters, generally helping to get her settled safely in the Cross. Natalie had quit the Pussycat gig about six months after Pepper started working there. She wanted bigger bucks and, having received enough lucrative offers to make her realise she was sitting on gold, Natalie decided to open the mine and go on the game. At first she tried to go it as an independent, but after a couple of hidings from vicious Johns and several heavies by the coppers, she realised she needed some protection. What she needed was a handler, a pimp—or a 'hoon' as they're affectionately monickered in the Cross—and guess who Natalie's hoon turned out to be? Joey the punk from the front desk of the Canberra Oriental. Turns out the reason Joey was doing the straight and narrow there was so some of his girls could use the rooms in the back for tricks, and he could keep an eye on their cummings and goings like any good hoon should. After all, that's why he got 50 per cent of the slash stash.

Like all fledgling hookers, Natalie went strolling naively into the game with both legs open and both eyes closed. Money was all that mattered, and she gave no thought to the dirty nature of the business she was getting into. A few carefully picked customers a night and—pow!—500 tax-free quid in the kitty. She was a real good sort and knew it. She also knew she could ask top price and get it. She never worked the streets, only the high-class hotels like the Menzies and the Sheraton, and that's all she needed. She was in the big game was Natalie, firing big time. An apartment in Rushcutters Bay, clothes, car, jewellery . . . firing. Then came the beatings and the coppers shaking her down, wanting her to cut the lag out in trade, which of course she'd had to do. She freaked but was hooked on the life and like a fool didn't take the chance she had to quit while she was ahead and still an independent whore.

So Joey the Hoon became Natalie's hoon of choice. Although at first hating to give half her hard-earned swag to him every night, she had never been hassled since, so she figured the insurance was paying off. Natalie and Joey had lived together for a time and, like all whores, she saved her love pussy just for her man. The Johns were biz and didn't count as sex. Joey was Natasha's only sex, her exclusive main man and, again like most whores, at first she thought she loved her protector.

She believed all the gooey bullshit he spun her about her only working the game until they could get enough big bucks together so that she could quit, retire to their house in the country and live happily ever after raising rug rats. One night a casual conversation with another hooker brought reality screaming into Natalie's pipe fantasy. Some nights around midnight, after she'd finished her first shift of tricks, Natalie would take a break and get something to eat. She and Joey would go to Vadim's, the Spaghetti Bar, the Cosmopolitan, whatever was handy. Sometimes they'd go over to the Hasty Tasty for a graze. Something to eat to sustain her through the next shift of tricks before drying the slops bucket and hanging up the towel for the night. One night after Pepper had made dinner, we were lying on the bed talking and she told me a story as told to her by Natalie shortly after it happened.

'Natalie and Joey were in the Hasty Tasty one night when one of Joey's mates comes running in, panting, verballing somefing about some John beating up on one of Joey's uvver girls. See Natalie wasn't his only source of income. Joey had uvver girls, but they were just whores according to him and he had no personal relationship wiv them. It was just business, or so he told her, the silly moll. So Joey takes off out of the restaurant to sort this bloke out, leaving her sitting there alone in all her callgirl finery. Some drunk starts ragging her about the way she's dressed. You know, black stockings, black skirt and a black top that just manages to cover her boobs. Anyhow, anuvver pro named Josie was in the place. She spots Joey take off and sees this mug hassling Natalie, goes right over and plonks herself down next to her in the boofe. Now Josie's a big old girl. Looks like she eats bullets with her cornies and one "piss orf" from her and this mug is gone. The second he leaves Josie starts rabbiting to Natalie at a hundred miles an hour in a full-on speed rave.'

Pepper went into a great impersonation of Josie on speed, firing words out like machine-gun bullets, hardly stopping for a breath.

'"That prick Joey, watch him, he's fuckin' low. Yeah . . . I used to work fer 'im fer a bit and there's nuffin' he won't do for a quid. Before working fer 'im I worked on me own and 'e kept leanin' on me to join up but I just kept tellin' 'im to fuck orf. One night some arsehole I picks up beats the shit outta me, put me in fuckin' 'ospital fer a week. A coupla weeks later I gets rumbled by free fuckin' coppers and have to do 'em all in the back of the fuckin' paddy-wagon to get out of the lag. Then the next night Joey gets me aside at the Stacatto 'n' puts it on me again. Swears he'll look after me and all that shit so I signed up. Yeah. I was wiv him fer a year, then he sold me to big Tony and I've been pushing it six nights a week for him ever since. Don't trust that bastard Joey, mate, he's a fuckin' mook!"

'Well before Josie'd got the fourff sentence out, Natalie

put two and two togever and came up wiv arsehole. She realised Joey had set her up with the coppers and manipulated her into his stable and her brain snapped on the spot. She was still sitting there spewing when Joey comes waltzing back into the restaurant. Before he could open his mouff, she's given him an atrocious verbal and frew her plate of food all over him. Anyhow, Joey's blown up, punched her in the face, then dragged her into the street, kicked her up and down Darlinghurst Road, not giving a shit that people were watching. Jean-Pierre hadn't arrived for work yet and nobody had the balls to step in and help her. Joey had her in the gutter, kicking the crap out of her when the coppers arrived in the paddy-wagon. First they grab Joey, then guess what?'

'What,' I said. 'I have no idea. What?'

'Well, the next fing they've let Joey go and they book Natalie wiv loitering wiv intent to solicit for prostitution, cuff her and frow her battered and bleeding into the back of the paddy-wagon, then take her away in custody. She had a fractured jaw and busted ribs. Spent two days in a coma and two munfs in St Vincent's. Turns out that Joey had this deal wiv some of the local coppers and kicks them back part of the swag. That's how he gets them to set up the girls to work for him. Then the coppers never mess wiv them once they're on wiv Joey. What a prick, eh?'

Pepper went on to tell me that Natalie had gotten a little taste for morphine in hospital. After she got out she'd turned to smack, but quit the game and had been living at the Hampton Court trying to kick her habit, living off what she made waitressing at the Silver Spade room at the Chevron Hotel. Realising he'd cooked his golden goose, Joey sent her flowers every day in hospital and came slithering around after she got out, sliming on her shoulder and apologising, swearing it would never happen again.

'Natalie gave him the coat, mate,' said Pepper. 'Brushed him and told him to piss off or she'd get her bruvvers to pull his slimy head off and Joey knew she meant it. Her bruvvers are bad buggers, built like two Russian concrete shithouses,' she said, laughing.

'Joey the Hoon, as tough and connected as he finks he is, knew he would be very dead very quick, so he backed off. Still hustles her a bit if he sees her on the street or somefing, but nuffing serious. Natalie's been a real good friend to me, Bill, even after she went on the game. I was short my rent money once 'cause the Pussycat shut down for repairs and I had no work for a munf. I got this letter in the mail wiv two hundred pounds in it and no signature, just a big red lipstick kiss in the middle of the page. I knew right away it was from Natalie. When I went back to work and had some donero again, I fronted her about it but she wouldn't take it back. Absolutely refused to discuss it. Just said, "Maybe I'll need some help one day, mate. That's what friends are for," gave me a big hug and a kiss on the cheek. Natalie's got a heart of gold, mate. She's the best girlfriend I've ever had. When we're togever she's just like a kid again and we talk and laugh and tell each ovver girl stuff, you know.'

No, I didn't know, but I'd met Natalie a couple of times with Pepper and I liked her a lot. The first night we met, Pepper took me to a party at the Hampton Court and we had a ball. Natalie was a beautiful and gracious hostess and made an obvious big fuss of Pepper and me. I could tell they were really close friends. I also got the distinct impression that night that she was coming on to both of us. Nothing heavy, just the little looks and subtle innuendos. The occasional low bend to reveal just the right amount of boob and the sexy glances from across the room to see if either one of us was looking. All very innocent but nevertheless happening. Pepper seemed to either not notice or ignore it.

Pepper and I sat like this a lot and talked about stuff. I got to know all about the people she knew in the Cross and she loved to tell me her Cross stories, getting a big kick out of my questions.

That same night she told me about Natalie, she asked if I liked her.

'Yes, mate, I think she's great,' I replied.

'That's good,' she said, ''cause she finks the world of you. She fancies you, you know that, don't you?'

'Well no, I didn't until you just told me. I do remember that night at her party, I thought she was coming on to me and you a bit, but I thought I was imagining it. I just put it down to the drink and flirting.'

'No mate, you weren't imagining it. She gets a bit like that sometimes. Likes to flirt wiv people, women as well as men.'

'Is she a lesbian?' I asked.

'Sometimes, I guess, but not very often. She prefers men, but goes wiv women sometimes. Just now and again and only wiv someone she falls in love wiv for a while. She gets head over heels sometimes, you know, just dotes on a girl and they sometimes give in. She tried it wiv me once. I went home wiv her one night just after she got out of hospital. We'd had a few drinks and ended up sitting on her bed talking for hours. She was a bit wobbly from the drinks, just sitting there talking about boys and stuff and she kissed me and put her hand up my skirt, touched me, you know? I was a bit wobbly too and we fooled around a bit, just kissing and touching and stuff, but nuffing really serious happened. It was warm and loving. She didn't force herself on me or anyfing. Afterwards I told her that it didn't really interest me and that I wanted her to be my friend. She never tried it again.'

Pepper paused and looked at me. 'Do you fancy her, Bill?' she asked point-blank.

'Well, I, er, think she's gorgeous,' I fumbled. 'I'd have to be dead not to appreciate her, but I've never had any thoughts about, you know,' I lied.

Of course I thought about you know. No straight man alive looks at a girl as beautiful as Natalie and doesn't think about it, wonder what she looks like under her dress and comes up with 'SEX'. Any man that says otherwise is a liar. But that's just part of the private fantasy world we all have, male and female, and usually that's where it stays.

'You do, don't you?' said Pepper. There was no jealousy in the way she asked or acted. It seemed to be just an honest question between two really close friends.

'Well, as a male I fancy her—who wouldn't, mate?—but that doesn't mean I want to jump into bed with her,' I said diplomatically. 'She's beautiful and a great girl. Of course I find her attractive, but that's it, mate. I promise,' and I meant it. 'What the hell made you ask that?'

'Oh nuffing.' She was obviously fibbing.

'C'mon, Pepper, I know you too well. Why did you ask me that?'

'Well, she fancies you . . . has from the first time you met. When you and me first started to see each uvver, she asked me if I'd mind if she had a crack at you. Well, you don't belong to me and I told her to go for it. That night we went over to her place for the party she came onto you all night long and I know you knew, but you politely manoeuvred around it and made a big fuss of me. She told me that you only had eyes for me and she wouldn't try again. She also whispered, "If the two of you ever fancy having some fun wiv me, I'd love it", you know.'

This conversation was starting to arouse me to say the least. I knew Pepper well enough to know she wasn't gay and I'd have thought she'd want to keep all of this a secret.

I looked at Pepper and saw an 'I've got you now, you bugger' look on her face.

'Why are you telling me this?' I asked.

'Oh, just curious to see your reaction,' she fibbed again.

'C'mon, Pepper, I know you better than that,' I pressed, intrigued to see where this was going. 'What's up?'

'Well, I'd like to try everyfing wiv you, mate, and if you want us to, it's all right wiv me. I'm not funny or anyfing like that, but wiv someone like you and Natalie it might be fun. Would you like to see me kiss anuvver girl and, you know, make love to her in front of you?'

'Do you want to?' I asked, practically bursting my fly.

'Only if you do. I'm not into it on my own, but I'm starting to get real horny finking about it wiv you and Natalie.'

So was I!

'Well I'll tell you what,' I said. 'I don't exactly want us to make an appointment with her like a dentist or something, that would take the edge off the whole thing, but if it ever feels right, happens naturally, I'll go for it if you want me too. How's that?'

Jesus, what a bullshit artist, I thought. I was all ready to sprint, dick in hand and panting, up to Natalie's and knock her door down.

'OK, it's a deal,' Pepper replied, and we shook hands on it.

The conversation had us both hot by this time, and lying there on her bed we started touching and kissing. Pepper started nibbling my ear and whispering in her sexy voice.

'Just imagine Natalie and me wearing sexy dresses and high heels. We've got stockings and suspenders underneaf and we're sitting on her bed kissing and touching each uvver while you watch. Would you like to watch her undress me, Bill? . . . Watch her put her hand up my skirt and touch me? . . . Watch her slip off my panties and make me all wet while you kissed me? . . . You would, wouldn't you?'

'Yes I would,' I answered, and reached over and turned out the light . . .

The only things that broke Natalie's reverie at her window was the nagging thought that she had to go to work soon and she was out. The supply she'd been counting on for the weekend hadn't arrived yet. *Fuck Manny*, she thought. *He's probably slammed himself too hard this arvo and is lying out cold somewhere with my eight ball in his pocket. Jesus, he better get here soon or I'm fucked.* Manny was one of the few dealers around the Cross. He had a number of stash places and to Natalie's joy one of them turned out to be the room next to hers. She'd already banged on his door a dozen times in the last half hour but no Manny. 'C'mon, Manny, cuuum onnn!' she said out loud to the street below.

The neon was lit now, but Natalie, lost in her worst nightmare, hadn't even noticed it come on. The marks from the suburbs were starting to get off the buses in droves, pay packets burning in their pockets, busting for the lunacy to begin. In half an hour or so Natalie would have to start getting ready for work. She knew the routine only too well. Take a shower, get dressed, then get out her stash and have a little hit. Not too much, she wasn't greedy. She knew too much would have her nodding off at the tables. Natalie had only shot up a few times and it really freaked her because it was too good and, luckily for her, it made her violently sick afterwards. Now sprinkling some smack in a roll-your-own and smoking it seemed to settle ol' Mr Jones and got her high without the nod. She was never a scratching mumbling mess, at least not in public, and unless you knew how to read the poppy signs you would never pick she was high. None of the people at the Silver Spade ever picked it, or at least ever mentioned it if they had.

After her hit she would glide to work through the Cross, packed in her warm cottonwool glow. By the time Natalie hit the street she was on auto pilot. Up Bayswater Road, right on Darlinghurst Road, left on Macleay Street by the fountain and down to the Chevron for another night as head cocktail waitress in the Silver Spade. Natalie really loved working at the Silver Spade. It was the coolest room in town. Major international stars performed there regularly and she got to meet and serve them all. Although working, she also got to enjoy the shows and for the last two weeks the star had been American comedian Jerry Lewis, who she just loved. The first night she took his bottle of Jack back to him in his dressing-room he nicknamed her 'Legs'. Wouldn't accept any drinks backstage unless 'Legs' brought them.

He didn't come on to her, was very polite and tipped her heavily every night.

On the other hand, that same night as she was leaving Jerry's room, a hand came out of another dressing-room door and grabbed her straight on the tits. She turned around to slap the offender, jumping back in shock when she saw it was Mickey Rooney, who was the opening act for Jerry Lewis that run.

'Hey, babe,' Mickey said, 'I ain't seen a pair like that since Ava. What's your name, sweetheart?'

Before she could answer, the voice of the Delicate Delinquent came out of Jerry's dressing-room. 'Oh Mickeeeeeeey, ya ya ya ya, what are you doing Mickey, you old perveeert. Ya ya ya ya huuuuuahh. You be nice to my new girl Natalie or I'll smash your kneecaps. You heeeeeerrrree meeeee Mickeeeeeeey?' he yelled in his high-pitched comic voice.

'Ah fuck,' Mickey Rooney said. 'It's worse than being on the road with my goddamn wife. OK, Jerry baby,' he yelled back. 'Just checking to make sure they ain't sending us any goddamn fags back here.'

'If Legs is a fag, I'll turn, ha ha ha ha ha huuuahh,' yelled Jerry from his room.

Every night during the show Jerry would ask from the stage, 'Where's my best girl?' and the lighting man would hit Natalie with a single white spot and she would have to take a bow as he blew her a kiss. It embarrassed her a little but she enjoyed it and so did the crowd because it was all in good fun. Neither Jerry nor Mickey ever came on to her and one night, even though it was against Chevron rules, she and some of the other girls snuck up to Jerry's suite for a drink after the show. He treated them all like ladies and she and her waitress friends spent hours pissing themselves with laughter at the insane antics and pantomime schtick that Jerry and Mickey got up to. It was priceless stuff by two of the funniest men alive.

The day Jerry checked out of the Chevron to go back to

the States he left Natalie a package at the front desk of the hotel. 'Mr Lewis insisted I give this to you personally,' the concierge told her when she got to work that night, and he handed her a small gift-wrapped package. Inside was a simple little wooden box with 'Legs' written on the top in gold letters. To her amazement when she opened it, there was a man's solid gold Rolex watch. It was Jerry's. She had admired it one night in his dressing-room and he let her try it on, saying, 'Legs, compared to you, this is tin.' In the box alongside the watch was a note of some kind and as she read it she burst into tears. The handwritten message read: *Keep your chin up, kid. You can kick it. Big hugs, Jerry.*

She stood there crying her eyes out like a little girl. He had picked that she had a monkey on her back, but never once let on or said anything to her about it. Turning the watch over she saw inscribed on the back in tiny letters, 'Smile kid, life's much too short for tears. Love J.' It was the most precious thing anyone had ever done for her.

Like I said, Natalie loved her job at the Silver Spade. It was good honest money and sometimes she would make two or three hundred a night in tips. At times she wondered how the hell she could have ever gotten on the game, selling her body to anyone with the price. The thought disgusted her now and she swore that she would clean herself up soon, get out of the Cross and go to Europe or somewhere and start a new life. She looked at the Rolex on her wrist and saw it was seven-fifteen. She was just about to damn Manny the Man to burn in hell when there was a soft knock on the door. She leapt off the bed and opened it without bothering to ask who it was. It was Manny all right, standing there whacked out of his brain, eyes darting left and right like a lizard looking for the hawk.

'Aw sorry I'm late, maaan, I got a bit of China and slammed a little too hard, maaan. Fuck! The rush was incredible, maaan, but I couldn't fuckin' move.'

Manny said it all in one monotonal breath, punctuating his sentences only with 'maaan' and frequent rubs of his face and nose. The junkie's hand jive.

'Er, can I come in? It's a bit fuckin' public out here in the hall, maaan,' he said, eyes darting as Natalie let him into her room. He kept the rave going as he walked in and took in Natalie's pad. He'd been there plenty of times in the past, but was always so whacked he always said the same thing when he came in.

'Wowww, maaan, I really like your new pad. Er, what was I saying? Oh yeah, I remember, the white man knocked me flat on my arsemaaaan.' Rub, rub, scratch, sniff. 'Came to behind the fuckin' boatshed in Rushcutters Bay, maaan. Didn't know 'oo the fuck I was fer a minute. Then remembered I 'ad to be at the Paradise,' scratch, rub, rub, 'at eight, maaann. Yeah that's right, eight, come by on the way to fix you, maaan, you dig?

'You cool and everything? Now I got some brown or a little bit of the white if you wan' it, maaan, but it's not fuckin' cheapmaaan. 'Cause if you wanna work something out I can let you 'ave it for the right price, know what I mean?' He leered, his eyes glued to Natalie's crotch.

She had been so eager to get to the door that she hadn't realised that she was only wearing a black T-shirt and tiny black lace panties. After Manny came in Natalie had sat back in her chair by the window, turning it around so that she could face him.

'Is this what you like?' she said, opening her legs and rubbing her right middle finger up and down the centre of her crotch. 'Oh Manny, I bet you're a real tiger aren't you?' she said, putting her hand down the front of her pants, teasing him.

Manny was scratched out of his brain, but a taste of something like Natalie didn't come along to someone like him everyday and he thought he was about to hit the jackpot.

'You think you're maaan enough for this, Manny boy?'

Manny was a heartbeat away from the closest thing to sex he'd had in months.

'Well, it's tooo expensive for you, maaaaaan,' she fired at him. 'It'd take your whole fucking stash just for a squiz.'

Natalie got up and went over to the wardrobe, Manny's eyes glued to her arse as she walked across the room. She took out a black and gold batik print and wrapped it around her waist.

'Now let's stop playing silly buggers or I'll flatten ya, ya little prick,' she spat. 'Understand?'

'OK, OK, OK, maaan, no heavies, no heavies, maaan,' he whined. 'I didn't mean nothin' by it, maaan. It's just you used to . . . you know, and I thought you might still be open for business, maaan.'

'The only business I want is the eight ball. You promised me an eight ball of white, that's what I paid you for. You telling me you slammed my eight, is that what you're fucking saying?' said Natalie, starting to panic a little.

'Er, no maaan . . . er . . . not exactly. I just thought I'd 'ave a lil taste, ya know, a little taste before I laid it on me best people, maaan.'

'Stop bullshitting me, you little fuck. Give me my goods. I gotta be at work in . . .' She looked at her watch. 'Oh shit!'

'Wow, nice watch, maaan,' said Manny, looking at the solid gold Rolex on Natalie's wrist, already pawning it in his mind. 'You come into some bread or somethin'?'

'Mind your own fucking business! You holding or not?'

'Yeah, maaan, you know me, maaan,' he whined. 'I'm always flush. Just don't 'ave yer full eight is all, but I'll get yer through the night and get yer squared tomorrow. Ya know I always deliver, OK, maaan?'

'OK,' said Natalie, starting to get real anxious. Timing her hit was important. Too late before leaving and she'd have a hard time maintaining for the first dinner show.

'I need enough for a few joints,' she snapped. 'C'mon Manny, I don't have much time.'

Manny shot her an astonished look, his eyes bulging. 'Joints?' he said in absolute disbelief. 'Ya mean yer gonna smoke this stuff in fuckin' joints, maaan? Jesus, this is the best shit I've 'ad in months, maaan, and yer gonna waste it in fuckin' joints. Fuck maaan, that's fuckin' sacrilege, maaan.'

'What I do with my dope is my fucking business!' she yelled. 'Now hand it over. I ain't got all night.'

Manny took off his battered shoe and removed his grimy sock. He emptied its contents on the table between them and about half a dozen small aluminium foil packets fell on the table top. Rummaging through them he picked one up and gave it to Natalie.

'This one's on me fer the fuck-up, maaan,' he whined, scratching his nose and sniffing. 'OK? We fuckin' OK now, maaan?'

Natalie opened the foil and saw the gleaming white powder inside. She instantly felt better.

'OK, Manny, but you make sure you're here before twelve o'clock tomorrow, OK?'

'I'll be 'ere maaan, I'll be 'ere, Manny won't let ya Jones, maaan.'

'Sure, now get outta here so I can get ready for work,' said Natalie, rifling through her handbag to find her cigarette papers. Manny got up, said 'OK maaan I'll see ya,' and let himself out.

By the time Manny was through the door, Natalie had one rolled and lit. The glow of the smack hit her system like an orgasm and she shuddered as it kissed every nerve end in her brain, shutting down the ache as it entered her system. The other thing good smack always did to her was make her horny and that was a big part of Natalie's hook. She fell back on her bed feeling the warmth track all through her, the tingling running like electricity from head to toe. Something made her look at her watch and she realised she had to hurry if she was going to make it to work on time. She tore off her T-shirt and panties, staggered naked over to her dresser and pulled out a bunch of clean underwear which she dumped in a pile on the bedspread.

While Natalie fumbled in her candy padded glow on the other side of the door, Manny the Man stumbled fifteen feet down the hall and quietly let himself into a room. He quickly went to the wall separating Natalie's room from his and silently slid a dresser away from the wall. There, about a foot above the floor, was a small hole. He got down on his stomach and gently pulled a plug of paper out with his fingers. The hole went through the old wooden wall and came out in Natalie's room just below her dressing table. Lying there on the floor Manny had an almost perfect view of Natalie's room, but unless she got down on her hands and knees it was impossible to detect Manny's perve hole, even when it was open.

Putting his eye to the hole he watched Natalie standing naked in front of her bed, fumbling with a bunch of underwear. For five minutes Manny the scumbag lay there masturbating, watching Natalie as she tried on different sets of undies, stoned to the gills, trying to get herself dressed. When she finally got it together and had finished, she brushed her hair, not worrying about her make-up which she always put on at work. She carefully rolled herself another couple, stashed her swag inside the wire of one of her bras, then walked across the room and put it in the dresser directly in front of Manny. From his pozzie on the floor, Manny's eye was a foot away looking straight at Natalie's shins under her dresser. He heard her close the drawer and watched as she walked over to her door, turn out the light and float off to work.

12
Tony and the
Maracosa Trio

AFTER Valentine Jones left I ate, drank, slept and dreamed the band. Rehearsing at Surf City almost every weekday, performing Wednesday through Sunday, including weekend afternoons, we started to get tighter and pick up a strong following. The only bummer was both Vince and I felt that the band would be stronger if we had another rhythm guitarist. I loved to play guitar, but it restricted my ability to work the crowds and we all agreed that we should look for someone to join. While averaging about 350 punters an afternoon, Saturday and Sunday afternoons at Surf City were really casual and relaxed and, although performing, we used these afternoon crowds to try out and tighten new songs. I'd ask them over the microphone what they thought and if their response to a new song was strong, it stayed. If not, next! If it was borderline, we'd try different arrangements, play it again the following week and ask them again. In this way we started to build up a strong set and, more importantly, fiercely loyal fans, many of whom we were getting to know personally.

They felt they had a personal stake in, and influence on, the band and what we played, and there was no doubt they did. These kids became the hard-core fans who started turning up four and five times a week. We respected their opinions and at times even had open discussions with them about some song or another in the middle of the afternoon gigs. They loved the fact that we involved them, and when they came to see us on the main nights they were guaranteed to react very strongly when we played those numbers. Their enthusiasm always revved up the rest of the crowd and ensured a fantastic response. The situation was made in heaven and we got better and better and more popular as the weeks went by. So popular, in fact, that John raised our salary to a hundred pounds a week a mere six weeks after our first ever show. We were rollin' hard. But before that happened, one more crucial ingredient fell into place.

On Saturday and Sunday afternoons John booked some other fledgling bands to play between our sets. Because of what was starting to happen there, every young band in Sydney was busting to play Surf City and they lined up for the opportunity. Some of these bands also backed contestants who entered the talent quest which was held about every other weekend. One Saturday afternoon we'd taken our usual coffee break at the Spaghetti Bar, which had become the band's official hang. Walking back into Surf City, the first thing we heard was 'Zip-a-Dee-Doo-Dah.'

On stage in front of the support band, performing in the talent quest, stood this good-looking little bloke playing left-handed guitar and singing his lungs out. He was dressed in a tweed suit and waistcoat, cream shirt, black tie and black Chelsea boots. He had a pretty good voice, but what caught our attention was his rhythm guitar style and his crazy body movements. We all looked at one another and said, 'That's our rhythm guitar player!'

He received a good applause from the crowd and the next young hopeful took the stage. We all shot backstage and found him diligently putting his guitar away. He polished it about three times, held it up to the light, then polished it again. He took off the strap, wiped it, then rolled and rerolled it four times until it fit some predetermined shape. He carefully put the guitar and the strap in the case, which he also proceeded to polish. *This bloke's the neatest bloody musician I've ever seen*, I thought. His name was Tony Barber. Not the television personality Tony Barber from 'Sale of the Century' by the way. This Tony Barber had just migrated alone from Norwich, England, and was living in a migrant youth hostel somewhere out in Sydney's western suburbs. Tony had a broad Norfolk accent and any minute I expected him to go 'Arhh, Jim,' just like Long John Silver.

'So you're called the Aztecs, are you?' he asked. 'I like that name. Do you play here often?'

'Five nights and weekend afternoons,' Vince replied.

'My goodness,' he remarked, still rubbing his case down. 'You must be very popular then. How do you manage to play here so much then?'

'Our manager owns the fuckin' joint,' said Bluey. 'So yer from Pommyland, eh? What's it like?'

'Well, it's very nice really,' Tony politely replied.

'Oh yeah? If it's so bloody nice, what're yer doin' 'ere?'

Bluey really had a way with words. Here we are about to chat up this young bloke into joining the band and

Bluey's getting up his nose about being English. Tony didn't really have any reply and we all stood around for a second or two, shuffling our feet without saying anything.

Then Tony said nervously, 'I take it you don't like English people, Bluey?'

'Aw, some of 'em are all right, I s'pose. It's them bloody whingeing Pommy bastards that give me the shits, mate.'

'Well, I hope you don't think I'm a whingeing Pommy bastard,' I said.

'What, you're not a fuckin' Pom too, are you?' Bluey asked in disbelief.

'Yep,' I said, 'came out here when I was seven.'

'Ah fuck me,' yelled Bluey. 'Not two fuckin' Pommies in the same band! That's a bit bloody raw.'

Everybody except Tony cracked up. The best he could manage was a sort of nervous twiddle. He had no idea what Bluey was talking about and had this terrified look on his face. He must have been thinking he was in the company of one of those gangs of Pommy bashers he'd heard so much about in the hostel.

'Ah don't worry about him, mate,' said Col. 'He's just a bloody bass player.'

'Ah get fucked,' Bluey responded.

'No you get fucked,' said Col.

'No you get fucked.' 'No you get fucked.' The two of them went at it in their familiar little rant and Tony blushed red. He'd obviously never seen or heard anything like Bluey in his life.

Tony was this polite, immaculately groomed, handsome little Englishman. His hair was perfectly trimmed, his tweed suit pressed and his black Chelsea boots spotlessly shined. Well spoken and well mannered, he was shy, skinny and frail, with the delicate hands of a painter and body language that just bordered on the effeminate. He didn't, however, strike me as a shirt-lifter, his persona being more that of a quiet, precise, young English gentleman, who would be perfectly at home supping on tea and scones while discussing the latest techniques for buttercup pruning with his old Auntie Polly in some little thatched cottage in Devon.

Bluey, on the other hand, had the manners and demeanour of a water buffalo on heat, the hands of a brickie, mouth of a whore, a twisted and disgusting sense of humour, and the ruddy complexion of a Scotsman. His red curly hair was so thick and wiry you could buff the paint job on your car with it. He picked his nose and farted as a matter of course and didn't give a twopenny fuck what anybody thought, and would be perfectly happy sniffing the sheets and drinking the dregs from the leftover glasses at a whorehouse party. He also had a heart of gold and I adored him.

In short, these two were about as opposite as any two human beings could possibly get, and here we were about to discuss the possibility of them playing in the same band.

Oh well, I thought, *nothing ventured, nothing gained*, so I broke the silence and said, 'We're looking for a rhythm guitar player and we thought you might be interested.'

'How much does it pay?' Tony shot back.

'Well, we'd want you to try out with us first,' said Vince. 'If it works out then we'll start you off at fifty pounds a week. We rehearse every day and play seven shows a week.'

'I'd be happy to join your band,' Tony replied, and with that Billy Thorpe and the Aztecs became five-piece . . . and the real fun began.

Tony tried out with us a few days later and he was in,

though he only sat in on the afternoon shows until he felt comfortable with the band. He had a very unusual style, like nothing we'd heard before, and it seemed to fit perfectly. When we did our first gig together it was sensational. Just as the band had taken a quantum leap when I had joined, it did the same thing with Tony. His style and personality somehow made the whole thing click. His rhythm playing and vocal style took the band in an even more original sounding direction. It also gave us another voice and we started to get into some interesting harmonies. Tony moved into the Cross, renting a tiny room in the Hampton Court Hotel. *You and Natalie ought to make very interesting neighbours*, I thought. *When she gets a load of you she'll suck the flesh right off your poor little Pommy bones*. We got down to rehearsing hard and Tony introduced us to some songs he said were very popular in England. He also told us about the booming English music scene and, more specifically, about some band called the Beatles who nobody in Australia had ever heard of. Tony said they were the biggest thing in England and would become the biggest band in the world.

'Not with a fuckin' name like the Beatles,' quipped Bluey.

Ah well, we all make mistakes!

There were no music press or music magazines in Australia at that time. The elitist snobbery of the straight press put them far above reporting on anything as mundane as popular music and there was no way of finding out what was going on in the new music scenes around the world except through people like Tony. We all went merrily along in our ignorance, with no real influences other than those we chased up ourselves.

The first night Tony played with the Aztecs John Harrigan wanted us to introduce him with new songs and make a formal introduction of the new line-up to our fans. It had to be on a Saturday night when we'd be guaranteed a big crowd and all the loyal fans would be there. This was it.

I introduced Tony as the new permanent member and the crowd gave him a fantastic welcome. It was an emotional moment for him and for all of us. He had done no real professional performing before the Aztecs and all this from two thousand plus people was absolutely overwhelming for him. The first song we played was one Tony had written for the band called 'Blue Day'. We felt it would make a great first record for us and, using the crowd that night as the barometer, we knew we were right. They loved it. In fact the reaction was sensational for everything we did and it seemed we couldn't put a foot wrong. It was obvious that they loved Tony and it was also obvious to the rest of us, as well as the audience, that this was the magic line-up.

One afternoon we were rehearsing at Surf City as usual when three big blokes came waltzing in and sat down in the dark at the back of the room. Sometimes some of the regular fans who worked in the city would pop in during their lunch breaks and eat while we rehearsed. Apart from them we never let spectators come in during the day as John didn't want strangers wandering around the building when there was no security. We were in the middle of some song or another when they strolled in. I stopped the band and asked them politely what they wanted.

'Aw, we joost coom in ta see yer band fer a bit,' answered this voice in a thick Liverpudlian accent.

'Sorry, mate,' Col yelled, 'but we don't allow anyone in here while we rehearse.'

'Well we coom in last Saterdee when yous war on,' the voice answered again. 'An' we tort yers were fookin' gear, mate. Me an' me mates 'ere are off ta *Maracosa* an' we tort yous would'n' mind if we 'ad a bit ofva listen fer a minute. Der yer mind or what?'

'Where are you from?' asked Tony.

'Liverpool, mate. Me two mates here are from 'Amburg and ta States.'

We took a break and called them down to the stage for a chat. Two of them were white, the other as black as Sammy's humour. I'd met other merchant seamen who'd come to Surf City and they'd all been great blokes. Lots of laughs and lots of information about the outside world we just didn't get from any other source.

'Ya want a beer, mate?' yelled Bluey.

'Ta,' the talkative one replied. 'Me name's Jimmy,' he said, sticking out his hand. 'Jimmy Prescott from Liverpool, an' teese are me mates, Candy an' Laz.'

We all shook hands and introduced ourselves.

Jimmy was in his late twenties, about five-eleven. He had a deep, dark tan, blond hair, deep green eyes and wore the best looking clothes I'd seen. His jeans were bell-bottoms, but not as wide as normal seamen's bells. Faded to a light blue, the cuffs had been cut and left to fray. They were the coolest thing I'd ever seen. So were his boots. The style was similar to a Flamenco dancer's, with a Cuban heel and stitching that ran down the centre from top to toe. His denim jacket was the same faded blue as his jeans and had the name 'Levi's' on a little patch on the pocket. None of us had ever seen Levi's before. Underneath his jacket he wore a bleached white T-shirt. Jimmy Prescott looked like something out of a James Dean movie, and way cool. He was as fit as a prize fighter and I could tell from his confident stance and body language that Jimmy was not someone to fuck with. But his big friendly smile melted any kind of menace.

Candy was a huge black man somewhere in his early forties, well over six feet tall and 250 pounds of pure muscle. With his short curly hair, jet black eyes and round and friendly face he was a dead ringer for a young Satchmo. He wore burgundy gaberdine pants and jacket, the pants cut straight and narrow. Like his pants, his waist-length jacket had a cream saddle-stitch around the pockets and seams. The ensemble was topped off by a pair of cream patent leather loafers and a matching cream silk shirt. His outfit was tailored to the max and, as Sammy would say, sharper than shark shit. Offering his massive hand, Candy introduced himself through a huge pearly white smile. I'd never seen teeth that white in my life.

'Hi, Joshua Alonzo Clemends, Shreveport, Louisiana. Chief steward on the United States ship *Maracosa*. Please call me Candy. Pleasure to meet y'all.'

On both his pinkie fingers Candy wore huge gold rings, each set with a gigantic white diamond. On his right wrist was about a pound of gold, hand-beaten into an ornate bracelet. Around his neck hung about two pounds of 24 carat gold chain.

His voice was so deep it was hard to understand him at first. Along with the rest of the band, I caught myself staring at this huge black man. This was the first Negro I'd ever actually met and from the rest of the band's faces I suspected it was also their first experience. Growing up in the suburbs of Brisbane I'd gone to school with Aboriginal kids. One of them was one of my best mates until the government pulled him out of Moorooka State school and forcibly relocated him and his family in some filthy camp fifty miles from where I lived. Many of the Aborigines I'd met were so black they were almost blue. But Aborigines were nothing like this man. They were mainly small and very shy. I loved them as a people, but they were a totally different race physically from the black man standing in front of me. This guy was physically imposing to say the least. He was absolutely magnificent and I couldn't take my eyes off him.

The third seaman was obviously a Kraut. Standing around six feet tall with snowy blond hair, bright blue eyes and deeply tanned skin, he was the perfect Aryan specimen that Hitler's twisted mania had fantasised would one day rule the universe. Laz was handsome, with a strong imperious jaw. An old scar ran from just under the corner of his left eye to the middle of his cheek, reminding me of the classic duelling scars sported by many a Prussian aristocrat at the turn of the century. Like theirs, Laz's scar obviously hadn't come from a friendly game of tiddlywinks. His build was athletic but a lot slimmer than Jimmy's and he could have easily blended in with the surfers at Bondi or any other Aussie beach. He was dressed almost exactly the same as Jimmy, the only difference being a black T-shirt and light brown open leather sandals.

'Gerday,' he said in a deep German accent, shaking all our hands and bowing imperially. 'I am Laszlo Horstz, from Hamburg, Deutschsland.'

It must have been a great picture with these big, fit, nail-pissing seamen and this bunch of skinny little guys, none of us being over five nine. I wasn't that old to start with, but in this company I looked and felt like a little boy. We got them each a cold beer and sat down together at a nearby table. Jimmy was the first to speak.

'Yeah, we coom in ta oother night when yer were playing an' it was fookin' great, man. It's ta first fookin' band I've 'eard 'ere tat can play. Yer riminded me ov 'ome, lads. Where'd ya get ya songs from? Soom're really gear.'

'Thanks a lot,' said Vince. 'Most of the stuff we play we found on records but Tony's written a couple for us.'

'Where'd y'all pick up on the Isley Brothers?' boomed Candy.

'I found one of their records in a shop in Brisbane,' I replied, 'but I haven't been able to get any more. It's really hard to find that stuff in Australia. Nobody's ever heard of people like that.'

'Av y're 'eard of ta Beatles, mate?' asked Jimmy, 'They're ta fookin gear. Scouses from Liverpool like me. Real fookin' nutters tey are, eh.'

'Yeah, Tony told us about them,' said Bluey. 'He's a Pom too.'

'Where yer from, Tony?' Jimmy asked.

'Norwich. I came out here five months ago.'

'Norritch, eh? Yeh I bin tere. Loov ta Norfolk Broads meself.'

'I lurve any kinds of broads, man,' Candy said, laughing, ''specially if they blonde, baby.'

We didn't make the double entendre, but I noticed Tony blush a little.

''Ave yer 'eard of ta Searchers, or Brian Poole and ta Tremeloes?' Jimmy quizzed.

'Yes,' said Tony, 'they were just starting to play around London when I left.'

'Aw t'ere fookin' gear too. What aboot Rufus Thomas or Jackie Wilson? 'Ave yer 'eard of 'Owlin Wolf or Muddy Waters at all?'

We all just looked at one another. 'Who?' said Col.

'Yer mean yer never 'eard of em? Jaiseuzz t'ere ta fookin' gear, man.'

'Yeah, Muddy's ma main man,' said Candy.

This was another language to us and we had no idea what the fuck they were talking about.

'Can you get us any of their records?' I asked Jimmy, intrigued.

'Sure,' he said with a smile, 'I might even 'ave some ont ta ship. If not I'll get soom when I'm in ta UK. Bring 'em back fer yer on me next trip.'

'Yeah, we'll be Stateside in six weeks,' said Candy. 'I'll see what I can find. We'll be back in a few months an' I'll bring y'all some blues, OK?'

'OK, great,' we all chimed excitedly.

'Jimmy, where'd you get those jeans?' I asked.

'Oh tese're American Levi's. Frayed 'em meself an drug em behint ta ship to fade 'em. Why?' he asked, a little puzzled.

'Why? 'Cause I want a pair, that's why! They're bloody great and so are the boots. They from the States too?'

'Ah noo, tese're frum Loondun. All ta boys wear 'em back 'ome. T'ere gear aint tey, eh?'

'They're mighty,' said Vince. 'How can I get a pair . . . and some of those jeans?'

'Me too,' I added.

'And me,' said Col.

'Fuckin' oath,' said Bluey.

The three seamen laughed. 'I'll tell yers what,' Jimmy said, 'are yer playin' tonight or what?'

'Yeah,' we all answered.

'Well, if yer gimme yer sizes I'll get yer soom when I'm 'ome. 'Ow's tat, eh?'

'Great, beaudy, fantastic,' we chorused.

'Tell you what,' said Candy, 'We've all signed on for the next trip to Orstralia. If James here can find the mothers, I'll put them on the ship's manifest and you can pay me when we get back. How's that sound?'

'Great, fantastic,' we all responded.

'Well, we're goona find soom birds an av a bit a foon, lads,' Jimmy said. 'So we'll see yer tonight, eh?'

'Yeah, I wan' me a big blonde young thang with big ta-tas,' laughed Candy.

'Tanks fer ta beer lads,' said Jimmy as they got up to leave.

'I'll give them yer names at the front door,' yelled Col as they were walking out. 'Your money's no good 'ere from now on.'

Although meeting the three of them had been an interesting experience, at that time there was no way of knowing just how important that meeting had been and what a significant impact they would have on our music and our future.

13
Only a Matter of Time

THE first moment I saw Joey, my warning bell rang.

Black eyes stared coldly out of his face, like a cobra's sizing up its prey. They said it all. These were not windows to any soul. He didn't look through them, he fed through them, devoured. The long twice-over he'd given Pepper and me that time in the Canberra Oriental Hotel lobby was unmistakable. Trouble!

He was, I'd guessed, Slavic. Probably Yugoslav by the heavy-set features. His hair slicked back with a ton of Brylcream, sat atop his hard, craggy face like a wet black cat on a piece of granite. His face, even from the slight first glance I got of him, was etched into my memory as if my brain had pushed all the buttons in my trouble bank and filed him away for easy reference.

Below the hard cliff of his forehead hung a pair of thick black eyebrows that sat at right angles to his face. His large Romanesque nose started as grooves of flesh between his eyes, then fell and fanned out into two wide nostrils. The bone was straight as a knife edge from bridge to tip. Deep grooves ran from his jutting cheekbones and ended at the corners of his downturned, twisted mouth. His thick jawbones exploded on impact into a chin that resembled the first two battered knuckles on a prize fighter's fist. Dark, swarthy skin was stretched over the frame of his face without elasticity, like a shark's. A smile would have torn him from his scalp to the nape of his skinny neck.

Although obviously formed by a combination and inbreeding of gypsy peasant stock that dated back to the Tartars, his face seemed more the result of some bizarre industrial artwork. As if a strong hand had taken him by the scruff of the neck and repeatedly slammed his face into a grindstone until the right amount of fear and evil had been forged. He was ugly to say the least, but it was the ugly that makes men wary and women wet.

The first time I'd seen him he'd been sitting down, but I could tell he was a hard boy. Wiry, thin, maybe five nine or ten, early to mid-twenties with the build of a long-distance runner. He was wearing a short-sleeved, tight black T-shirt and from his arms I could tell he was body fat zero. Just lean meat. Taut, tight muscle over hard tough bone. A coiled spring.

I'd noticed some kind of tattoo on one of his arms. A dagger or sword, maybe, I really couldn't tell. What stuck in my memory was the colour and style. It was the dirty blue, rough design that only comes from one place. It was a boob tattoo. A prison tattoo and it told me right away he'd done enough time to get an emblem to remember it by. Joey was a real piece of work. I'd seen him a couple of times at the Canberra since he gave Pepper and me the stare, and whenever I came by he just followed me menacingly with his snake eyes. Never said or did anything, just looked. I said hi to him once, but he ignored it so I let it slide as just another would-be. Then one day he was gone and I hadn't seen him since. I figured he'd just up and quit and I never gave him another thought. It hadn't been until Pepper told me Natalie's story that I'd found out he was hooning round the Cross, occasionally using the Canberra Oriental for his girls on the sly.

Pepper and I had been constant companions since that first night at the Pussycat. Apart from the gigs and rehearsals with the band we'd spent almost every day and night together. She cooked for me, pampered, purred and mothered over me. Neither of us could get enough of each other. She loved sex, loved being my teacher and I her pupil. Her body was a beautiful work of art and she loved to be watched and touched, revelling in my admiration. There was nothing dirty about any of it. It was exciting, stimulating, erotic and natural. One night Pepper brought home a copy of the *Kama Sutra* and we laughed at the pictures, then tried them all, one by one. Some of the positions felt like they had been written just for us and we tried them over and over, at times taking an hour or more to reach an exhausted climax that left us completely drained, falling asleep in each other's arms only to wake, eat, drink, then start all over again. I'd never even imagined anything like it. It was pure and she was perfect. Pepper had no inhibitions and I felt totally at ease. To her everything was natural. We were simply partners in the oldest dance of all. There was no shame, only a completely open, uninhibited libido with no holds barred. For the first time in my young life I understood the pure joy of it all.

If Pepper didn't cook we usually ate together up the Cross. Mostly at the Spaghetti Bar, a small Italian restaurant in Darlinghurst Road that sat between a florist and tobacconist a couple of doors down from Surf City. I'd become friendly with the young Italian bloke who owned the place. I loved spaghetti bolognese and Angelo's was the best I'd ever eaten. Angelo was a happy little bloke who sang while he cooked. He then served the customers himself, standing proudly next to the table waiting for the inevitable 'mmmm' that ensued after the first mouthful went down. My rave reviews brought a huge smile to his chubby face and invariably resulted in extra free servings and garlic bread. I liked him and could tell he liked me.

Although I'd been spending a lot of time at Pepper's place I still had my room at the Canberra Oriental. One night out of the blue, Pepper casually asked me to move in with her. There were no strings, no promises made or favours asked. She simply said, 'Why waste your money on a hotel room you don't use? Come and stay here wiv me, mate.' So I did, but insisted on splitting the rent and food. Because I was paid up for another two weeks at the hotel, I decided to keep a few things there and use the room if I needed it. A couple of times I spent the night, but I went back mainly to pick up clothes and bits and pieces of my stuff which was slowly making its way to Pepper's.

Living in the rhythm of the Cross, I'd become tuned to a night-shifter's schedule. This meant doing everything at least five hours behind the rest of the city. Eat breakfast at noon, rehearse one till five, lunch at six, gig with the band till around midnight, dinner around 1 a.m., home and round again for the next twenty-four.

It was heading towards October and still cold, windy

and occasionally wet. Some days a freezing wind howled up from the harbour, cutting through Darlinghurst like a knife, probing the narrow streets and lanes, searching for the next victim to chill to the bone. During those cold patches punters were scarce in the Cross and pickings thin. Most business took place on weekends when, regardless of the weather, they just had to make the pilgrimage for that little taste of the bent. Just enough to get them through the week. Stories to tell and laugh about with their mates during the straight, boring hours back in the tedious reality of earning a living.

Pepper was only working Thursdays, Fridays and Saturdays at the Pussycat and one week, because the band had been working so hard, John Harrigan let us take nearly a week off. We only played the Friday and Saturday nights, so decided to take a break from rehearsals and make the most of it. That meant a week of free fun time, and Pepper and I hit the town. Most of the clubs and bars were owned or run by the syndicate and Pepper knew all the managers. They all liked her and she was always welcome. Through her I'd got to know all of the main characters in the play and we enjoyed an open-door policy at practically every joint in the city. This meant free admission and usually free food and drinks. Our clock was set to sundown when the door to the day slowly closes, that neon one opens and through it step the night-shifters, rested and ready for another roll of the dice. That week, with one exception, Pepper and I never got to sleep until well after dawn.

Monday and Tuesday we'd partied so hard we slept until 5 p.m. on Wednesday. We ate an early evening breakfast at Pepper's and decided to hit a club or two after midnight. It was about eleven-thirty, cold and raining. We had gone over to the Spaghetti Bar before going down to hear the last set at the El Rocco, which was a super hip jazz club in a basement just off William Street, about a hundred yards down from the Cross. Sammy was sitting in with the band for the last set and he'd invited us both down as his guests.

The Spaghetti Bar was only a small place. Maybe fifty feet long by twenty wide. Along each wall sat half a dozen padded wooden booths, each one large enough to hold four people. All were decorated by the traditional sign of Italian food—a red and white plastic tablecloth over a laminex table. Large bare lightbulbs had been hand-painted a deep, flat yellow and their mellow light bounced off the cream coloured walls, giving a simple yet warm charm and atmosphere to the place. The only hint at interior design were dozens of large, wicker-wrapped chianti bottles that hung like ancient bunches of grapes from various places on the ceiling. From around them green plastic vines crept across the ceiling like a floral spider's web, extending out to the corners of the room and hanging in long loops like streamers at a child's birthday party.

To top it off, half a dozen wood-framed Italian travel posters hung at various angles on the walls. It was the usual stuff. Shots of an Al Italia jet winging its way across the skies above the Colosseum or the Tower of Pisa. Above the kitchen door at the back of the restaurant, Angelo had proudly draped his *pièce de résistance* . . . the red, white and green flag of Italy. Below it on the door frame, carved by hand, was the word 'Mamma'. Regardless of how crude Angelo's interior design may have appeared to the over-educated, discriminating, sophisticated, snobbish eye of a society decor perve, to me it gave a warm home-grown Mediterranean feel to the room. It was a great place to eat.

It felt cosy, happy and festive. With Italian opera softly playing through the sound system, it always felt inviting and comfortable, no matter what time.

''Ello Beel, 'ow are a you tonight? Where's a ma beeeyutiful Pepper?' Angelo said, giving me a big-brother hug as I walked in. 'Ahh, there a she is,' he beamed as she walked in behind me.

Every pair of eyes in the room, male and female, shot to her. They always did wherever she went. People would stop dead on the street and watch her walk by, turning until she was out of sight. Pepper was a redheaded stunner! Angelo gave her a big friendly hug, pecking her lovingly on her left and right cheeks, European style, like family. She returned his affection by taking his chubby face in both her hands and planting a big wet kiss on his cheek, which made his face blush as red as the lipstick heart she'd left there.

'Ah Beel, Beel, thees is a madonna. She's a bella madonna, mucho bella, mucho bella.'

In the classic Italian gesture, he brought the thumb and fingertips of his right hand together, put them to his lips and kissed them with a loud smack before throwing his hand open and away from his face as if tossing a ball into the air.

'Bella,' he said again.

I smiled and nodded in agreement. *Yes she is, isn't she*, I thought as he sat us at a booth.

There was no need to order. Angelo knew exactly what we wanted and he took off full of purpose to his tiny kitchen to prepare our food. A record of Caruso's 'O Sole Mio' was playing on the sound system and we could hear Angelo singing along as he cooked. Angelo loved his little restaurant.

Pepper and I were facing each other in one of the booths. I had my back to the door. She was laughing about something when I saw the expression on her face change. She seemed to stiffen slightly, but it was enough to make me turn around just in time to see him come slithering over to our table.

'Ey baby, where ju been?' Joey said greasily. 'Hav'n zeen ju round latly. I eer ju 'ad zom fon at ze Canbeera, eh?' His voice was as slimy as the wet black cat on his head, his tone lurid and menacing, showing Pepper no respect. Pepper just kept looking straight at me, ignoring him.

With an almost imperceptible shake of her head, her eyes closed ever so slightly and spoke to mine. 'Don't!' they said. 'It's OK, I'm cool.' The look Pepper had given me told me she was, and not to get involved. Joey the Hoon acted like I wasn't even in the fucking room, let alone sitting opposite her at the table. He was dressed entirely in black. Black leather jacket draped around his shoulders, black T-shirt, narrow-cut pants with a patent leather belt and matching Italian loafers. He looked every inch a pimp, right down to the big diamond ring on his right hand and the gold-hilted knife tucked in the waistband of his pants.

He stood there leaning between us, ignoring me, his right hand on the table, the smudged blue dagger on his forearm now clearly visible. I was right, a boob tattoo, unmistakable. His left hand rested behind Pepper's head on the back of the booth and he leant over closer to her and repeated his question.

'I zaid, where ju been baby? Whats amata, cat got jor leetle tongue, baby?'

Pepper showed no fear and kept her cool, still looking at me, ignoring him. This was pissing him off . . . and he was pissing me off. He was a bully, and I hate bullies.

I had always been the little kid at school, the one who regularly got his arse kicked, and one day I just had enough. I was ten when I joined the Brisbane Judo Academy which was owned and run by a sixth dan by the name of Geoff Gurtz. Geoff was a big, tough, lovable German who had not only been a combat instructor to the Belgian commandos, but had also trained the Dutchman Emile Gesink. Emile went on to be world champion, becoming the first white man to ever take the title from the Japanese, which completely freaked them out. Geoff took a real shine to me and I learned fast. With him as my instructor and mentor, I never got my arse kicked again. By age fifteen I held the rank of black belt in judo and brown cherry blossom in jujitsu, instructing the children's classes at the academy three times a week and teaching a judo class at Salisbury High School where I was a pupil. Geoff taught me traditional judo and jujitsu, and he also taught me how to fight combat-style, showed me every dirty technique a little guy like me needs to know to survive, and this prick Joey was rapidly becoming a candidate for a private lesson.

'She's been with me, man,' I said, trying to keep it cool. I didn't want to start a brawl in Angelo's restaurant, but I knew if Joey boy kept this up there was only one way it was going to go.

Without changing his stance, Joey moved his head slightly in my direction. 'And 'oo za fugg es zis lizzle cunt?' he said, his accent thick and guttural. ''E's a bit yong for ju ant he, baby?'

He looked me over and his snake eyes met my stare, then he turned back to Pepper and leant in even closer. It was then my alarm bell rang. His look had sized me up. Took in my age, size and baby face and figured I was a pushover. Thought if I stuck my head in he'd kick me around for a while. Be a big man. Impress Pepper by beating up on a kid. It's funny all the shit that goes through your head at a time like this.

Christ, I'm in a booth sitting down, can't get to him with my feet. What's his first move going to be? Forget that shit, keep your eyes on the knife! I know I can take it, but Pepper might get cut in the scuffle. What have I got I can use? No bottles on the table. Fuck! No knife on the table. Pepper's got a nailfile, but it's in her bag. Fuck! What? . . . What? Relax, relax!

It all went shooting through my brain in a couple of nanoseconds. I slowly undid my belt under the table and slid it out of the belt loops, wrapping it round my hand. The buckle was in my palm with the long buckle tooth sticking out between my first and second knuckle. I waited.

Joey kept it up. 'C'mon baby, ju still werin' zose lizzle white panties ju flash at Joey in the hotel, baby? C'mon baby, leeft up jor skirt unt give Joey a lizzle look. C'mon.'

He made a quick grab under the table but before his hand got to her crotch, or I could get at him, the plate Pepper had been holding in her left hand smashed flush into his face! It hit like a bus and rearranged Joey's nose forever. The sound on impact was like that of a wet bag of cement being dropped onto a water bed from ten feet.

The force of the blow shattered Joey's nose along with the plate and that once-straight nose was now sitting across his left cheek with jagged shards of plate sticking out of it. Slivers of plate were also sticking out of his face and right eye.

'Ju fuggin' beech,' he screamed. He staggered back from the table, moaning from the pain, both hands to his face. Blood was streaming from his eye and broken nose.

His right hand groped for the knife and I pulled myself out of the booth, but Pepper was already on her feet and quick as a flash, wham! She kicked him square in the nuts with her right foot. The shock wave hit Joey's balls first, bulging his eyes, then shot straight to his brain like a fucking freight train. The knife fell from his hand and Pepper kicked it out of reach under one of the booths. He dropped forward, gasping for breath, landing on all fours on the floor at her feet, groaning.

Joey was finished. Pepper wasn't!

Without missing a beat she grabbed a fork from an adjacent booth and brought it down from high over her head. Using both hands, she plunged it into Joey's back, screwing it a couple of times before letting go. The whole head of the fork buried in his flesh and he screamed in agony as it ripped the muscle and ligament high up on his right shoulder. She then stepped back and, with all her weight behind it, kicked him flush in the face with her right foot. His jaw shattered under the force, breaking with the sound of a bullwhip crack. His head shot back and he did a reverse flip and landed flat on his back, out cold. At this moment Caruso hit his crescendo with a high C, underscoring Joey's fate, and he lay there looking like a fresh black trophy rug on someone's living-room floor.

'You want to see my panties, you prick?' Pepper spat out. 'Well, here they are, see.'

With this Pepper turned around, lifted her skirt and gave him the arse, then stepped over him like the piece of shit he was.

'Come on, mate,' she said, taking my hand. 'Let's get out of here.'

I just stood there with my mouth open. I'd seen some

tough boys go at it from time to time, but I'd never seen anything like this. She sounded completely calm. It was as if we were just getting up off a park bench to go for a stroll. Joey was flat on his back, moaning. Blood poured from his face, forming a pool beneath his head. The front of his black T-shirt had now become a purple mess of blood from the fork, the prongs of which were now sticking out the front of his right shoulder, having been pushed through and up by the force of his fall when Pepper had drop-kicked him into a back flip. It had all happened so fast that nobody in the restaurant had moved. Like me, they were mesmerised, stunned at the speed with which this gorgeous young girl had reacted and dropped this street thug. She was magnificent. Shit, she was magnificent!

The sound of Joey's scream when Pepper stabbed him must have cut through the music and alerted Angelo that something was wrong. He came running through the restaurant just in time to see Pepper deliver the *coup de grâce* with her foot.

'Oh sheet, sheet,' he kept saying over and over. 'Oh sheet, sheet.' Then he said, 'Beel, you get 'er outta ere quick! I take care of . . . Go! Queeck! Before de coppas. *Go now!*'

I grabbed Pepper's hand and, along with the other dozen or so people in the restaurant, bolted out the door. The late-night clientele in Angelo's was not the kind who relished hanging around answering coppers' questions, especially about something like this. As one we just up and scattered in a dozen different directions.

It reminded me of a 'flying feed'. When I was a kid a group of us would go into a restaurant and eat, then get up and scatter out the door in different directions, leaving the bill on the table and the waiter pulling his hair out.

Hand in hand, Pepper and I belted down Darlinghurst Road, running full tilt past Surf City, around the corner, across Victoria Street, and into the lobby of the Canberra Oriental. Thank God I still had a room there. In the background I could hear the distant wail of police or ambulance sirens getting closer, but before they hit the Cross we were safely inside the hotel. There was nobody on the desk and we sprinted up the stairs to my room. My hand was shaking so badly I couldn't get the key in the fucking keyhole.

'Here, let me help you wiv that,' Pepper said coolly. 'Give me the key.'

She calmly opened the door, then strode across the room and sat on the edge of my bed by the window. Her hands between her legs, palms together, she rocked slowly back and forth, staring out at the street below. For a few moments, only the sounds from the streets broke the silence in the room. Car horns beeped, dogs barked and the sirens wailed louder and closer.

The lights from the flashing neon sign outside the window danced around inside the room like Puck in the forest. The colours backlit Pepper's form as she sat on the bed, making her red hair glow like the moon through the neon clouds, casting a flickering profile of her figure on the white walls and ceiling of the darkened room. It could have been the cover shot of a movie magazine. She was so beautiful and the star of the scene. For a moment I was carried away by the overwhelming sensuousness of the picture. Her beauty was always grabbing my attention at the strangest moments and for a second I forgot how we got here. Then my brain shot back into focus.

'Jesus Christ,' I yelled at her. 'You could have killed him!'

'Mate, if I'd wanted to kill him he'd be cold as yesterday's breakfast,' she replied, calmly lighting a cigarette. She took a long, deep pull, then blew out a cloud of smoke that caught the neon and added to her aura.

'Where the fuck did you learn to handle yourself like that?' I asked, still stunned by fighting skills that would have given Cassius Clay a fat.

'Raised on a farm wiv five bruvvers,' she said. 'Learnt how to protect myself real early on. Had to.'

It was the first time Pepper had mentioned anything about her past. Every time I'd asked she had quickly changed the subject. I figured she'd buried it for a reason and didn't want it dug up, not even by me. So I never pried. I was about to ask her if she was OK when she burst into tears and began sobbing violently.

'Oh shit,' she moaned. 'Oh shit, that greasy pig! That fucking greasy pig! He treats all the girls like they're his whores and some of them are so terrified of him they give him whatever he wants. And he likes to belt them around afterward. What a prick! What a low-life prick!'

I went over and sat next to her on the bed, putting my arms around her. I could smell the sweet scent of her breath as her warm tears trickled down my neck. I lay back on the bed holding her while she got it all cried out. She must have cried for five minutes without a word. The sobs came from way down deep and something about the way she cried told me that not all of her tears were for what had just happened, but for something in her past that it had brought screaming back. Something or someone had really hurt Pepper, and she couldn't keep it in any longer.

'They were always at me, putting their filfy hands up my dress or grabbing my boobs whenever Mum and Dad weren't around. Even when I was a little kid my big bruvver Mick tried to screw me! The low pig! I was only eight years old. Eight fucking years old . . . a child!' she sobbed. 'He was eighteen!

'One evening I was in the barn brushing my pony. He came up behind me and put his hand over my mouf. He was groping me wiv his filfy hands and holding me so tight I couldn't move. He got my pants down and was just about to do it when Mum called out from the house for dinner and he shit himself and let me go. He freatened to kill me, said he'd drown me in the dam if I ever told anyone. At the dinner table I started to cry uncontrollably. I couldn't stop. Mick was shitting himself. When I wouldn't tell Dad what was wrong he sent me to my room. I can still see the smirk on Mick's face 'cause he knew he'd got away wiv it. The pig! He never tried again and I never told anyone, even after he left home. One of my uvver bruvvers, Brian, tried it a couple of times too. I always managed to fight him off, but the grabbing and perving never stopped. I lived in a fucking nightmare for years.'

We lay there in the darkened hotel room with the neon light dancing around us. Naked rainbows of colour licked Pepper like fingers of fire, gently caressing her body and kissing her face. The lights seemed perfectly choreographed to the moment. Like some twisted lighting director was outside the window adding his own bizarre effects to the already dramatic scene. Pepper kept talking. I just sat in silence and listened.

'One night when I was just fifteen, Brian and a couple of his mates came home from the pub pissed as snakes. I was fast asleep upstairs but they woke me up wiv all their racket. It was raining hard but I heard them come into the house, stumbling around rotten drunk and they went into the kitchen. Drank some more.'

She paused, trying to catch her breath between the deep sobs.

'Mum and Dad were still at the pub watching some show and my bruvver and his mates kept on drinking and yahooing for a while, then it got real quiet. I knew what was coming. First I heard the stairs creak and their drunken giggling. Next minute they were outside, tapping on my bedroom door.

'"Pepper we got shomefing for ya. C'mon, we know ya wannit. C'monnnnn, have a drink with us, eh? We just wan a little Pepper on our eggs. Ha ha ha ha."

'I recognised the uvver voices as Paul Gillings and Jimmy Bretton, my bruvver's best mates. I could hear him revving them up saying, "She's got a beaut body 'n' tits, mate" and fings like that. I was dry retching with fear. I didn't know what to do. I pushed my dresser against the door and leant against it wiv all my strength, but it was no use. They forced it open and came staggering into my room, laughing and swearing, cans of beer in their hands, my bruvver still goading them on.

'Paul Gillings said, "C'mon, Pepper, show ush yer big tits. We jus wanna little perve. We won' hurt ya. C'mon, get her fuckin' gear orf." He creamed.

'I couldn't scream! Couldn't move! I was frozen scared. You know?

'The free of them circled me like wolves at the kill. I had no chance. They were saying awful disgusting fings to me and said "C'mon, we won't tell anybody." Then they grabbed me and frew me on my bed and tore off my nightie and pants. I tried to cover myself wiv the sheets but they

yanked them out of my hands and frew them on the floor.
They were grabbing my boobs and touching me wiv their
filfy hands, trying to get my legs open, all the time telling
me what they were going to do to me. I was terrified,
naked, and helpless. My bruvver just stood there laughing.
I pleaded wiv him to make them stop. I was screaming,
"Please, Brian, don't let them do this to me! Please make
them stop! I'm your sister! Make them stop! Make them
stop! Pleeease!" But he did nuffing to help me. Jimmy Bretton took his pants off first. He stood there swaying, rubbing himself and swigging beer from his can at the same
time. He said, "C'mon Pepper luff, ish time you 'ad a good
fuck. 'Oo yer saving it for, eh? We won 'urt yer, will we,
boysh?" They all laughed.

'My bruvver went round the uvver side of my bed and
grabbed my wrists, holding my arms over my head. I was
kicking wildly, struggling to get away, but Jimmy grabbed
my legs and dived on top of me. His weight knocked the
wind right out of me and I couldn't breave. I was pinned
down. His stinking booze breff was so rotten it made me
want to vomit. With his rough hands he pried my legs open
then rammed it in.

'I was a virgin and the pain was unbearable. I nearly
passed out! Oh God I wished I had! I wish I had! Then I
wouldn't have felt any of it. I wanted to die.'

Her tears were gushing now and she was gasping, trying
to talk in between the sobs.

'I was struggling, screaming for help, but wiv Brian
holding my arms I couldn't move. I just had to lay there wiv
my eyes shut tight wiv Jimmy on top of me, raping me and
grunting like the filfy pig he was. Then I stopped struggling
and the pain disappeared. A kind of numbness came over

me. I could feel him grunting and moaning on top of me but I felt like I was watching from somewhere else. I knew it was me, yet it wasn't, you know?'

I just nodded. There were no words to say.

'Then I felt somefing on my face. I opened my eyes and saw my bruvver was kneeling on the bed wiv his pants off, and he was trying to get it into my mouf. My fucking dirty filfy bruvver wasn't just helping his mates any more . . . he joined in himself to gang bang his young sister.

'That's when I lost it. Somefing snapped in my head and I just went off. I bit down on it really hard and held on. Brian was hitting me, punching me, yelling "Don't! I'm sorry, I'm sorry", trying to get away, but I still didn't let go. The harder he pulled the more damage I did. He was screaming in agony. Finally I couldn't hold on any longer and I let him go. I hurt him really bad and he fell off the bed half-unconscious from the pain. In all the noise and confusion Jimmy Bretton had stopped humping me. He was so drunk he didn't know what the fuck was happening. He was still laying on top of me, pinning me, looking over the bed trying to see what was the matter wiv Brian.

'By now my head was really clear on getting out of there and I didn't care what it took to do it. I reached up and grabbed Jimmy by his ears, then dug my fumbs into his eyes, right up to the joints. The bastard screamed like a stuck pig and fell off me, groping at his face wiv his hands as he fell. I rolled off the side of the bed and headed for the door on my hands and knees, but there was Paul Gilling swaying in front of me.

'Shit, he used to sit next to me in school! We were real good mates when we were kids. Now there he was, ready for his turn, blind, staggering drunk, standing naked between me and the door, wiv a hard-on. He grabbed me by the hair and forced my face against him.

'"While you're down there, luff," he laughed. I grabbed it like I was going to give him somefing and I was nice to him for a few seconds, then slowly got up wiv it still in my hand. He let go of my hair and tried to kiss me. I'll never forget the look on his face when I stepped back, still holding it, and kneed him full force in the balls. His eyes rolled back, he frew up all over himself and went out cold at the same time, felled like a tree wiv his dick in his hand.' She laughed. 'He looked so pafetic it was almost funny. He fell straight back and his head hit the corner of the dresser he'd help push away from my door.'

Pepper was laughing and crying at the same time by this stage. *Jesus, you've got heart,* I thought.

'Then I ran. The uvver two were still moaning, so I bolted out of the house. Ran stark naked frew the rain to my girlfriend's farm a couple of miles away. The branches and scrub cut me to pieces, but I didn't feel it, just kept running and running. I woke Shirley up by frowing stones at her window and she let me in. She wanted to call the cops but I wouldn't let her. I just wanted to get away from that place forever. She gave me some money, clothes, shoes and a bag and I walked ten miles in the rain and slept in the railway station all night. I caught the morning train to Sydney and I've never been back, and I'm never ever fucking going back. Those bastards! Those fucking dirty rotten bastards! If I ever went back I'd get a gun and kill 'em all! I swear. Even my bruvvers!'

I lay there flabbergasted, not knowing what to say. Pepper was shaking like a leaf and I was in tears. She had lived in hell for half her life but had escaped. The Cross had become her refuge. Unlike me, she wasn't here by choice. She simply had nowhere else to go. She had been a sexually abused fifteen-year-old country girl on the run from the worst enemy a person can have . . . the past. As beautiful as she was, God knows what horrors she'd gone through working at the Pussycat, when every leering glance and sexual innuendo must have brought it all back night after night. No wonder she seemed so streetwise for her age. She'd had the strength to confront her worst fears every night and in doing so had honed her attitude to a fine edge as her only defence mechanism against the one problem she knew was never going to go away as long as she was beautiful. Men!

In the short time we'd been together I'd never once seen any sign of anger or violence in her. Nothing. Not even a hint. I'd never heard her raise her voice in anger to anyone, even the couple of times I'd seen people piss her off. Pepper loved life, loved to have a good time and to party, but in my experience she was second to none when it came to gentleness and kindness. Sure she lived alone in the Cross and worked in a strip joint, but she was no rough tart. Far from it. If it wasn't for her inability to pronounce 'th', I wouldn't have been surprised to have first seen her starring in a Hollywood movie, or on television at some grand function on the arm of the King of England. Pepper was a princess.

All the ferocity, all the anger I'd witnessed in the restaurant now made sense to me. Joey had pushed the one button in Pepper that turned her primal. It was her brothers and their rapist mates that she'd attacked so violently. Joey had lit her fuse and she'd exploded. He never had a chance from the second he started his slime on her. Her tears were all gone now and she smiled at me.

'That was free and a half years ago,' she said. 'Except

for Shirley and Natalie you're the only one I've ever told. Apart from that night, which doesn't count, I've never been wiv anyone until you. Most men always treat me like shit. Joey's typical. Finks he's a big man. Comes in the club, orders a few drinks, tips me big and finks he can get into my pants. He's never got anywhere wiv me, mate, and that's what's pissed him off. They fink because I look like this and work in a club I'm an easy quick screw, that I don't have any feelings. But I do!'

'Then why the hell do you stay there?' I asked.

'Because I'm safe there,' she answered instantly. 'I like Wayne and Last Card. I trust them. They've never come onto me. They know I've had problems, even though they don't know what they are. They never asked any questions, just gave me a good paying job when I had nowhere else to go. They've always protected me like a daughter, looked after me when any mug goes too far.

'I've never had a boyfriend before. Until I met you, most men made me sick. Half the girls at the club fort I was a dyke because they'd never seen me wiv a man. I know you don't remember much of that first night after the Pussycat. You and Sammy got so pissed you could hardly scratch yourselves. But I do.'

She smiled at me.

'I remember every minute of it. Even when you got drunk you treated me like a lady and kept calling me miss. No-one ever called me miss before, my whole life. You were so polite. Never came on to me, never made the usual corny remarks. You were real shy and Wayne got a couple of the young strippers who fort you were cute to go over to your table and flash you, rub your leg and stuff to embarrass you, and they did. You don't remember any of it, do you?'

I was starting to wish I could.

'You and Sammy were having a great time. You were no trouble and had everybody in stitches. When it came time to leave all you wanted was to go home alone to get some sleep, but you couldn't remember where it was. You were really funny, mate. You fort you were still back in Brisbane living wiv your parents.'

She was laughing now and making me laugh too.

'You were so legless I told Sammy I'd take you to your hotel. But instead I took you back to my place. It was my choice, mate. I picked you. Even if I never saw you again I wanted you to be the *real* first. Jimmy Bretton may have taken my cherry when he raped me, but I *gave* my virginity to you. Nobody has ever treated me so gently. You're always such a young gentleman. You've made me feel like someone special for the first time in my life and I'd do anyfing for you, Bill, anyfing. I love you.'

She stroked my hair back off my face then kissed me so gently and lovingly that I felt a shudder go down my spine.

'Please don't ever hurt me, Bill, will you? I couldn't let anybody ever hurt me like that again. I know we mightn't stay togever forever, what wiv your music and everyfing. But as long as you want me I'm yours. If you want me.'

I thought my heart was going to burst. I was just seventeen years old. No woman, no girl, nobody had ever talked to me like this. To be saying these things to me after the story she had just told me touched me deeper than anything I had ever known. Pepper was very, very special.

I'm not going anywhere, I wanted to say, but the words just didn't come.

That's the first time Pepper ever mentioned love and the first time she had called me Bill instead of Billy. The way she'd said them both gave me a feeling I'd never had before. What could I say? There were no words. How could I respond to such honesty and depth of emotion? No amount of sympathy could assuage that kind of hurt. Only love eased such a deep pain and in the neon-filled hotel room, lying with Pepper in my arms, I realised in that moment that was exactly what I felt for her.

'I love you too, Pepper,' I whispered.

I felt her body shudder and go limp in my arms as she took my words inside her. It was as if she'd never heard them before and I realised that, given her miserable child-hood, she probably never had. We lay there in each other's arms for the rest of the night exchanging soft kisses and touches. No sex, no words, just loving caresses. It was magic. Moments a lifetime of experiences will never erase. The only intrusion into our bliss came and went like a scream in a child's dream. I heard the wailing of a distant siren and for a moment our perfect peace was shattered and the Spaghetti Bar came flashing back. Along with it came the thought that we hadn't seen the last of our friend Joey and I knew Pepper was smart enough to know it too. Joey couldn't go around the Cross acting tough Joe Cool with people knowing he'd been flattened by a young girl. To his kind it was the ultimate insult.

The word would have already spread round the vine. Joey had to save face. One way or another there had to be some payback. He was hurt bad and might be out of the picture for a while, but it's coming. Guaranteed. Only a matter of time . . .

14
A Wolf Amongst Lambs

EVERYTHING seemed to be happening so fast. New people, friends, events. The troubles with Jackie Marsh and Joey seemed long gone and everything was sweet as a nut. It was late October and I'd been living in the Irish just over four months. I'd met a great girl, joined four young blokes to form a hot new band that was packing them into Surf City and I was making some bucks. The roll was on!

As the weeks went by the crowds got bigger. One by one, some of Australia's famous older rockers and band members starting sticking their heads into Surf City to see for themselves what this thing was they'd all been hearing so much about. The undeniable reality they confronted must have scared the living shit out of them, because by its very nature it embodied every element of that unstoppable process called change. It undoubtedly shook the very foundation and heart of their trend- and youth-related stability. In a few short months they had become yesterday and they knew it.

Something new was happening, not only with the band and me, but in general everywhere. It was in the air and in the hearts and minds of the teenagers who came to see us night after night. It was the feeling of being a part of something indefinably new. We didn't know it at the time, but what we were all feeling was the strength of our numbers. We were many and just starting to get a sense of it and of the fact that we had our own tastes and the power to satisfy them. The baby boomers were going to have their say and, once we discovered the right words, it was going to be one of the loudest statements ever heard. In late 1963 the word forming in the minds of everyone between the ages of twelve and twenty was 'US'. We just hadn't said it yet. There seemed to be an electricity to everything. No connection to past or future, just the inescapable, unpredictable excitement of the new now. The times they were definitely a-changin' and everyone could feel it, whether they liked it or not. We felt like lead riders on an electric wave that had an energy and power all its own. It swept people up as it rolled, carrying them and us at a dizzying speed with an intensity that seemed to build weekly. The wave was nowhere near ready to peak and miles from some unknown future beach where it must eventually crash in a spectacular display of violent energy and beauty, finally dumping all but the most serious or lucky riders back on their arses into the boring depths of normality.

Of course no-one caught up in such a wave has any time to consider its direction or eventual end, only the luscious, heady euphoria of the ride itself. It's better than sex and, believe me, with someone like Pepper to make the comparison vivid, I didn't come to that conclusion lightly.

Pepper was great to be with, so supportive and as

excited as I was about the way things were going. She understood I needed to work hard and, more importantly, that I needed the two things she always deprived me of— my strength and sleep. We both worked nights, came home and got up late. I rehearsed all afternoon, so our personal lives seemed to be squeezed into the spare moments in between. I still spent most of my non-working time with Pepper and she popped into Surf City most nights on her breaks, always escorted by her new admirer Ivan the Ox.

Pepper had never once treated Ivan like the bumbling oaf most people took him for. Ivan was not used to kind and respectful treatment from women, especially from one who looked like Pepper. It was obvious he adored her, but not in any complicated way, just as a kind and beautiful friend. The way Pepper looked, she was guaranteed a hassle coming into Surf City alone at night to watch me play. I don't mean she would get heavied, just hit on by every unattached bloke with a dick. Without being asked, Ivan became her unofficial protector and although I hadn't realised it, in his mind he'd also become mine.

It was Saturday night at Surf City. We'd played two one-hour sets and were taking a break before the third and final performance of the night. As usual we had a quick beer in the dressing-room, then went out and talked to the punters. I knew a lot of the regulars on a first-name basis and some were becoming good friends. The audience in general loved the fact that we obviously weren't up ourselves about all that was going on. They got a big kick out of the fact that we hung out with the crowd, and that they could come up and talk about songs, music, racehorses, midgets, whatever. We were one of them and they loved it, and we welcomed their acceptance.

American and French navy boats were in port, docked down at Woolloomooloo. Business was booming in the Cross and there were quite a few sailors in Surf City that week. White American gob caps and French sailor hats with their red pompoms danced frantically around the room in the purple-black light, looking like fluorescent fireflies on speed. I was about to go back on stage when Jacky Pie, one of the regular young knockabouts, told me he'd seen Pepper down at the Darlingston Police station about twenty minutes earlier. She'd asked him to let me know when he came in. Now I couldn't just waltz out of the gig and leave the band dick in hand in front of a couple of thousand people, so I went on stage, did the last set, changed my clothes, then headed off to see if I could find Pepper. It was about one-thirty when I got to the Darlingston nick but Pepper was gone. The first person I ran into as I walked in was Sergeant Brian O'Malley.

'You looking for Pepper?' he asked. 'She left nearly two hours ago. She was pretty upset, poor girl . . . Bloody horrible thing.'

'What happened?' I asked. He grabbed my arm and pulled me over to the corner of the room.

'Son, we found the body of a young girl in the harbour yesterday and I thought Pepper might be able to help us with our enquiries. She's not in any trouble, just a routine identification.'

'What made you think Pepper could help?'

'One of my constables thought he saw the dead girl talking to her a few weeks ago.'

'What!'

'Yep,' O'Malley said. 'It's the first break I've had in a year.'

'A year of what?' I asked.

'Murders,' he answered matter of factly.

'Shit!'

'Shit's right, son, that's exactly what it is, some deep, diabolical shit to say the least. Look, I'd rather not talk about it here. Why don't we go somewhere quiet. I'd like to talk to you about it too. Maybe you knew the girl. Maybe she came into Surf City. Seeing you're here, would you mind taking a look before we go? It's just downstairs. Won't take long. You got a weak stomach or anything, son?' the big sergeant asked. ''Cause this isn't going to be very pleasant for either one of us.'

I'd seen a couple of dead bodies in the past. One the victim of a motorbike accident with his handlebars jammed through his head; the other, what was left of a man after the fish had got to his eyes and face in the Brisbane River. But nothing had prepared me for what I was about to see.

I followed Sergeant O'Malley down a flight of stairs and into a morgue of some kind. It looked exactly like the ones I'd seen in so many Hollywood movies, all squeaky clean with dissection tables, drip trays and big silver wall fridges set one atop the other like drawers in a Kafka-esque filing cabinet. We were met by some guy in a white coat. I don't remember his name or what he looked like, my heart was beating two-twenty, my mind already in shock from the smell of formaldehyde and whatever I was about to see. We went over to one of Kafka's fridges and the assistant opened it and pulled out a long tray, revealing a semi-clear plastic bodybag with a naked corpse inside. He pulled back the zipper and my lunch hit the floor.

'It's all right, son, happens to most people, even me now and then,' the sergeant said, handing me a roll of paper towels. 'Here, why don't you go into the bathroom and clean yourself up? We'll be here when you're ready.'

When I got back, I took a deep breath and another look. The autopsy had obviously already taken place because what had once been her chest was now a gaping cavity extending from her throat to below her navel. Her ribs were separated down the centre, the gutted interior looking just like the torsos of cattle I'd seen on hooks in butcher shops. My head started to swim again and I leant against the table to steady myself.

'I know this isn't easy, son,' said the Sarge. 'You OK?'

'Yeah, I'll be all right. It's just bloody horrible, that's all.' I took a couple of deep breaths before having another look.

Even in her shocking condition I could tell the dead girl had been young, very young, and had once been pretty. I say once because her beauty, like her life, was now a thing of the past. The right side of her face was almost gone. From her lip line up, only a fish-eaten eye, torn cartilage and cheekbones remained. It looked as if some huge hand had taken a handful and ripped it away. Even though she'd been in the water, thick congealed blood stuck to her pale blonde hair and face like honey to a blanket. The left side of her face was unmarked except for a bruise around her eye, which was frozen wide in a terrified stare, witness to the final horror she had endured. A deep, clean cut ran from just below her left ear, clear across her throat to the top of her right collarbone. The wound was clean and so deep it revealed the inside of her throat, larynx and wind pipe, right through to the top of her spinal column. Her murderer had almost decapitated her.

'Fuck!' I said, horrified.

'That's not all,' said the Sarge.

The assistant carefully pulled the tray all the way out and peeled the bag partly back, gently turning the naked body over on its left side. The skin on her back was covered with cuts and bruises. The wounds reminded me of those I'd seen in photos of concentration camp victims, the flesh literally torn from their bones after they'd been whipped to death by sadistic guards.

'Jesus, she's been whipped, hasn't she?' I said.

'Looks that way, son. Now take a look at this,' O'Malley said.

The assistant lifted one of the corpse's arms, turning it slightly for me to get a better look. I saw a deep, dark, bluish bruise or burn mark encircling the wrist.

'What's that?' I asked him.

'Looks like cuff marks or rope burns. The medical examiner seems to think she was strung up by her wrists when she died. They think she was killed sometime last Thursday night. They also found traces of heroin and amphetamine in her blood.'

'Did Pepper see all this?' I asked.

'I didn't show her the back or wrists. She didn't need to see any of that, but she was still pretty upset. A constable took her up to St Vincent's for a tranquilliser shot afterwards, then dropped her at her flat. She seemed to be OK by the time she got home. She's a tough little sheila, isn't she?'

I just nodded. I was still in shock myself. 'Did she know the girl?' I asked.

'Yep,' said the Sarge, 'but not well. Seems to think her name's Brenda Cox or Coggs. Used to hook from time to time. Pepper only met her once or twice. Have you seen her before?'

'No, sergeant, I don't think . . . Wait a minute, I did meet her once. She was hangin' around outside the Spaghetti Bar late one night and said hello to Pepper as we left.'

'OK,' the sergeant said to the assistant, 'that will be all.'

We walked up towards the Cross together and I was grateful for the fresh night air. How the hell anybody can wake up, have a family breakfast, kiss the wife and kids goodbye and go merrily off to work everyday in a joint like that is beyond me. I'd rather shovel shit. The big sergeant and I walked without saying a word to each other. We headed along Darlinghurst Road, past St Vincent's Hospital and down a narrow lane, entering a little bar by the back entrance. He seemed to know the place and nodded to the barman.

''Ow ya goin, Sarge?' the bloke said, nodding back.

'All right, Norm.'

As we entered a couple of knockabouts deftly took it on the toe out the front door. They must have spotted O'Malley come walking in and suddenly remembered they'd left the iron on at home.

'I'll be seeing ya real soon, Frankie me boy,' the sergeant shouted at one of them as he shot out the door. 'Bloody mugs,' he said to himself.

We sat at a quiet table in the back and he ordered a couple of cappuccinos and a large cognac. Norm brought them over, put them on the table and told O'Malley that they were on the house.

'Thanks, mate, appreciate it.'

'No worries. Just give us a yell if you want another.'

'Here son, I know it's after hours and you're under age and all that,' the Sarge said, pushing the cognac over to me, 'but it's sweet. You look like you need it. This will fix your guts. I fancy one myself but I'm still on duty.'

I shot the whole glass. The warm liquor hit my throat, its kick and aroma clearing the fog I'd been in since the zipper went down on the bodybag. The sergeant handed me a brown manila folder and asked me to take a look inside. I opened the top and pulled out about a dozen colour photos, all of them gruesome after-death pictures of two young girls. I scanned the shots. They seemed to be roughly the same age as the body I'd just viewed, but neither of the lifeless, cold, death-mask young faces rang a bell.

'Do you know either of them, son?'

'No, Sarge, I'm happy to say I don't, but I notice they're blondes like the one we just saw. Is there some connection or what?'

'Some people don't think so, but I do. It's more than bloody coincidence that over the last fifteen months, approximately four to five months apart, the bodies of three pretty young blondes turned up in the harbour. 'Course there's some bloody connection! Has to be. None of them have been reported missing. None of them appear to have any immediate family. And they've all been seen around the Cross and Darlinghurst area. We've had quite a few bodies, male and female, turn up in the harbour over the years. That's not unusual in a harbour as big as this. So mix these girls in with those others and it doesn't seem that peculiar, but I dunno. My right ear gets itchy when something's not right and I started scratching the bludger the minute I saw Brenda's body. They could have been bloody sisters by the look of them.'

He scratched his ear absent-mindedly as he spoke.

'The homicide boys think these girls are just random.

You know, kids that have gotten into the game or something. Got with a tough crew or boyfriend. It happens in a city the size of Sydney. Those two don't appear to have been beaten or murdered. "Could've been the sharks," one young mug detective said. So they are officially recorded as suicides.

'Suicide and sharks my Irish arse!' he said. 'Something stinks here, I bloody know it! Don't know what yet, but it'll come . . . it'll bloody come. I think we've got a bloody wolf on the prowl. Anyhow, I've got to get back to the station. Thanks for your time and thank Pepper again for me, will you? And don't talk to anyone about these photos, son. No-one, not even Pepper! After what she went through I didn't want to scare the shit out of her right now. I'll ask her about the others in due course. For now this is between you and me, so let's keep it that way, OK? I want you to do something else for me, son.'

'What?' I asked.

'Look, I think I can trust you. You're not like the mugs that hang round this neighbourhood. I just want you to keep your eyes and ears open, eh? You're in the Cross every night. You may see things you don't know you've seen. So stay on your toes. I think there's a real dangerous bastard on the loose out there and I need all the help I can get. Some of the lazy bludgers I work with couldn't find their dicks in the dark. I'm sticking my neck out telling you some of this, but now you know you might pick up something I'd never get to.'

''Nother round, Sarge?' Norm asked from behind the bar.

'No thanks, mate,' O'Malley said, then turned back to me. 'Look, son, I'm not asking you to be a fiz. You know what I mean, be a grass.'

I nodded.

'Some of the young blokes who hang around Surf City are petty crims but they're harmless. I'm not interested in them. I'm not asking you to give up ya mates, but it's murder I'm talking about. So keep your eyes and ears open. And let's keep this little talk between us?'

I nodded again. 'OK, Sarge, whatever you say.'

'You all right now, son?'

'I'll be fine Sarge, but . . .'

'But what?'

'Well, I wouldn't mind another one of those cognacs if that's OK.'

'Not some Irish in you is there, boy?' He laughed, then ordered me another drink, gathered up the photos and left through the back door.

I sat there for a while, sipping my cognac. *Now I'm an undercover fucking rock singer*, I thought. *Jesus, this is getting weirder by the minute.*

By the end of the second cognac I felt much better and I headed straight home to see how Pepper was. The TV was blaring and every light in the place was on. Pepper was out cold on the couch, sleeping like an angel. I went to the bedroom, pulled the cover off the bed, covered her with it and let her enjoy her peace. I turned everything off, poured myself a beer and sat in the dark by the window, watching the late-night stragglers making their way down Bayswater Road five floors below. As I sat there trying to get the image of the dead girl out of my mind, something occurred to me. This was the second time in a couple of months that Senior Sergeant Brian O'Malley of the Darlingston police had asked me to keep something a secret. Why?

At some stage I happened to look up and caught sight of

someone at a window on the eighth floor of Bayswater Courts across the street. I couldn't tell who it was, or whether it was a male or female. I gave them a casual wave and they quickly closed the blinds. I didn't think any more of it, just someone having a stickybeak.

The next day Pepper woke at around one in the afternoon. She seemed fine when I asked her about the previous night.

'I freaked out when the coppers arrived at the Pussycat,' she said. 'I didn't know what was happening and neiver did Wayne. He fort they were going to nick me, but Sergeant O'Malley came in and explained and everyfing was all right. Jesus, she looked awful, didn't she? How sad, how terribly sad . . . a young girl like that. It could have been me. Oh God, it's awful. It wasn't the way she looked that upset me as much as the fact that I knew her. I've never known anybody before that's been murdered. Gives me the bloody willies. Makes you feel like you're connected or somefing. You know what I mean?'

'Yes, mate, I do. It gave me the creeps too, but you told the Sarge everything you know and he's happy, so just get it out of your head.'

'I'll be all right,' she said.

I knew she would. She had balls of steel.

'But there's one fing I didn't tell him, Bill.'

'What do you mean?' I asked. 'Something about the dead girl?'

'Well, yes.'

'What?'

'She came into Surf City now and then,' Pepper said. 'She used to take her breaks and come in and listen to the band. I saw her there the night they fink she was killed.'

'Oh shit! Why the hell didn't you tell the Sarge?' I asked.

'Didn't want to involve you, that's all. You know, have the coppers sniffing round the place and the band and stuff.'

'Well, I told him I saw her once. Remember, outside the Spaghetti Bar.'

'Shit, I forgot about that.'

'He has to know, mate,' I said. 'You never know, it could have been someone she met at Surf City that topped her. This is some gruesome shit and I don't think we should screw around with the sergeant on this. He seems like a real straight bloke. What do you think?'

'Yeah, he does, doesn't he,' she said. 'Have you got the phone number? I'll give him a call right now.'

Pepper called him and told him the rest of the story. At first he was really pissed off that she'd lied, then he cooled and took it all down. Said he wanted to talk to her again.

'He asked me not to tell anybody else, Bill,' she said.

'Yeah, he asked me to keep it quiet too. I wonder what he's up to.'

'Don't know. Expect he knows what he's doing. Don't you?'

'Hope so, mate,' I replied.

15
Welcome to Candy's Place

IT had been a while since we'd seen Jimmy Prescott and the boys from the good ship *Maracosa* and the band eagerly looked forward to their next visit. In the few days they'd spent in Sydney on the last trip they'd come to Surf City every night. Their exotic tales and knowledge of musicians we'd never heard of both fascinated and intrigued us. In that short visit they'd helped establish our first real connection to the outside world. A world that, according to their stories, was changing as fast as the one we knew in Australia. I'd had a couple of cards from Jimmy from places like Turkey and Mexico. The last one I'd received was dated 2 August. He'd sent it from San Francisco and said he'd be back in Sydney soon.

Time had been flying by for all of us and we were no longer an unknown band working on a sound and looking for an audience. All the work had turned us into a tight rocking unit and our style was starting to attract more and more attention as the weeks sped by.

The new English music scene had started to impact on Australia. The Beatles' 'From Me to You' had been a hit and it was obvious Tony's prediction about them would come true. Some of the other bands that Jimmy and Tony had told us about had also started to become popular in Oz. For the first time we felt a connection with the rest of the world and a pride in knowing we were part of a revolution that was changing the face of music. We were the first in Australia, but other young bands started to spring up.

The new influences not only came from people like Jimmy Prescott but from other young European migrants like Tony who were now bringing the new styles with them. Bands were forming in migrant camps in places like Elizabeth in South Australia and, although they didn't form until later in 1964, five young Scottish and Dutch kids who later became one of Australia's most popular '60s groups, the Easybeats, had been getting their thing together in a migrant hostel. As fate would have it, when we met for the first time Tony recognised them from the same place he'd been living at before he joined the Aztecs and we both ended up on the same record label.

The emergence of other bands not only contributed to the growth of the local scene but made for healthy, friendly competition that only made us all strive harder to be the best. One afternoon we were packing up after rehearsal when in strolled Jimmy and Candy. 'G'day, boys. 'Ow are yer?' Jimmy yelled from the back of the room.

We ran down the stairs from the stage, dying to see what the two large boxes they were carrying contained.

'Is that our stuff?' I asked like a little kid.

''Ang on! 'Ang on!' laughed Jimmy as we gathered

around them. 'Don't we git a fookin' 'allo and 'ow arya, boys? Would yer like a beer fairst or nuttin'?'

'Damn right,' said Candy. 'We swam a long way to get here with this shit and the goddamn sharks nearly got my black ass a coupla times on the way.'

We all broke up and shook hands while Bluey raced off to the fridge and got a couple of cold ones for them.

'Tat's a bit fookin' better,' said Jimmy after taking a long pull on his stubbie.

'Goddamn mother's milk,' Candy sighed, 'Outside of Germany this is the best Goddamn brew on the planet. Now let's see what we got here, shall we?' He and Jimmy undid the two big boxes they'd brought with them.

'Now Candy got yer soom Levi's 'n' jackets in San Fran and I got yer boots when we wuz in Loondun,' said Jimmy. 'We dragged ta fookin' denims behint ta boat all ta fookin' way from Colombo ta fade 'em nice fer yers. So if tere's fookin' 'oles in 'em yer can blame ta fookin' sharks.'

From the happy looks on their faces we could tell they were as excited about this as we were and couldn't wait to see us in the stuff they'd brought.

We all grabbed our new things and started unwrapping them.

'Fuckin' grouse,' said Bluey as he unfolded his Levi jeans and jacket.

'These boots are fantastic,' Vince shouted as he eagerly tried them on.

I swear we were like a bunch of kids on Christmas morning as we all tried on our new things. Tony was excited too, but of course had to go to the dressing-room to drop his daks. No public showing of the crusties for him. Not like the rest of us who had dropped our gear on the spot, unable to wait to get into our new stuff. Everything was the right fit and we all stood there admiring each other.

'You look so smooth, if a fly lands on ya it's gonna break it's leg,' Candy said and we all broke up.

'Yeah yer look fookin' gear in tem outfits,' Jimmy added. 'Ta fookin' sheilas will cream. Do we git ower cut of ta leftovers or what?'

It was unbelievable how different the new clothes made us look. Apart from Jimmy, we'd never seen anyone wearing bell-bottom Levi's and Spanish boots before.

'Now yer'll 'ave ter fray ta bottoms of tem bells or yer'll be squares,' said Jimmy. 'It's all ta rage in Loondun and yer've got to 'ave 'em frayed if yer wanter be in, like.'

Tony came waltzing down the stairs in his new gear and we all whistled and laughed, but somehow it didn't look right on him. The clothes made him look like he was trying to get a look. They seemed perfectly natural on everybody else, but a work outfit didn't seem right on Tony. We told him how good it looked anyway.

'Listen, boys,' said Candy. 'We're having a little wingding on the *Maracosa* tonight and y'all are invited if you wanna come as my guests.'

'I'd love to,' I said. 'We're not working tonight either.'

'Ah shit,' Bluey moaned. 'It's me mate's twenty-first and we're throwing him a party in Hornsby. What a bastard.'

'Yeah,' said Vince. 'Col and I are going as well.'

'What about you, Tone?' Jimmy asked.

'You're fuckin' kidding, aren't ya?' said Bluey. 'Tony at a party! Shit, he might have a good time.'

'Oh no, thank you very much,' Tony said politely. 'I'm not much for parties. I'd like to have a quiet night at home tonight, I think. We've been rehearsing hard and we've got a big weekend coming up. But thank you anyway.'

'Suit yourself, brother,' Candy told him, 'but you're most welcome if you decide to change your mind.'

'Thank you,' Tony said again.

Candy shrugged. 'Well, Billy, looks like you'll be holding the fort for the boys.'

'Ah fuck!' said Bluey in disgust. 'Fuck! The *Maracosa*! Shit!'

'Now Billy, there's just one little thing,' said Candy. 'Can you organise some broads? Let me tell you what's happening. The first officer is an old navy buddy. We served together in the Pacific during the big one. A lot of people have dead-ended on this trip and there's a lot of cabin space. The captain's ashore and we've got permission to throw an upper-deck crew party. Jack Little, that's my buddy, is going to let us have one of the big rooms and it should be a gas.' He rubbed his hands together. 'You ain't been to a party till you been to one of the Candy man's champagne parties.'

'Ah shit!' Bluey said again.

'Now some of the other guys are bringing broads but there's gonna be a shortage. Do you think you and Pepper can organise any or what?'

'For a champagne party on the *Maracosa*?' I laughed. 'You're fucking kidding, aren't you?'

'Whatd'ya mean?'

'I mean if Pepper drops this one on the girls the bartenders will be the only ones working in the Cross tonight, that's what.'

And so the plans were laid. Candy organised a password for us, which would get us on board with no hassles. Pepper hit the phone to some of her girlfriends and it was on! She had to be cool who she asked because if word about this hit the streets there would be a line a mile long and we could blow the whole thing. So Pepper swore everyone to secrecy and told them, 'no stray blokes or boyfriends.'

The *Maracosa*, a huge luxury liner of some 50,000 tons, was moored at her usual spot at the Woolloomooloo docks, just half a mile down from the Cross. She was equipped to carry about a thousand passengers plus crew but tonight, except for a few stay-aboards, we would have the ship to ourselves.

We arrived at about eleven-thirty and 'I'm looking for Candy's place' got us straight on board. No hassles. A handsome black American seaman in an immaculate beige suit and loafers introduced himself as Buddy Bronson and escorted us up to the sports deck, where the party was already well under way. As Buddy took us along the deck and through one of the big hatches into a small, elegantly decorated lobby I could hear some great blues music playing and the sound of people having a ball. We then went through two floor-to-ceiling, mirror-shined brass doors into the nightclub. The place jammed with over a hundred laughing, chattering people.

With the club positioned at the rear of the upper sports deck, the view that greeted us as we entered was the most spectacular I had ever seen.

The far edge of the semicircular room, which was about sixty feet wide at its axis and seventy feet long at its straight inboard centre, was rimmed with floor-to-ceiling French doors which allowed an unobstructed view out onto the main aft deck below and, beyond that, to the harbour. Through the left side the magnificent Sydney Harbour Bridge stood out like some giant alien dirigible hovering silently in the night sky. Ahead of us, over the stern, lay Sydney Harbour and the twinkling lights of the north shore; to the right, the brightly illuminated Woolloomooloo docks and naval yards, the lights of Macleay Street, the glow from the dancing neon of Kings Cross and the lights of Elizabeth Bay.

The rear section of the club was about two or three feet higher than where we stood and separated from the lower part by an ornate, brass rail and three wide sets of stairs. Inside the brass railing and around the far edges of the room, laughing people sat sipping cocktails on plush velvet chairs and large, red-leather, studded Chesterfield couches.

We stood just inside the entrance. To our right, a huge semicircular bar, packed with people, stretched to the far side of the room. On the second level, couples danced on a raised, circular dance floor which was also surrounded by a brass rail. From beneath its smoked glass floor a rainbow of lights danced in time with hundreds of tiny coloured spotlights around the edges of the ceiling, all moving in perfect sync with the pulsing rhythm pumping out of the sound system.

The *pièce de résistance* was a magnificent, domed glass ceiling. From light years away, through a cloudless, deep blue Australian night sky, shone the heavenly light of a million twinkling stars. It passed effortlessly through the ceiling to find its final resting place in the eyes of the happy revellers in the *Maracosa* nightclub.

The overall effect was breathtaking and Pepper and I stood there trying to take it all in.

The club was elegant, spectacular like nothing I'd ever seen in my life, and happening big time. As soon as we got inside Buddy shot off to find Candy and Jimmy. Pepper and

I wandered around the club with our mouths open and slowly made our way over to a couple of chairs by the doors on the upper level. The boys came dancing through the crowd, drinks in hand and looking sharp. Candy was dressed in a cream wool suit, black shirt, black tie and cream loafers. Jimmy was in all black with a black tie.

'Welcome to Candy's Place, great you could make it,' said Candy as he shook my hand. 'Hi, baby,' he said to Pepper, kissing her hand.

'Great to see yer, Pepper,' Jimmy gave her a peck on the cheek.

'What about me, you arsehole?' I said.

''Oo notices an oogly ponce like you wen soomwun tat looks like Pepper cooms in ta room?' laughed Jimmy. Pepper was dressed in a tight-fitting, over-the-knee, strapless, dark green, shantung evening dress and matching shoes. Looking gorgeous as always.

Candy took off for the bar and brought back a bottle and some glasses. 'Here you are, my friends.' He put a bottle of Dom Perignon and two glasses on the table. 'Time's a wastin'.'

'Did you organise some broads?' Candy asked as he popped the bottle. 'We're a bit short on females.'

Just as she was about to answer I heard 'Pepper! . . . Hey Pepper!' and turned to see Natalie standing down near the bar, beaming at us with about fifteen of the best sorts in Sydney.

'Goddamn! I am in lurve!' Candy called out, letching at a gorgeous young blonde with huge tits. 'Scayoos meee,' he said as he shot over to her.

'Jeezus,' said Jimmy. 'when yer deliver, you fookin' deliver!'

'Christ, Pepper, who are they?' I asked.

'Well, you know Natalie of course, and that's Penny, Jasmine and Monica from the club,' she said, pointing to the group. 'And those free are models from June Dally Watkins. There's a few working girls too, but they're having a charity night tonight.'

'How come you never introduced me to any of them?'

'What, and have you raced off?' She laughed, squeezing my bum.

They were all knockouts! Guys started milling around them, offering them drinks and one by one they paired off. Natalie swayed over to Pepper and me and, keeping her eyes on mine, gave Pepper a big hug and a kiss on the cheek.

'Are you gonna share him tonight or what?' she said, rolling her tongue round her lips and winking at me.

Oh boy! my dick said.

'Down, boy!' I heard Pepper say and we all hugged and laughed.

Pepper and I could tell that Natalie had her warm, cotton-candy buzz going, but she didn't look stoned and nobody else would notice. Natalie didn't pair off with anybody, preferring to hang with Pepper and me, which was just fine. She was a million laughs to be with. Of course she kept getting hit on by hopefuls, but either politely manoeuvred around them or dragged me onto the dance floor and made like we'd just come back from a dirty weekend in a sleazy motel. Sometimes the three of us danced together and I was the envy of every bloke in the room. They were all wondering who the hell this young kid was to have not just one, but the two best sorts in the place all over him. I lapped it up.

By 2 a.m. the party was kicking hard and loud and Candy was the life of it. Several times he took a girl onto the dance floor to give an impromptu performance. *And Candy could dance!* He jived and jitterbugged like a pro, spinning the girls and expertly throwing them up in the air and catching them. The crowd applauded wildly and the vibe was fantastic. I spotted Jimmy from time to time slow dancing and smooching with one of the models, both lost in their own private little reverie. These girls were a long way from the type that either Candy or Jimmy normally met when ashore but they acted like perfect gentlemen and the girls obviously loved them. Champagne was flowing like water and the whole place, including us, had a real buzz going. As the champagne got to Pepper and Natalie they got more and more lecherous with me and the game Natalie had been playing started to get serious. She was dressed all in black as usual, looking ravishing in her short, black, crepe, strapless evening dress, black stockings and black silk-covered high heels.

I was sitting on a stool at the bar, talking and laughing with Candy and some of his shipboard mates when Natalie came up behind me, pressed herself against my back, put her arms around me and held my hands.

'Tonight's the night, Billy boy,' she whispered. 'I dressed specially for you.' She brought my right hand around behind me in the dark and slipped it up under the front of her dress. I felt a garter belt, stockings and . . . no panties.

Oh oh! said my dick.

'I'm going to make your eyes water tonight,' Natalie whispered as she squeezed her legs closed on my hand.

They were watering already! Pepper must have been watching Natalie coming on to me because the next minute she was behind me, kissing me passionately on the neck.

'Where's your hand?' she asked and I whispered that Natalie was naked under her dress. When Pepper heard this she took off.

'Oh shit,' I said. 'She's spat the dummy.' I pulled my hand back.

'Bullshit,' Natalie replied.

Pepper came back about a minute later.

'Neither am I,' she said.

'What?' I asked.

'Wearing any undies,' she whispered. Squeezing in beside me she took my hand and put it between her legs. 'See!' she giggled.

Seeing Pepper do this, Natalie squeezed in on the other side, grabbed my free hand and put it back in its original position. There I was sitting at a bar full of people, grinning like a fucking idiot at the bartender, Pepper hard against me on one side and Natalie on the other, with my hands between their naked thighs.

My dick couldn't think of anything to say. I was dick-tied!

They both had their arms around my neck and their heads on my shoulders, making little mmmming sounds in my ear as I stroked their nakedness. I thought I was going to pass out on the fucking bar stool and Pepper whispered, 'You're making me horny, Bill.'

Natalie heard her, wiggled her hips and giggled. 'What do you mean making?'

'Ooh doesn't this feel good, Bill?' Pepper asked sexily, kissing my ear.

I started to mumble something, then caught my reflection in the mirror behind the bar. It was packed and dark and nobody could see what was really going on. In the mirror it just looked like two girls coming on to some lucky grinning fool.

'Well, I think little Billy's about to burst his trousers,' Natalie whispered, looking at Pepper in the mirror and winking. 'Now it's only early, Bill, and you better save your strength,' she giggled. 'We're going to have a dance and you can just sit here and think about us out there on the dance floor together with no undies on. Be a good boy.'

'O-O-OK,' I managed to whimper.

They kissed me on the cheek and took off giggling. Here I am, seventeen years old with two of the most beautiful girls in the world, both naked under their dresses and letching over me like I was Steve McQueen. *Where did I go right?*

'Having a good time?' asked Candy, snatching me back to reality.

'Having a fucking great time, boss.'

'Yeah, I thought so.' He laughed knowingly. 'Listen, I've got something down in my cabin I'd like to show you. The girls would probably enjoy it too. Why don't you grab them and follow me down. Meet me over at the door in five. Cool?'

'Cool,' I replied.

After a lot of giggling, whispering and arse-grabbing, I finally got the girls off the dance floor and we waited for Candy who appeared a short time later with his little blonde. Jimmy had his model and two couples I didn't know with him. We took an elevator down to F deck, then walked down through a series of walkways and hatches to get to Candy's cabin. All the way down in the elevator, Natalie and Pepper were grinning at me like Cheshire cats. We were the last ones out of the elevator, with me at the rear of the pack. As we walked along the dimly lit cabin-way Natalie slowly lifted the back of her dress revealing her black suspenders, stockings and gorgeous white bum. Seeing Natalie doing it, Pepper lifted hers. I crept up and flicked them on their bare arses with the backs of my fingers and they both screamed, dropping their dresses.

Jesus, Candy, I thought, *whatever you've got to show me had better be bloody good to beat this.*

Candy's cabin had none of the luxury of the club we'd been in. It was a barebones, basic crew cabin, painted flat grey with a bunk, sink and small porthole which must have been underwater when the ship was loaded. I supposed it very similar to the other crew quarters on the giant ship. The eleven of us squeezed in and I ended up sitting on the end of the bunk with Pepper on one knee and Natalie on the other. The soft nakedness beneath their dresses was obvious as they pressed against my knees.

'Mmmm, this is a good start,' Natalie whispered as she wiggled her bum on my knee.

'Behave yourself,' Pepper whispered back as we tried to keep from cracking up.

Candy went around to various cupboards and pulled bits and pieces out of each one. The pieces all seemed to fit together and when assembled made a hookah with a water bowl and four long pipes. I'd only ever seen one in pictures and the significance of what it was didn't hit me at first.

'Oh goodie,' said Natalie, excitedly wiggling her bum again.

Candy half-filled the water bowl with some Jack Daniels and began to pack the little bowl on top with some red looking stuff. He then lit it by puffing like a maniac on one of the tubes. Smoke poured through the jack and into his lungs as he took several giant hits, then passed the other pipes to Pepper, Natalie and me.

Well I've never been backward at being forward so I followed Candy's example by taking a gigantic hit off the pipe. The smoke hit my lungs and I thought I was going to die. I burst into a coughing fit and the whole room started laughing.

'Easy there, Cool,' said Candy. 'That's some of the best Afghan red money can buy. You ever smoked before?'

'No-ho,' I choked.

'Shit, son, I thought you had. Sorry! Now take it easy, Cool. Just some gentle puffs and you be feelin' fine.'

I took another puff. This time Pepper and Natalie joined me on the other two pipes and away we went. It's impossible to describe the sensation it gave me, just as it's impossible to describe the feeling of climaxing. All I can say is I loved it and by the look on her face so did Pepper. Natalie had obviously done it before and expertly took several hits, passing the pipes around to the others. The whole room seemed to take on an eerie glow and a beautifully warm feeling engulfed me. I looked at Pepper who was sitting on the floor, swaying gently from side to side and grinning. Natalie was sitting next to her. She glanced over to me and licked her lips seductively. Pepper got up and came over to me.

'Have you ever done this before?'

'Nope,' I managed to say.

'Neither have I . . . Bill, I feel great, don't you?' She asked and gave me a squeeze.

'Yep,' is about all I could manage. I was totally fucked-up on one hit. We both started giggling like little kids and so did half the room. The feeling was so contagious we all ended up laughing until we cried. I couldn't stop.

'OK, folks, we better get back to the party,' Candy said. 'Now y'all are my special guests and I want you to keep this cool between us. Cool?'

'Cool,' we all replied.

'Now listen! I've got some keys here to four staterooms. Billy, you take one. Here Jimmy, here's one,' and so on to the others. 'Each of these rooms has a couple of bedrooms. If the party goes late I've OK'd it for you guys to stay aboard, but nobody else. Unerstan'? If the captain finds out bout this it's my ass! I've organised visitor passes for y'all and they'll be in the cabins. If you stay on board don't leave till after ten-thirty and be cool! One of my buddies'll be on the watch and y'all will have nooo problems. So enjoy, my friends, the night is still young and there's a helluva party up there a-waitin'!

'Now come on, y'all,' said Candy. 'Let's party!'

We all giggled our way back upstairs to the club. Natalie letched all the way and Pepper flashed me once when nobody was looking, but I was gone and just grinned through the hash haze like an idiot. The vibe upstairs hadn't changed and people clapped when they saw Candy walk back in.

'Ah, my public lurves me,' he laughed and took off for the centre of the dance floor, dragging Natalie and Pepper with him. It was fine when he spun Pepper because her dress was tight, but every time Natalie went around her skirt flew high, you could see the lot and a giant cheer went up. I was laughing my arse off and so was Pepper. Natalie didn't give a shit and just danced away, having an absolute ball.

'Jesus, my son, that's a fucking a bayutiful bum,' said the voice. I looked around.

'Sammy!' I shouted, happy to see him. 'Where have you been, man?'

'Well Sir Gil, my brother knight,' he said. 'I, Sir Ponson, have been sailing on a similar vessel prrrotecting the high seas from marauding pirates with acts of naktie naktie with a crap handle and malik.'

'Wwwhhaaat?' I laughed.

'My son, I've been on the good ship *Fairstar* entertaining for the last six weeks. Bloody great gig. Went all up round the islands. It was a fuckina greata, my son, and it's a bloody good to see you. I hear you bin killin' 'em with the band, you bludger.'

'Yeah, mate, things have been great. How the hell did you get here?'

'Ah my son, de bayutiful Pepper she called and invited me as a surprise a to you.'

I looked over at Pepper and she blew me a kiss. Both she and Natalie were slow dancing with Candy to some blues song I'd never heard before. She looked beautiful and blew Sammy and me another big kiss.

'Eh Bill, you look shitfaced, my son,' Sammy laughed. 'You gotta eyes like a two pissholes in the snow.'

'Ah just too much champagne, Sam,' I lied, still ripped to the gills from the hash.

'Jesus, there's some very serious crackatorious here! What's the story?' He gazed around the room.

'Hang on,' I told him. 'I'll be right back.'

One of the girls Pepper had brought was sitting in a corner surrounded by horny blokes. I could see she was no street hooker, more like a five hundred quid a night callgirl. The guys weren't exactly hassling her but I could tell she'd be happy to be rescued.

'Sammy's here, babe,' I shouted as I walked up. 'He's over by the bar.' She picked it up in a heartbeat and jumped up, giving me a kiss on the cheek.

'Thanks, mate. My name's Nikki. You're Billy, aren't you?'

'How did you know that?'

'Oh, Natalie told me all about you.'

I explained that Sammy was a good friend and invited her to come over and meet him.

'Billy, I'd be delighted!'

'Sammy, my son,' I said, 'this is Nikki, and she just told me that she's got a thing for men of the cloth. So if you've got that back-to-front collar, whack it on, 'cause Nikki wants to see God tonight.'

'Bless you, my son. Bless you,' he said, crossing me and grinning from ear to ear. 'Come, my child, let us partake of the festive spirit followed by some serious quaffing of the liquid elixir,' he said to her and whisked her onto the dance floor. Natalie came over to me and said Candy had given her a joint and why don't we go and smoke it.

'What's a joint?' I asked. She burst out laughing and told me.

'Oh,' I said, 'a joooiiint.' Like I knew. I'd never heard of a joint before in my life.

'No thanks, mate, I'll pass. I'm buzzing like a lightbulb as it is.'

'Ah come on,' she said, pouting. 'Let's get high.'

'If I get any higher, mate, you'll have to scrape me off the bloody ceiling.'

'OK.' She smiled. 'Suit yourself, mate, but I'll be outside if you change your mind. Now you keep your hands to yourself.' She grinned and walked through the large French doors onto the deck.

The party had hit fever pitch and a couple of girls from the Pussycat started doing their thing on the dance floor. It must have been contagious because other girls got up and started grinding out of their gear. Before I knew it there were about a dozen ripping sorts dancing naked. One of them was Nikki. She climbed up on a table and stripped stark bollickers down to her high heels and, to my amazement, Father Sammy climbed up with her and started getting his gear off as well. Soon he was down to nothing but his shoes, socks and vicar's collar and the whole place was in hysterics, cheering and clapping him along. He was such a funny character there was nothing lurid about his display. He was hilarious wiggling his fat little bum at the crowd with his little dingle bouncing in time to the music. Someone handed him a bottle of champers which he proceeded to skol. That put him right over the top and with Nikki in his arms he fell off the table into the laughing crowd. Everybody in the place was crying with laughter. Clambering back on the table, naked Father Samuel began blessing the crowd, the ship, Candy, me, Pepper and anybody he could think of, yelling 'My father beat your father at dominoes! . . . Bless you my son, bless you my daughter' at the top of his lungs. Pouring champagne on his hands he crossed the air, anointing us all pontifically. He was ridiculously funny. By this time Pepper and Natalie were with me, laughing and clapping along at Sammy's antics.

'Jesus, Sammy's having a good time, isn't he,' I yelled at Pepper.

'Ssshld be,' slurred Natalie.

'Why?' I yelled back.

''Cause h'smoked most of that bloody joint on 'is own. That's why. He's never smoked a joint in his li-i-i-fe,' she mumbled. By the way Natalie was talking I could tell that the other half of the joint was not the only thing she'd had in the last fifteen minutes. She was whacked out of her mind.

Sammy and Nikki were now giving a full performance, arms around each other's waist, doing Rockets-style high kicks in unison while turning in circles. Every time one of Sammy's legs went up his balls bounced along in time, which was breaking everybody up even more. Suddenly Sammy stopped dead. As if prompted by some divine inspiration, he threw his arms up in the air and leapt off the table. 'Yehaaaah!' he screamed with a rebel yell and, bottle in hand, he ran through the cheering crowd, squirting people with champagne. He ran right around the club, bounced off a Chesterfield couch and then shot up in the air, hurtled through the French doors, bounced off a deckchair between two amazed couples and flew straight over the side of the fucking ship!

The place went silent, then into hysterics. Candy got on a microphone and told everybody to quieten down and stay inside. Pepper, Jimmy, Candy and I ran out onto the deck expecting to see a dead Sammy floating in the water. As we looked over the side we all went from a state of terror to shitting ourselves laughing. There, backstroking around like a baby in his bathwater, bottle still in hand, swam little Father Sammy. He looked up at us waving frantically, shouting.

'It's the fucking cacko pestorious in here, my son! Come on in, my children. I Sir Ponson shall baptise thee! This is the fucking cacko!'

He was backstroking around in the dark water like a drunken Esther Williams. Candy was in hysterics at first, then freaked and called someone on a deck phone to get Sammy out of the water and into a cabin to dry him off before someone reported a crazed, naked, swearing, drunken priest swimming around in Sydney Harbour. It was now about four-thirty and obvious that Candy's Place had started to get out of hand. Given the amount of champagne flowing, it didn't surprise me one bit. We went back inside and Candy got on the microphone again, politely asking everyone to finish up because 'Candy's Place be closin' in fifteen.'

'Aaaaawww,' went the crowd, and then applauded. Candy took a bow.

'My pleasure, folks. Now goodnight y'all.'

Pepper and I were both really wobbly, but managed to go with Candy to check on Sammy. He'd been put to bed in one of the staterooms and we found him sleeping like a baby, still clutching his empty champagne bottle like a teddy bear.

The next morning I woke up in a stateroom bed with Pepper on one side of me and, to my surprise, Natalie on the other. We were all dreadfully hung-over, moaning and holding our heads. Pepper and Natalie started playing grab arse with me under the sheets, but it was just fun and games. I felt so bad I'd never felt less like sex in my life. To do it would be to die in pain. I was sure that nothing had happened between us because we were all so far gone by the time we got to the cabin. I seemed to remember Natalie being so out of it Pepper had to undress her and put her to bed. Pepper and I had sort of letched drunkenly at each other for a while, but we had passed out cold in the middle of it. Natalie must have woken up alone and crawled into bed with us at some stage and I assumed we'd all slept together like innocent babes.

Then Natalie started saying things like, 'C'mmmonn, Bill, you didn't play hard to get a couple of hours ago! You loved it.' From the grin on Pepper's face I could tell that I must have, but I couldn't remember a thing.

'You two took advantage of a helpless, innocent, unconscious young boy and didn't even have the decency to wake me up?'

'Yeah, and you loved every bloody second of it too,' Pepper said. She was laughing but holding her head in pain.

Think! think! said my dick, but nothing. I was so hungover I couldn't remember a bloody thing!

We got ourselves together, got dressed and searched the ship to collect Father Samuel. When we finally found his bloody cabin, the bludger had already left. Struggling blindly through endless corridors, suffering a dreadful champagne hangover, we managed to find the exit, only to experience near death as we walked out into the painfully blinding midday sun. Hands desperately shading our eyes, and half-crawling down the gangway, we mumbled some sort of goodbye to the watch. Then arm-in-arm, the three of us staggered through the 'Loo, up Macleay Street to the Cross, and fell into the first chemist we came to for a hangover draught, which in 1963 was a legal over-the-counter liquid combination of amphetamine and aspirin guaranteed to bring even the deadest brain cell back to life.

Powww!

We finally made it to Darlinghurst Road and cut through the rest of the fog with mondo cups of steaming black coffee, followed by a huge greasy breakfast at the Hasty Tasty. By one-thirty we were raring to party again.

That night Natalie moved in with us.

16
Hormone Heaven

I'D thought about Jackie Marsh, the murders and Sergeant Brian O'Malley a couple of times, but as the Sarge hadn't contacted me I had no reason to call him. I assumed that all was sweet and he didn't need my help after all. The day after the morgue incident, Pepper had gone to Darlingston and gave him a full statement and a description of the guy she'd seen with Brenda Cox at Surf City, then spent a couple of hours looking through mug shots, but she had no idea who he was and hadn't seen him since. The Sarge showed her the other two girls but she didn't know them and that seemed to be that. The last time I'd seen him was up the Cross one afternoon about a month back. He'd only spoken briefly about the murders, telling me, 'no more bodies have turned up, thank God,' but to still keep my eyes and ears open.

It was mid-December 1963 and Christmas was almost here.

Apart from a couple of brief love affairs, Natalie had been living with Pepper and me since the *Maracosa* party and the times she spent with us were fantastic. No, not just that! Although there was plenty of that! Some fun and games of course, but we were best mates. Pepper and Natalie had never had anything sexual going on between them in the past and they didn't now. It was never suggested and just seemed to be that way. As Pepper had said, she wasn't gay. It didn't interest her on her own, but with Natalie and me it might be fun . . . and it was. *Oh it was!* Natalie understood Pepper and I were ultimately a couple and didn't try to get between us emotionally. For all of us it was a first-time experience living as a threesome and it definitely had its moments. Outside of the band I was a very private person and none of the Aztecs had any idea what was going on. As far as they and most other people were concerned, I simply shared a flat with two girls.

I was still really a kid, but I sure felt like I'd grown up fast since I'd hit the Cross only six months before. Living with two girls can do that to you. It's one of the greatest experiences any male can have. Particularly with two girls as funny, entertaining, street-smart and drop-dead gorgeous as Pepper and Natalie. I never got used to waking up in the morning between these two stunning girls and had to pinch myself to see I wasn't dreaming. As soon as they woke up I knew I was awake all right! I also never got used to them being around the apartment just in their underwear. It drove me crazy.

It was an incredibly hot December and the apartment was humid day and night. As a consequence, neither of them wore very much and I was in a constant state of arousal. This must have been obvious to them because all I usually wore was a T-shirt and bathers and there was no way to camouflage my perpetual erection. They both knew I loved to see them in sexy lingerie and they loved to wear it and show off. It turned into a sort of private game. Pepper and Natalie went to great lengths shopping for silk stockings, suspenders, bodices and lingerie to please me, and themselves, and we all got off on it. It was la théâtre erotique. *Oh I do love the theatre!*

I believe most women have this side to their personality and it's healthy to act it out once in a while. Pepper and Natalie had no inhibitions whatsoever about living the fantasy and expressing that side of themselves whenever they felt like it. If that was seven days a week sometimes, well Hell Hoss, it was j-u-r-s-t fine by me, boy! They were so damn healthy they near killed me. We were kids having fun together and we knew that this relationship wasn't going to last forever. We simply decided to enjoy it all to the maximum while it did.

I'd get a phone call during rehearsal at Surf City. 'Hello,' I'd say. 'Who is it?'

'Hi, Billy. Um, it's me,' Pepper's sexy voice would reply. 'I'm finking about you. I've just rubbed myself all over wiv oil. I'm sitting here wearing a new, white lace, silk bra and panties wiv a matching garter belt, and I'm putting on my stockings and heels. Are you going to be long?'

'Whaaaat?'

'White lace . . . oil . . . stockings and heels,' she whispered down the phone. 'And what would you like my girlfriend to wear?'

'Er, guys,' I shouted to the band. 'Got an emergency! Gotta go! Can you rehearse without me for a while? See you tonight!' Zooom!

Other times I'd be sitting on the couch watching television and out they'd vamp without warning, dressed in some new skimpy lace outfit or another. They'd slow dance erotically together until none of us could stand it any longer. I'd often come home from rehearsal to find them both dressed in lingerie, stockings and heels, either making dinner or just sitting around reading the newspaper like it was perfectly normal. There's not a straight man alive who wouldn't swap ten years of his life for one month of the experience I was having. Money definitely can't buy the real thing. This kind of ménage à trois is every honest, straight man's deepest fantasy and I was living it twenty-four-seven! I was seventeen years old and in Hormone Heaven.

We didn't need the outside world much and when not working spent most of our time together at home. Whenever we did go out it was usually to a club like Checkers, the Latin Quarter or some upmarket restaurant and they both dressed up like fashion models. Sometimes Natalie would wear a black, tailored man's suit with a shirt and tie. That really fucked people up bad. Many times they went to the ladies room and came back and dropped their panties in my lap. I'd find myself sitting between them in a booth in some fashionable restaurant full of people, with my hands between their legs and theirs between mine. We'd all get so hot we'd sprint out without touching our meal and grab a cab straight home. It was a thoroughly disgusting way to act and I loved every second of it! The rosy glow never wore off and I felt like a lucky bookmark pressed contentedly between the two best pages of a *Playboy* pictorial.

It was a very sensual experience to say the least, but also so much more. The relationship between us helped us all grow as people. As an only child I'd had no experience living with brothers and sisters or of sharing in that respect. Sharing had a different connotation to me, but this all felt perfectly natural and in a way the three of us had become a family. We ate together, bathed together, slept, lived and made love together. We shared everything. Pepper and Natalie were great friends with no hang-ups or petty jealousies about each other. We were so relaxed around each other that sometimes they were oblivious to the fact I was even there, let alone a male. At times watching either of them just pottering around being girls, I felt privileged to be a witness to the female of the species at its absolute finest. They were great people. I was their closest friend and they mine. I was included in all their girl talk and learnt what made them tick. I learnt about, and how to appreciate, women on a completely different level. In fact that time with Pepper and Natalie taught me how to relate to, relax with, and be myself around females for the rest of my life, and it taught me to respect all women.

Natalie was still getting high but she never let it intrude into our lives. She never took a hit around us. None of the greaseball dealers ever came around the flat and she never tried to get us into it. I never saw her as out of it as she'd been that night on the *Maracosa*. She was often in her gentle little cottonwool world but it didn't bug us. We talked with her a lot about her habit and she genuinely wanted to kick but didn't know how. She cried about it to us sometimes and we would hold her and soothe her pain, but we knew that her future was a bleak old campaign, and she knew it too. If there is such a thing as the devil, it's smack. It's one of the purest forms of evil and robs you of your very soul. Smack controls you like an evil master and you'll do anything to please it. I'd never seen pain until I'd watched a junkie suffer and there's only one cure for it, that's why they're junkies. They don't shoot to get high, they shoot to stay sane.

So it was a great moment for Pepper and me when we finally convinced Natalie she had to go into a clinic to kick clean. And she did. She never touched heroin from that day on and didn't need any substitutes. She was loved straight and began working her arse off at the Silver Spade to save enough money to go to Europe, which had been her dream since long before we'd met. Like I said, Natalie had a couple of affairs during all this. Both times she was convinced she was in love, only to come home aching. After she got straight Natalie seemed to lose the need to chase after love and was content being with Pepper and me. We occasionally had some old friends around, but not that often. Some people found our relationship weird, so we were very cool about who we brought into it.

I'd run into old Dulcie from time to time and bought her a drink or a meal. She filled me with rich information about her life in the Cross and not long before Christmas the girls invited her over to dinner. She was a sweet old girl and both Pepper and Natalie loved her. I knew she had a house in the 'Loo and wasn't living on the street, but dressed in her trademark old baggy jeans, sweatshirt and beaten-up sneakers she was a sad and lonely old soul and looked impoverished. When we asked her over her eyes welled up with tears. 'Oh yes please!' she said. 'Oh you darlins.'

During the dinner she had us in stitches about the old days in the Cross. She'd lived there all her life and knew its history back to the settlement. She knew where all the bodies were buried, sometimes in the literal sense. There was nothing happened in the Cross that Dulcie didn't know about. Other people heard the street drum, but Dulcie heard the whole bloody band! She'd been telling us for the second time about when Peter Finch lived up the Cross in the late 'thirties. It was one of her favourite stories.

''E lived on eleven different couches in eleven months, mate,' she said. 'An' one of 'em was mine.' She laughed. 'Ooh 'e was a pretty boy. 'E made love like a stallion. Couldn't believe it when I 'eard 'e was a poof! Still don't. Jesus, 'e didn't act like no poof when ole Dulcie tinkled 'is winkie!' Cackle, cackle, cough, cough, belch. 'Oh dear! They was great times, great times, me darlin's. Ya mind if I 'ave another scotch? Hey hey hey, I think I'm sobering up. Tried to quit drinkin' once years ago. Worst bloody three hours of me life.' She laughed.

Dulcie was a classic and had us all rolling around in stitches.

''Ow's them sailor friends of yorn, Billy? You know, the ones off that *Marcoota*?' she asked.

'*Maracosa*,' I said.

'That's what I said, *Marcoota*. Well 'ow are they, eh, nice blokes or what? I 'eard they brung yous some stuff with 'em last time. They sounds like nice boys, eh?'

Jesus, how good's your radar?

'Saw one of 'em in a pub with an 'ore one night. 'Aving a great old chinwag they was. Over price, looked like. No 'fense, Natalie. You never belonged on the game in the first place.'

Dulcie had the pulse all right!

'None taken, darl,' Natalie said and she meant it. She knew Dulcie had done her time on the boardwalk too, a long time ago, and some of it was for food.

'Which one was it, Dulce?' I asked.

'Which one was it what?' she asked, eyeing the second bottle of Cutty.

'Which seaman did you see?'

'Oh darl,' she said, 'I ain't seen no semen in years! Past all that.'

'Not s-e-m-e-n, Dulce!' Pepper spelt out, pissing herself. 'You know, s-e-a-m-e-n, sailors.'

'Oh sailors. Why dinya say so? It was that big blond bloke with the snowy 'ead.'

'Oh, Laz,' I said. 'Yeah, he's always after some Theodore.'

'No, not the Kraut, mate, t'other one.'

'Jimmy?'

'Yeah, 'im,' she said knowingly. 'Must've come ta terms cause 'e left with her, 'e did.' She nodded her head. 'Speakin' of 'ores, that reminds me. I 'eard that ratbag Joey rattled Angelo's cage a coupla times afta you giv 'im an 'idin',' she said to Pepper.

'What do you mean, Dulce?' I asked.

'Aw, threatened to kick 'is 'ead in fer 'elpin' out that night. You know, when 'e straightened it with the coppers fer yers.'

'That figures,' I said. 'Might have to ask Ivan or Jean-Pierre to stick their heads in on Angelo from time to time. What do you think?' I asked Pepper.

'Yes,' she said. 'If that prick ever does Angelo any harm, I'll *kill* him.' She was close to tears.

It was the first time since that night in the Spaghetti Bar I'd seen that side of Pepper come back and I knew she meant it.

'He won't,' I told her, hoping it was true. 'Don't worry, mate. It's just talk.'

The three of us had run into Joey the Hoon once or twice. He was still hooning molls, still kicking back dirty coppers, still the same low greaseball. His once proud gypsy nose now hung sadly flat on his face like a half-filled condom and he was no longer a pretty boy. When he saw me with not only Pepper, but Natalie as well, his black eyes spat fire, veins stood out on his skinny neck, and his granite face twisted, distorted with rage.

Remembering Natalie's giant brothers, knowing Ivan's reputation, and that Jean-Pierre would kick his head off his shoulders, seemed to keep his arse in line and he never really hassled us. Just the occasional cursing in a tongue we didn't understand anyway. We were all part of the Cross family. Everybody knew what had gone down and Joey was smart enough to figure that if anything happened to us there were some very heavy people who would immediately shove his wet black cat of a hairdo in his slimy hoon arse. I'd expected some sort of payback after he got out of hospital but none had come, at least not so far. Still, Joey definitely was the type with a long memory.

'What about a nice cold glass of champers, Pep?' Natalie asked. 'How about you, Bill, and Dulce?'

'Yes please,' Pepper and I replied.

'No thanks, darl. Mind if I 'ave another scotch instead?' said Dulcie and finished the first bottle.

Natalie poured us a glass each and Dulcie kept talking.

'Ya know 'oo else I seen creepin' around?' she asked.

'No, who?'

'That ugly fuckin' dyke Jackie Marsh.'

'What! Where?' I asked.

'Oh, mostly on Victoria Street. Can't stay away from 'er old place'f employment, I s'pose?' Cackle, cackle, wheeze.

'Oh dear! She's a bad'un, she is. Shot her old 'oon's dick right bloody orf in the street just fer talkin' to anotha sheila. Then sat on the steps 'n' watched the poor bludger bleed ta death. Bad business all right. I always stay clear of 'er. She likes to trip old girls like me just to watch 'em fall an 'urt 'emselves.' She shook her head.

'It's an ill wind I tell yas. An ill bloody wind wot brings that bitch back round. She's upta summit, I bloody know it! Wouldn't be 'angin' round 'ere if she weren't!'

'Keep your eyes open, Dulce, and let me know if you see her again,' I said.

'Always open, darl.'

'I might have to give our friend Mr O'Malley a call,' I said. 'He'd definitely like to know.'

'Yeah, 'e wants 'er tits in a jar,' laughed Dulce.

Christ! I thought. *Is there anything she doesn't know about in the Cross?*

'You're more of a prize than we ever realised, Dulcie my darling,' I said and gave her a big hug and kiss on the cheek. 'Now close your eyes, the girls have got a little surprise for you.'

'What . . . What surprise?'

'Oh it's not much,' lied Natalie, 'It's just that it's nearly Christmas and we got you a little present, that's all.'

'Now close your eyes and put your hands out,' said Pepper. 'There's a good girl.'

Old Dulcie, all eighty-seven years of her, put her arms straight out with her palms up, scrunching her face up tight like a four-year-old. Her expression touched us all and when Natalie put the present in her arms Dulcie could hardly lift it. She opened her eyes and the look on her old face brought us all unstuck.

'Oh my Lord. My Lord. Oh sweet Mother of Jesus! What's this?' she said as she unwrapped the big package. When she saw all the new clothes inside she was speechless. Nobody had given Dulcie anything but heartbreak for most of her life and she just sat there staring at us in disbelief, with tears rolling down her face. We were all crying too.

'Now there's three new pairs of shoes there,' Natalie said. 'I think they're the ones you like to wear. There's some slacks and a couple of pairs of the jeans you like. Blouses and a couple of pullovers, some undies, talc, soap . . . and perfume as well.'

'And there's a card too,' Pepper managed to get out through her tears. 'Go on, open it,' she said excitedly.

Dulcie's hands were shaking so much from excitement she could hardly open the envelope. When she finally pulled out the card and opened it up, I thought she was going to have the big one right there on the spot. In the middle of the card were twenty-five neatly folded twenty pound notes.

'Merry Christmas, Dulcie,' cried Pepper and Natalie.

Dulcie was dumbfounded. She just sat there gently stroking her new things and the money like they were made of fairy web that might disappear if she touched them too hard. She sat like that for five minutes or so, not saying a word, just gently stroking and petting her new things. It had been so long, so long, and the look on her face was the only one we needed. It had all been Pepper and Natalie's idea. We'd all chipped in for the clothes but I didn't know anything about the money. They had done that on their own. None of us were made of dough. Pepper worked hard for hers and Natalie was saving for her precious trip, so it made the gift all the more meaningful. I looked at them both and wanted the moment to last forever. What a fantastic thing to do.

I guessed Dulcie had never had that much money in her hand at any one time. Five hundred quid was a heap of scratch in 1963 and could buy an old girl like her a lot of food and necessities. Dulcie was so shocked she didn't even want another drink before she left. I called her a taxi and went with her to her little house down off Cathedral Street in the 'Loo. Helping her with her presents, which she insisted on carrying, I walked her to her door and wished her a Merry Christmas with a big hug and a kiss.

'Come in fer a minute, darl. C'mon. 'Ave a quick one with me 'fore yer go 'ome, eh?'

'Sure, Dulce, I'd love too. Don't want to stay too late though.

'Don't worry, darl', ole Dulce won't try ta race yer orf or nuthin',' she laughed and we went inside her old house.

I'd never been inside before and as I entered her living room I was taken completely by surprise. I felt like I'd stepped back through a timewarp into another world somewhere around the turn of the century. The furniture was hand-crafted from various Australian hardwoods, beautifully grained and stained dark brown. All the pieces were polished to a mirror shine and in immaculate condition. Over the small stained-glass window hung a pair of deep green velvet drapes with a plaited gold pull cord at one end. A pair of Queen Anne-style boudoir chairs with matching green velvet covers sat at either side of a small Edwardian table placed under the window. There was a matching velvet-covered love seat and a pair of lead glass and crystal lamps sat on two other small tables.

On the flocked green wallpaper covered walls hung

dozens of old paintings and photographs. Some of the paintings were landscapes of what looked like Sydney Cove in the settlement days. Others were portraits of people I didn't recognise. Some of the faded brown photos contained groups of people smiling and laughing at me from some long-ago, washed-away, forgotten beach or now-concreted picnic spot. Quite a few of them were of a beautiful young girl.

There was a small fireplace with an ornate Victorian cast-iron grille, jarrah or ironbark surrounds and a thick, pink marble mantelpiece which was covered with small portraits and nicknacks. The room itself had taken me by surprise. It was spotlessly clean and seemed to be a perfectly preserved Edwardian sitting room, but it was something else that caught my eye and riveted my attention. Above the fireplace hung an old, ornately framed oil painting some five feet high by four feet wide. It was a nude and the subject was the same girl in the photos. Suddenly I realised I was looking at Dulcie Maysberry maybe seventy years ago.

'God, Dulcie,' I said, staring at the painting of the beautiful young girl languishing casually on a wooden chair with her right arm draped loosely over the back. Her left hand lay gently in her lap and in its open palm a single red rose petal glowed against her pearl-white skin. Her right leg rested on a small table to the left of the picture, her left leg loosely crossing it at the ankle to reveal just a hint of upper thigh and buttock. Curly blonde hair framed her smiling face, fell to her shoulders and over the back of the chair, almost touching the floor. Her strong passionate eyes had looked straight into those of the artist and now they stared unashamedly right back at me. She was beautiful, sensuous, innocent and captivating. In that silent moment I felt the soul of the painting touch me and I shivered. It was as if I had just walked into a secret room and interrupted this naked nymph in her silent gaze out of a window, her head casually turned as if to greet a lover.

'That's you, isn't it?' I said.

'Yeah, Bill,' she laughed. 'I was seventeen when George Lambert painted me. 'E used ta paint all the toffs in Sydney in them days, 'n' got paid a bloody fortune for 'em too! 'E use'ta fancy me a bit. Give it to me fer me eighteenth birthday, 'e did.' Dulcie proudly nodded her head. 'I 'ad a good figure back then, eh?' Cackle, cackle, cough, wheeze.

'You're not kidding,' I replied, stunned. 'Dulcie, you were absolutely gorgeous. Boy!'

'Easy, darl,' she said. 'You might bust a nut or somethin'.' Cackle! Wheeze. 'I'd 'ave 'ad you in the needle and thread in an 'eartbeat, young Will. Wouldn' 'ave cost yer a razzoo neither.'

I was transfixed by the painting and the fantasy of how Dulcie must have been seventy years ago. If she was this fiery at eighty-seven, what must she have been like when she looked like that at seventeen? It was impossible for me to put the scotch-swigging, swearing, belching, dear old Dulcie that I knew in perspective with that beauty in the painting and the spotless, sophisticated elegance of the room in which it was contained.

Age is a bastard, I thought. *God, look at her! So young, beautiful, alive, full of fire and dreams. The world at her feet and life by the balls.*

'Ya wanna scotch or brandy, darl?' she said, snapping me back into reality.

'Oh, er, a brandy please,' I replied, still staring at the

beauty in the painting. 'How long have you lived in this house?'

'Oh I wuz born 'ere,' she said matter of factly. 'In the bedroom upstairs. Used to be an 'ore 'ouse. Me old mum was on the game 'n' one of 'er old customers left it to 'er in his will.'

'And you've lived here all this time?'

'Yeah, darl, 's'wicked init? I seen it all.' She laughed. ''Ere's yer brandy. Good bloody 'ealth and God bless the three of yous.' She raised her glass.

'God bless you too, Dulce,' I said and we both took a drink.

'Cross used ta be beaudiful once,' she said. 'So did the 'Loo. You shoulda seen all them lovely mansions up around 'Lizabeth Bay 'n' Potts Point. Gorgeous they was. When I was a kid, me mum used to 'elp clean some of 'em frum time ter time. Got too old fer the game. Did allsorts o' things. I used ter play in the gardens of Clarence 'Ouse. Huge bloody mansion with ballrooms 'n' the like. The gardens run right down ter the water in big carved stone terraces. Shoulda seen it with all them pink 'n' red camellias in bloom. I saw that flick, what's its name . . . *Gorn on the Wind* or somethin'?'

'*Gone with the Wind*, with Clark Cable and Vivien Leigh.'

'Yeah, 'im. Gorn with the bloody Wind. That's the one. Well, everyone wus sayin' 'ow beautiful that was. You know the scenery, 'ouses 'n' all. Nothin' compared to what it looked like round the 'arbour when I was a kid. All them lords 'n' ladies in their finery ridin' in carriages pulled by teams o' whites. It was bloody beaudiful, darl. 'Lizabeth Bay Road, you know the one wot runs down past that new 'otel.'

'The Sebel Town House,' I said.

'Yeah, that 'un. Well, that use'ta be the bloody driveway to Macleay 'Ouse. Macleay 'Ouse 'ad lawns that run the whole shore of 'Lizabeth Bay. Bloody beautiful it was. Made them 'ouses in *Gorn with the Bloody Wind* look like toys. 'Nother brandy, darl?' she asked, filling my glass again.

'Yeah, I seen 'em all. Told yer 'bout Peter Finch, did I?'

'Yes, Dulce.'

'What about Nellie Cameron, Tilly Divine or Kate Leigh?'

'No, Dulcie. Who are they?'

'Those three sheilas run the bloody Cross in the 'twenties. Kate run all the sly grog shops when six o'clock closin' come in. Tough as bloody leather. Mum Leigh they called 'er. Always carried a gun. Killed Snowy bloody Pendergrast stone dead she did. An' Tilly Divine. Tilly run 'alf the brothels in Darlin'urst. I worked fer 'er fer a bit up at 191 Palmer Street. 'Ard moll, er. Still alive. Lives up in Surry 'Ills somewhere. Gord she was tough. Jeez, those were 'ard days, darl. The Darlin'hurst Push run East Sydney in them days.' She threw down another scotch. ''Nuther brandy?'

'No thanks, Dulce, I'll sit on this one. What's a Push?'

'Aw Pushes were gangs, darl. They was round 'ere 'n' all over Sydney since 'fore I was born. Carried razors, guns, any bloody thing. Bad bastards some of 'em. Used ter drink with a few of 'em up the Tradesman's Arms a bit ... 'N' Bea Miles. Caw, Bea was crazy as a loon. Lived in a bloody storm pipe in the Rushcutters Bay in the 'forties. Used ta sprout that Will bloody Shakespeare an' catch cabs ter bloody Perth 'n' Mount Isa, then would'n' pay. The cabbies were bloody terrified of 'er.' She coughed and wheezed again, laughing at the same time. 'Oh dear. Knew 'em all, I did. Just about all gorn now. Dear, they was great times. Would'n' swap em fer me tits back.' Cackle, cackle, wheeze! ''Nuther drink, darl?'

'No thanks, Dulce. It's been a long day and I better get going. Thanks for the drink and the stories.' I paused, then gave her a big hug. 'We love you, Dulce, I hope you know that. If you ever need anything you know where to come.' She started to sob gently and held me tight for a good minute. 'Oh, darl,' she said at last, 'what a lovely evenin'. Bless yer, God bless yer all.'

Walking through the 'Loo back up to William Street, the whole area seemed to change. I was transported back to the Woolloomooloo and Darlinghurst that Dulcie had described and it overcame me. I saw a beautiful young Dulcie Maysberry dressed in her bustle and bonnet as she walked the same streets and lanes I now walked. In the half-lit streets I could feel the street ghosts walking beside me and heard the laughter of children who had been dead a hundred years. For a split second I felt their memories and longing for life and it moved me near to tears. Lost in that emotion, completely oblivious of anything that was going on around me, I walked home to the Pagoda.

The girls were still up when I got home. I told them all about the portrait and Dulcie's stories and that their surprise gift of the money was the kindest act I'd ever witnessed.

'Aw mate, it's Christmas,' said Pepper.

'Anyhow, Dulcie could be any one of us years from now,' Natalie added. 'What's it all about if we can't do things like that from time to time?'

They were right and even though no-one had said it we all knew that, but for the grace of God, Dulcie could be any of our mothers years from now. Although the subject never came up we all missed our folks in our own way. It was Christmas and I know we were all feeling it. In a way our little dinner with Dulcie had been like a family celebration. Those moments when she opened her presents had been golden and had taken us all back to some Christmas when we were little kids.

It's funny, it doesn't matter how old you get or how tough you think you are, from time to time something like this goes down and you'd just love to be able to give your Mum a kiss and a hug and you curse yourself for all the times you could have and didn't.

17
Happy New Year

CHRISTMAS week had been incredible. The weather was perfect and Pepper, Natalie and I had spent practically every day at either Bondi Beach or Camp Cove. As usual the sand next to us must have been particularly soft because dozens of guys were packed in so tight they were nearly suffocating. At Bondi some tanned young German tourist came up ogling and started coming on to the girls. 'Vould du like ein beer mit me?' he said. 'Jour young bruzzer cand shtay here und vate till ve come back.' Pepper and Natalie responded by nearly raping me in front of him and he wandered off mumbling some sort of Kraut obscenities to himself.

What a shitty life this is, I thought. There's got to be something better than wasting my days on a perfect beach drinking ice-cold beer, eating fresh prawn and mayonnaise sandwiches with two gorgeous half-naked spunks rubbing me with oil, and nothing to look forward to at the end of the day but a hot shower together followed by four hours of rock 'n' roll in front of a full house of cheering fans! *Woe is me!*

When the neon door opened, the streets around the Cross were packed with fat-walleted punters eager for sport. The weeknight crowds at Surf City had swelled to over a thousand and on the weekend you couldn't move. We played a fantastic Christmas Eve gig and I spent a quiet Christmas Day with Pepper and Natalie, opening presents and eating a wonderful meal they'd been preparing all week, which included some traditional Russian dishes and a home-made Christmas pud. I invited Tony to join us but, as usual, he decided to eat fish and chips alone in his room. Col had invited me to take a drive with him in his old, blue '38 Hudson and I decided to use the trip to see my folks in Brisbane. Seeing we weren't scheduled to play until New Year's Eve we decided to leave on Boxing Day. We figured we could make the 600 miles to Brisbane overnight, stay a couple of days with my folks, and be back in Sydney in plenty of time for the gig.

Col decided he wanted to take the inland route, which in those days passed through the university town of Armidale and about three in the afternoon we set off on our adventure. The old Hudson was a powerful, American beauty and Col opened her up once we hit the open highway. The big Detroit V8 purred like a kitten and, riding on sponge rubber suspension, we cruised effortlessly at eighty-five miles an hour. The '38 Hudson was a huge old classic car, big enough to hold a family of eight no problems. With just the two of us on board she flew through the landscape like a thoroughbred on speed. It had been dark for quite a while and in the beautiful, bright, clear, moonlit night the countryside shot by in a silver glow and we hit the outskirts of Armidale about 2 a.m. We hadn't seen another car for about an hour and were happily chatting away about the band, girls, music and life, when we turned a long curve to find ourselves hurtling down this one-in-five grade doing about seventy-five. Suddenly out of nowhere we saw this old man on his pushbike, and I mean old. He must have ridden out of a gate or something because all of a sudden he was directly in front of the hurtling beast.

'Fuuuuck!' we both yelled as Col pulled the wheel to the right to miss him. The old fella must have heard us yell or the motor or something, because he turned, saw us and started pedalling flat-out like he was in the lead of the Tour de France. Col swerved to the right as the old fella pedalled frantically back to the left. We shot past, missing him by an inch, but the wake from the huge car hit him.

'Aaaaagheeee . . . shiiiiit!' he yelled and he and his bike took off like a trick cyclist over the side of the steep hill, landing in the treetops below the road.

Then bang! The car started weaving all over the road with Col wrestling with the wheel, trying desperately to keep control.

'What was that?' I yelled.

'The bloody torsion bar's snapped!' Col yelled back.

For those who don't know, the torsion bar is a device that connects each side of the body to the chassis at the rear of the car to stabilise the body sway. Without it the rear is floating loose, sitting unanchored on the suspension. The body sways uncontrollably in every direction and that's exactly what was now happening as we hurtled downhill about to literally hit bloody Armidale in two tons of V8-powered, out-of-control Motor City steel. We were about halfway down the steep grade with Col still fighting to keep control, but managing to keep us in a fairly straight line down the centre of the road. As long as nothing came up in front we would be . . .

'Oh shit no!' Col yelled. 'It's bloody cows!'

'How can it be cows at this time of the bloody . . . Oh shit, it is too!'

About 300 yards ahead of us were about a dozen bloody cows, a farmer at their rear, all oblivious to the flying death hurtling down at them. Col hit the horn, leaving his hand on it as he wrestled with the wheel, and we flew straight at them like a mobile, air-raid siren, shattering the tranquillity of the country morning. When he saw us the farmer started frantically beating the cows on the arse with his stick, but it was too late. We ploughed into them, the farmer shot up in the air over the side of the road into a gully and we made hamburger meat out of about three poor, dumb unsuspecting cows. One hit the front of the old Hudson, then flew clean over the top. Another shot into the air and landed somewhere near the farmer. It was raining bloody cows. The old beast of a Hudson hardly felt the impacts and ploughed on like a Sherman tank that had just flattened a squad of sprinting Germans at the Battle of El Alamein.

The up side, if there was one, was that the impact slowed us down. The down side was we drifted sideways into a slide, crashed through a fence, bounced across a small field and slammed flush into the side of a shed at the bottom of the hill. At this stage I've got the crown jewels in one hand and my arse in the other. I had both my legs planted firmly on the dash and the only pain I felt came as the bloody dresser I'd bought for my Mum, that had been sitting in the huge back seat, hit me on the back of the head.

I went out like a light and came to still in the front seat with Col standing over me, accompanied by the moaning farmer who's giving him a terrific serve.

'You bloody city bastards speedin' through the bloody country without any thought to life and limb,' he shouted. 'You bloody near killed me and what about me flamin' shed and dead flamin' cows? The rest of 'em 'ave gorn flamin' bush! It'll take me a bloody week ta find the bludgers.'

'Fuck ya cows,' said Col. 'What about me fuckin' 'Udson. 'Ave a look at the bastard, will ya?'

'Fuck the both of you,' I said. 'What about me?'

'Ah, you're all right, son,' the old farmer said. 'Just a bit of a knock on the 'ead is all.'

The glow from the Hudson's powerful headlights illuminated the inside of the shed like daylight. I sat there in the front seat nursing my head as Col and the old farmer went at it over whose fault it was. Gradually I started to focus on my surroundings.

The right front of the car was sitting a good six feet inside the old building. Bits of tack, chicken wire, boxes and broken eggs covered everything and there on the bonnet, squashed flat like a magician's rubber props, lay about a dozen freaked-out dead chickens. We'd killed three cows, nearly flattened the farmer, demolished his bloody chook-house and killed half his chooks in the bargain. No wonder he was spewing.

'Listen, old fella,' Col shouted. 'The bloody torsion bar snapped on the back of the bludger! We swerved to miss some silly old bugger on a pushbike ridin' without any flamin' lights at two o'clock in the bloody mornin'. It was a bloody accident! So just bloody calm down.'

'What silly old bugger?' the farmer asked.

'I dunno,' said Col. 'I'm not from round bloody 'ere, am I? Just some silly old bastard come out of nowhere into the middle of the bloody road. He went hurtling into the bloody trees about five 'undred bloody yards back up the hill.'

'Christ, that must've been old Kenny Stroud. 'E's about bloody eighty not out. Always ridin' round 'alf pissed at all hours of the bloody night. We've warned 'im about it an 'undred bloody times but it don't sink in. Jesus, we'd better take a look to see if 'e's all right. Quick, boys, help me get me bloody cows off the road then we'll 'ave a look at 'im.'

So that's how we came to be wandering around in the dark at two-thirty in the morning, scraping dead cows off the highway, combing the scrub and climbing bloody trees on the outskirts of Armidale looking for some eighty-year-old codger who'd taken off like a rocket when the wake of the Hudson hit him. After about an hour of scrub searching and tree climbing we finally found old Kenny out cold in a tree with his bike. He stank like the public bar at the Mansions and must have been pissed rotten when he pedalled out in front of us. Miraculously he'd landed unharmed in the branches of a big tree and that's where we found him, snoring his head off, dead drunk about ten feet from the ground, perfectly unharmed except for a bent bike and a few scratches. The farmer's name was Bob and considering the fact that we'd near killed him and half his livestock, he was very friendly. By the time we got old Ken out of the tree and back to Bob's house it was nearly dawn. He stuck the old guy in a bed, made us some breakfast and we went to check out the extent of the damage to the Hudson and the shed.

One side of the old shed was kindling that now sat

underneath the huge car. Although most of the shed's contents had shot up in the air when we hit, apart from the chooks, most of it was intact. After about half an hour of chicken scraping we managed to get most of Bob's stuff stacked and Col went over the Hudson. The right front fender and door were pushed in and the right front tyre was blown. Egg yolks had taken a lot of duco off the bonnet and the windscreen was covered in chickenshit. The poor chooks must have literally shit themselves when they heard us come flying into the shed, and died of a heart attack before we flattened them. We got the car cleaned up as best we could and Col checked to see if it would start. When he hit the ignition the old V8 fired first time with a roar like it was ready to do it all over again. Bob helped us change the tyre and used his tractor to get the car back onto the side of the road. Over breakfast Col had placated him by giving him insurance information and telling him it would all be covered. Nobody had been hurt except the cows and chooks, so it was sweet. Bob told us the name of a good mechanic and we limped off to Armidale in the dented, swaying beast.

The locals couldn't believe their eyes when they saw us bouncing through Armidale. We found the garage and the mechanic told Col that he'd have to forge a new part to fix the torsion bar and that his brother-in-law could fix the body damage if we wanted. Said the whole thing would take about four days. The only problem was the repairs would eat up most of our cash, leaving us just enough for food and the gas to get back to Sydney. I called my folks and Pepper and told them what had happened. Then Col and I spent the next four days sleeping in the bloody car out the front of the garage, washing and shaving under the service-station hose in full view of the customers and passing traffic. Five days later we headed back to Sydney, hitting the outskirts at about 5 p.m., New Year's Eve.

By the time we got to the Cross I had just enough time for a shower and headed up to Surf City with Pepper. We played the New Year in on the huge theatre awning which overhung the footpath on Darlinghurst Road. Fifty thousand people danced and partied in the streets below us and counted down to midnight. Backed by Billy Thorpe and the Aztecs, thousands of happy voices sang 'Auld Lang Syne' and we all welcomed in 1964.

18
We Nearly Killed 'em in Wagga

IT was January and all of Sydney bathed in the heat of a sweltering Aussie summer sun. The open-air restaurants were full, the harbour was covered with bobbing, white sails and the beaches were packed as holiday-makers from all over Australia and the world visited Sydney for a taste of one of the best summer experiences to be had anywhere. The Cross was a buzz of activity day and night. Each evening when the sky had rolled its golden red blanket around the sun and neon bathed the streets with its enticing glow, many of the younger tourists began making their way into Surf City. For the first time our music was being exposed to a completely new group of people. We started to make new fans and get offers to do outside gigs. John felt that it was premature for the band to go interstate, feeling that we should wait until we had a record, then start doing other shows to promote it. We all agreed.

Prior to my joining the band, the Aztecs had released an

album on the Linda Lee label. One side had been surf instrumentals and the other with Johnny Noble on vocals. It hadn't done much, but the owner of the label approached John about making a record with the new line-up and John made a deal. Linda Lee was distributed by Festival Records and it was at Festival's recording studio in Pyrmont, not far from the city, that many artists, including Australian rock legends Johnny O'Keefe and Col Joye, had recorded most of their hits. Through Linda Lee's relationship with Festival it was arranged for us to make our first record there.

In 1964 making a record was an extremely primitive process. Sophisticated multi-track tape machines didn't exist and studios all over the world were mainly equipped with two-track tape recorders. This made the recording process both simple and efficient. The band was recorded live on one track and the vocals were recorded simultaneously on the other. No mixing afterwards, both straight to tape at the same time. For all intents and purposes it was a live recording and, given that we were so well rehearsed, the songs went down in practically one take. The only sophistication was reverb and tape echo. These effects were generated live as the band recorded, mixed in with the sound and recorded to tape.

Festival had an all-brick bathroom downstairs from the studio and had a pretty good natural reverb. The live sound from the studio was sent to a speaker in this toilet, a microphone was placed in the room and that was the reverb! The only problem was the toilet had a habit of flushing itself in the middle of a take and we had to start again.

It took about four hours to record two songs written by

Tony called 'Blue Day' and 'Broken Things'. I sang the vocal on 'Blue Day' and Tony on 'Broken Things' and by the end of the night our first recording was completed for a total cost of fifty quid. Ah, the good old days!

The plan was to release the record some time in late February and in the meantime stay on our usual regimen of seven gigs a week at Surf City. One night after the show John Harrigan came down to the dressing-room and told us we'd been offered a gig in Wagga Wagga, a country town in southern New South Wales. Seems the place was having some sort of festival. One of the promoters had been into Surf City a few times and when he bandied our name around Wagga he was surprised to find a lot of local kids knew about us so he called John to see if we would perform. John asked us what we thought. Thinking a small show in a country town would be a good chance to try our songs on a completely different crowd, we said yes and it was organised.

Two weeks later we packed ourselves and the gear into a brand new Volkswagen Kombi van John had bought for us and off we trotted. After a hilarious, nine-hour fart-filled trip we found the Wagga Town Hall, set up our gear, did a sound check and booked into a small pub on the edge of town. I'd been on the road since I was a kid but for the band and Tony in particular this was a brand new experience and everybody was excited.

The headline act that night was the Dave Bridge Trio. Dave was a well-known and popular Sydney guitar player who'd made some successful instrumental records. He'd performed on many tours with people like Johnny O'Keefe and major overseas acts since the late 'fifties. Dave was a fantastic player and a really good bloke. He and his band were older than we were and, unlike us, a well-seasoned act with years of road experience. Wagga was just another town to them, but when they heard us at the sound check, and saw our enthusiasm, they took an immediate liking to us.

In 1964 Wagga was no different to any other small Australian country town. These were down-home, good ol' country folk, and a city the size of Sydney represented the real big smoke. It was New York City as far as they were concerned.

When the local DJ introduced us and we walked out on the stage the place went absolutely silent. Some of us had started to grow our hair long and we were dressed in our new Thai silk band suits and Cuban-heeled boots. The crowd just stood there with their mouths open, staring at us like we'd just arrived from Mars. Some of the local spunks shot down to the front of the stage and started coming on to us, smiling and making suggestive comments, and the local studs took an immediate dislike to this young bunch of city poofters who looked like they were about to race off every girl in town.

Then it started. 'Fuckin' poofs!' 'Yer look like a bunch of fuckin' sheilas! 'Get yer 'air cut, ya mug!' and on it went.

I'd played plenty of country towns in Queensland and all the audiences were pretty much the same. In the main, the Saturdee dance was a real social event and everyone got dressed up for the big night out. Of course there were always a few half-pissed local lads who loved to blue, but it usually didn't amount to any more than a couple of them having a go at one another, getting thrown out, and the night's festivities continued. I figured it would all die down once they heard the band could play, so I ignored the cat-calls and counted in the first song.

One, two, three, four . . . Splaaat! An egg sailed through the air and hit Col right between the eyes, then another hit me and about a dozen more rained on the stage, hitting us all. The crowd took one look at this egg-dripping bunch of city boys in their shiny suits and burst into hysterical laughter. After the first egg hit I spotted the two young mugs throwing them, about halfway up the hall. Bluey saw them too and said to me 'Let's get the bastards!' We both leapt off the stage and pushed our way through the packed crowd. The egg-throwers were both so caught up lairing to their mates that they didn't see us coming. We got there just as one of them was about to launch another barrage. As he pulled his arm back about to let loose, I jumped in front of him and head-butted him flush on the nose. Down he went, broken eggs and all. His mate just stood there with his mouth open, staring at me, his hands full of eggs, then whack! Bluey dropped him with a right hook to the chin. It took everybody by surprise and nobody else even tried to have a go at us. The whole joint just stared in silence, so we got back on the stage and I took the mike.

'Hey, listen,' I said. 'We just drove nine bloody hours from Sydney to come here and give you a bloody show. Now does anybody else wanna have a go or what?'

Nobody said a word.

Now I'm not trying to come off like I thought I was the next lightweight contender. It seemed to be the right thing to do, and it seemed to have worked. I could see only too well that there were some very serious looking big cockies in the crowd, who looked like they spent their breaks between shifts of hay-bale throwing chucking tractors around for a bit of sport. If the place had really gone off we were in for some serious shit that would probably end with the words

> Poof musician
> Born?? Died 1964
> from complications while having
> his head removed from his arsehole

hand-painted on a plank of wood in the Wagga cemetery.

The confrontation seemed to freak them out. They didn't know what to do and neither did we. We were standing there silently wiping the egg from our faces, staring the audience down in a 750 to 5 Mexican stand-off when this big police sergeant jumped on the stage. He was about six four, 300 pounds, beer gut, a twenty-five inch neck, with arms that looked like he bench-pressed Brahman bulls for a hobby. I could tell from the expressions on the local wankers' faces that this big local copper had split the odd head and kicked more than one arse around town.

'All right! All bloody right!' he said, taking my mike. 'Now that serves you two bloody right! Yeah, you Tommy Millen *and* you Jacky bloody Egan.' He pointed at the two blokes we'd hit who were now being held up by about a dozen big mates.

'Now yous can 'ave it one bloody way or the other,' the big copper said to the crowd. 'One more bit of bloody larrikinism and I'm closin' the dance! All right? And no bloody refunds! I'll lock the next mug up that even farts! Now any of yas that wanna have a go will hafta deal with me and Constable Reilly.' He nodded to another giant copper I hadn't noticed in the scuffle. 'And we both need a bitta bloody trainin' for the tournament next month! So what der yer wanna do? Act like mugs and fight, or have a good time?'

'Have a good time!' yelled the crowd.

'All right then,' he said. 'Give these young blokes a fair go then. We asked 'em to come here in the first place and they've come a bloody long way ta be here tonight, so give 'em a bloody go! No more bloody eggs or trouble.

'All right, son,' he said to me. 'Play ya bloody songs!' And walked off the stage. I counted off 'Walkin' the Dog' and the whole place started dancing.

By their immediate reaction I could tell they'd never heard anything like us before. They got straight into it, clapping and shouting as we finished the first song. By the looks on the egg-throwers' and their mates' faces, I felt sure we were in for a kicking after the show but it never came. Blow me if half of them didn't end up down the front dancing their arses off, and after the show some of them and their girlfriends even came around the back to the dressing-room. We were expecting a stink but they turned out to be OK. A couple of them had drunk a few too many grogs but they were fine. Just wanted to meet us. Wanted to know about the band, did we have any records and even offered us a beer which we gratefully accepted as a sign it was all sweet. The local crowd had loved the band and new-sounding music. It was so different for them it seemed to melt the whole hassle away and our first road gig had been a tremendous success. So much so that the promoter asked if we would come back again soon. We said we'd love to. Dave Bridge and his band were booked into the same pub as us and after watching their act we decided to have a beer together when we got back.

The hotel was a typical old Aussie pub with a main bar

and ladies' lounge downstairs. The guests' rooms were on the first floor, and most had French doors which opened onto a wide verandah trimmed with Victorian ironwork trellis and railing. As we left the dance there were about a dozen young spunks itching to see our big city etchings, but some of the local guys were hanging around them and we thought it would be lunacy to pull the girls off them and start the whole bloody thing going again, so we passed. When we got back to the old pub we were surprised to find the big sergeant and some of his mates drinking in the closed bar with the owner.

He spotted us as we walked through the lobby and invited us in for a beer on the house. They were all very friendly and wanted to know about the band, Sydney, did we know Col Joye or Johnny O'Keefe and the like. We'd been sitting there about fifteen minutes and in strolled Dave Bridge and his two players, followed by a couple of the girls we'd left outside the hall. We all sat drinking and laughing, listening to Dave's many road stories and as the session progressed it started to get more and more rowdy. Most of us were under age but the sergeant didn't even look sideways.

I hadn't seen Bluey or Col drunk before and after numerous beers their antics became even more hilarious. The coppers, publican and his wife loved them and the more they drank the louder it got. Bluey did his Baltic for the sarge and the sergeant laughed so hard he fell off the bloody bar stool. Finding a willing audience, Bluey decided it was time for a real show and he, Col and Dave Bridge got into a huddle, then shot out of the bar laughing their heads off.

The first thing I heard was Da da da da dah dah . . . Da da da dah dah dah . . . Da da da da da da da dah dah dah dah dah like an old Spanish refrain coming from the lobby.

Then Dave and Col came singing and dancing through the bar, stark naked with a saucepan lid in each hand, which they rotated from their arses to their crotch in time to the chant like Gypsy Rose Lee doing her famous fan dance. They danced slowly through the bar, out the other door and everybody lost it. A few seconds later the lights went out and two naked flames sprinted through the room laughing and cheering. Dave and Col had rolled up some paper, stuck it in their bums, set it alight and sprinted through the bar and straight out the other door.

I'm shitting myself laughing and so is everyone else in the room when out of the corner of my eye I spot Bluey outside the door in the old lobby, lighting a huge roll of paper that he'd stuck in his bum all ready for his version of the legendary 'dance of the flames'. I saw him strike a match, put it to the paper and whooosh! a giant blue flame about two feet long shot out of his arse with a blinding flash. The lobby lit up like broad daylight and Bluey was jumping around with his arse on fire.

'Yyyyoooooowwwwww. Fuuuck!' he screamed and came hopping into the bar trying to fan his flaming arse out with his hands. He was jumping up and down, spinning in circles like a shitting dog, when the publican grabbed a soda siphon and sprayed Bluey's flaming bum which hissed and started smoking like the exhaust pipe on a '55 Holden.

It seems the silly bugger was so drunk he'd thought he'd give the fans a little something extra. He went to the kitchen and ripped off some greaseproof paper which had gone up like a bonfire the second the match hit it. When the lights came back on there's Bluey sitting on the floor of the old bar with his legs up in the air frantically throwing beer on his smouldering arse and balls, trying desperately to put out the remaining embers. Never before or since have I seen people laughing that hard. The big sergeant and the publican's wife were both rolling on the floor screaming crying. I was on the floor as well and the young girls from the dance were absolutely beside themselves. It was the funniest thing I've seen in my life.

The pub owner's wife soaked a bar cloth in ice water and gave it to Bluey. Covering his old boy with one hand and holding the wet cloth to his scorched arse with the other, he limped naked out of the bar with his legs wide apart like a kid who'd just shit in his pants. The sight of him limping off set everyone going again and the publican shouted us all another round. He reckoned it was the greatest thing he'd ever seen and Bluey's flaming arse was destined to become legend in those parts for years to come. We stayed a while longer, thanked everyone for their hospitality and went up to our rooms. I opened my verandah door to find Bluey standing stark naked out on the verandah, beer in hand, still holding the wet cloth to his scorched bum.

'How's your arse?' I asked him, cracking up.

'Ah me arse's all right, mate. Bit fuckin' scorched!' He laughed. 'It's me fuckin' nuts I'm worried about! 'Ave a look at the bastards,' he said, limping into his room.

I was already laughing back the tears, but when he got up on the bed he pulled the cheeks apart and said 'Jeeezus, 'ave a look at me fuckin' nuts, will ya?' I completely lost it again. There wasn't a hair anywhere on his crotch or bum. His arse was swollen up like a baboon's and both his balls were scorched jet black, looking remarkably like a couple of old prunes hanging between his legs. I was holding my gut laughing and in walked Dave, Col, Vince and one of the guys from Dave's band. When they saw Bluey with his cheeks spread and got a look at his prunes, they all burst into laughter again.

'What? What?' Bluey was asking us.

'Aaaaaghhh . . . Nnnnnnn!' was all any of us could get out.

'Your arse looks like a fuckin' monkey's bum, Bluey,' Dave screamed and we all fell down again.

'Ah get fucked!' said Bluey, wheeling himself around on the bed for a closer inspection of the damage in the wardrobe mirror. 'Ah fuuuck!' he exclaimed, seeing the glorious sight.

There was a knock on the door and I answered it. It was the publican's wife with some ointment for Bluey.

'Tell 'im to put some of this on it and if it's still bad in the morning, he'd better have someone at the hospital take a look at it.'

Hearing this set us all off again. The thought of Bluey in an emergency room pulling his cheeks wide for some young nurse to bathe, while explaining how it happened, was more than any of us could handle. I could just see her reaction and hear the whole hospital in hysterics with Bluey yelling 'Ah get fucked!' at the top of his lungs. We sat with him for a while, then one by one we drifted off to bed. Tony of course had gone straight to bed with a comic the minute we got to the pub and had slept through the whole thing. Loved to read comics, did Tony.

I was just getting off to sleep when I heard Col whisper 'Thorpie! Thorpie! You asleep, mate?'

'No mate, just drifting off,' I answered. It was hot and we'd all left the verandah doors open and Col, Dave and Bluey came wandering in, chuckling. Bluey was wearing a towel and his boots.

'Mate,' Bluey said excitedly. 'Dave's bass player's got one of those sheilas in his bloody room and we're gonna frighten the shit out of them. You wanna come?'

Why not? I thought. *After Bluey's escapade, why stop now?* And off we went like the Keystone Cops, tiptoeing down the verandah to a room at the other end. About halfway along Bluey spotted an old fire hose sitting on the wall.

'Dave, Dave!' he whispered, laughing like an excited schoolkid. 'Turn the bloody thing on when I get in the room, will ya? I'll freak 'em right bloody out!'

We crept down to the room with Bluey in the lead, hose in hand. Suddenly he leapt through the open door, yelled 'Now!' and squirted the hose full blast into the room. We're all pissing ourselves because all we can hear is shouting and screaming as Bluey rampages around the room in the dark, creating havoc, then comes flying out, drops the squirting hose and runs straight into his room. The loose hose darted and swished around the verandah like a pissed-off snake, soaking us all before Col managed to capture it and turn it off. Half-drenched, we all shot into our rooms and locked the doors. I lay in bed with a pillow over my face trying to muffle the sound of my laughter. When I finally stopped I listened but all was quiet outside. It was late, I was tired, I'd had more than enough sport for one night so I went off to sleep. The next morning I was awakened by a loud thumping on the door. Opening it I was confronted by an old cleaning lady, rag around her hair, roll-your-own hanging from her mouth, and mop in hand.

'If yous want some bloody breakfast, yer better get down there quick, 'fore the bloody kitchen closes!'

And a very good morning to you too, madam, I thought

as she went along to the other rooms, waking them with similar politeness.

Back in 1964 there was no room service or late breakfast sessions in hotels. In country pubs breakfast was normally served between six-thirty and eight and all guests ate together in the dining room. We got ourselves together and headed down to eat. When Bluey appeared we all cracked up at the way he walked. He must have had ointment all over his arse and some sort of bandage or something stuffed all around inside his underpants. He was hobbling like he was carrying a twenty-five pounder in his trousers. The second we entered the dining room I knew all was not well in Wagga! The publican's wife was eating breakfast by herself and the look she gave me would have split a diamond. I said good morning to her but she turned away. Everybody else noticed it too, so we went and sat quietly at a table in the corner. There were also two old couples eating breakfast and the instant they saw us they took off out the door like someone had rung a bloody fire alarm.

This is a bit weird, I thought, but I figured Bluey's hosing trick and accompanying racket had pissed them off and left it at that. Then an old waitress came waltzing over to the table with the same pissed-off attitude.

'Well, what do yous bloody want?' she fired at us.

Thinking we'd leave well enough alone we politely ordered and waited. As she left she mumbled, 'You boys should be ashamed of yer bloody selves.'

We sat there wondering what the fuck was happening. We had started to describe Bluey's escapades the night before to a bewildered Tony when this old bloke in his late sixties came shuffling into the dining room. Bluey immediately started laughing saying, "Ave a look at this silly old bugger, will ya.'

I watched as the old Digger struggled desperately to get to a table. The publican's wife gave us a filthy look, then went over and helped him into a chair. He was wearing a dark brown three-piece suit, a shirt and tie. What was weird was the way he was wearing them. His shirt was hanging out of his pants, his fly was half undone and his shirt and waistcoat were buttoned on all the wrong holes. He had the first button through the third buttonhole and so on and the tension was pulling his head down as he walked, making him shuffle along like an old hunchback. To top it off his tie was knotted outside his collar and he was only wearing one shoe! Of course we all started to giggle at the table. Just then the old bitch of a waitress lobbed back with our breakfasts and tossed them on the table like she was dealing a hand of poker. Seeing us all looking at the old fella and breaking up, she launched into a terrible verbal, calling us a few things I'd never even heard before.

'Excuse me, madam,' Tony said, 'do you always treat your guests like this? You are extremely rude, you know.'

'Don't bloody madam me,' she fired back. 'Extremely rude am I? Extremely bloody rude. Why, I've got a good mind to tan your bloody hides, the lotta ya! You should be bloody ashamed of yerselves laughing at 'im like that.'

'Aw, fair suck of the sav, love,' said Bluey. 'We're only 'avin' a chuckle. 'Ave a look at 'im. 'E's pretty bloody funny the ways 'e's going on.'

The old boy had a menu in his hands and it was shaking uncontrollably like someone had hit him with 240 volts.

'He's 'ad a real bad turn, the poor old bugger,' the waitress said. 'You should be ashamed of yourselves!'

'Why? It's not our fault,' I tossed in.

'Oh no!' she spat.

'Why?' Vince asked indignantly.

'Why? 'Cause one of you young bludgers ran through 'is bloody room last night, jumped all over 'is bed and hosed 'im with a bloody fire hose and 'e 'ad a bloody stroke! That's bloody why! You should be bloody ashamed of yourselves!' she said and stormed off.

We sat there with our mouths open like stunned mullet. Then the picture of Bluey in towel and boots running amok through the poor old Digger's room at three in the morning hit us and we all fell about laughing. Well, that did it. Next thing the publican and his missus are at our table.

'Get ya bloody stuff and get outta me pub now!' he screamed. 'I don't want the bloody likes a you in 'ere! Go on, get!'

'It was a terrible mistake,' I said. 'We didn't mean to . . .'

'Shut yer bloody trap before I shut it for ya!' he screamed again, shaking his fist and lunging at me. 'Bloody get out of 'ere before I call the police. You're bloody lucky you're not locked up already. Now get, I said. And don't ever bloody come round 'ere again!'

It took us about a minute to get in the van and gone! Nobody said a word for about ten miles, then Bluey chirped, 'Well, we nearly killed 'em in Wagga, eh boys?'

We all looked at one another, then pelted him with magazines, drink cans, whatever we could get our hands on.

'Ah geeet fuuucked!'

'No you get fucked!'

'No you get fucked! Get fucked! Get fucked! Get fucked!' went Col and Bluey.

Ah, only eight more fart-filled hours to go.

19
The Wedding Photograph

AS well as the punters who came for the strip clubs, bars and seedier red-light entertainment, young people from all walks of life started making the weekly and sometimes nightly trek up to the Cross and Surf City. By early 1964 it had become *the* place for young people to hang. Something was always happening and it was a far cry from the depressed, impoverished, boring life in the lower-working-class neighbourhoods that surrounded Sydney's inner city in 1964. It was a number of these suburbs, in particular those relatively close to the Cross, that produced the regulars who frequented Surf City and became our first and most loyal fans.

These suburbs were Bondi, Maroubra, Mascot, Redfern, Paddington, Surry Hills, Bronte, Coogee, Bondi and even some further away such as Glebe and Leichhardt. Many of these neighbourhoods were practically identical, with row upon row of Victorian look-alike shoe-box terraces stacked together like toytown. With their wrought-iron fences, tin roofs and tiny front verandahs, they were distinguishable only by the personalised paint job or plant arrangements and ornaments that hung from the guttering above the small concrete patio or garden at the front door.

These residences were inhabited mainly by labourers and their families. Men and women who worked hard to eke out a living. Some of the men worked on the docks if they were lucky, a wharfie being a prized and sought-after job that came with many perks, rorts and benefits. By and large most of these blokes were factory workers, road-workers, navvies, bus drivers, groundsmen and the like. Some were on the dole or surviving through child endow-ment. All were scraping by and many played the horses. From time to time more than one dabbled in the odd, small-time, fell-off-the-truck deal or shifty scheme in order to sur-vive. They weren't professional crims, just ordinary blokes who couldn't get a break to save their lives, doing the best they could to feed their families and buy the odd beer. It was the children of these neighbourhoods, with limited education, in their mid to late teens, who frequented the Cross and Surf City on a regular basis and became the regulars. Although a definite demographic, for some reason they didn't acquire a label like 'Mods', 'Sharpies', or 'Rock-ers', so for the purpose of the story I have named them 'Crossies'. I know they won't mind.

Two regular Surf City Crossies were Mulatto Mick and his girl Sally.

Mick looked like he could easily have been the son of Odd Job from the James Bond movie *Goldfinger*. A little bloke, maybe nineteen years old, five foot six, about 200 pounds, he was built like a brick shithouse with calves and forearms the size of Popeye's. His face was round as a ball, his features an Oriental–Polynesian mix with caramel skin and black, slanted Chinese eyes. Mick talked fast with a heavy Sydney street accent, and when he laughed a high-pitched cackle came out, his whole face seeming to roll into itself as his eyes disappeared into his face. In summer he wore tight, tailored to-the-knee shorts, brown or beige, held up by braces. This was usually accompanied by a burgundy or green Alligator short-sleeve shirt, always buttoned to the neck, a Kangol cap and leather thongs. In winter he wore the same, except the pants were long. Sometimes he swapped his Kangol for a bowler. Oh, and rain or shine, Mulatto Mick always carried a black umbrella.

This was Mick's variation on the way a lot of the Crossie boys, or 'Mark Foys' as they were known on the street, dressed. The only difference being they usually wore long tapered pants with sixteen-inch cuffs that fell to just an inch above their spit-polished, triple-D pointed brogues. Like Mick, their pants were usually supported by braces. They wore the trademark cap, Alligator shirt, and many carried their brolly which doubled as an effective weapon in a stink. Although working-class poor, the Crossie boys and girls, or 'Twist and Twirls' as they were street-monickered, took meticulous pride in the way they dressed and what little money they earned was spent on clothes and dancing. The sight of 250 immaculately turned-out couples on the dance floor at Surf City, jiving or doing the Wellington, was something to behold.

As stocky as a Brahman, as tough as horsemeat, a wharfie, street fighter and part-time street hustler, Mulatto Mick was always involved in some scuffle or another inside or outside Surf City. It was usually over some perceived insult to Sally or himself from some poor innocent mug who happened to be in the right place at the wrong time. Mick and Sally had become regulars and we got to know them both quite well. He was as rough as sandpaper but a nice bloke all-round. At least he was to us. Mick worked on the wharf in Woolloomooloo. The 'Loo, as it became known in the early settlement days, dates back to the original land grants of the early 1800s and is situated half a mile down a steep hill from Victoria Street at the back of Surf City.

Out of the blue Mulatto Mick started to pop into our rehearsals around lunchtime during the week. It was only a fifteen-minute walk up the century-old McElhone steps, all 103 of them, to the Cross and he simply decided that was where he wanted to eat lunch. Sure as shit, I for one wasn't about to tell him every day was a bit much. The way he ate looked like one side of his ancestry had had a lot of practice eating each other. So for a while Mulatto Mick became a regular Surf City lunch guest, rain or shine.

It was a Thursday in the last week of January and we were rehearsing as usual. We'd taken a break, just sitting around out in the lobby talking band shit. I don't remember the exact circumstances, only that Bluey and Tony were having some sort of disagreement over something relatively unimportant, but it was starting to heat up because Bluey kept calling him 'a little Pommie cunt', which was infuriating Tony. Can't understand why.

By this stage the personality lines that always cross in any band had been pretty much defined, the boundaries had been drawn, and we had all become great friends in our new adventure together. Vince was always quiet and shy, Bluey and Colin were always hilarious and Tony was so prim, proper and fastidious he squeaked. He had funny little quirks and habits—routines that he went through to do the most ordinary things. You know, dusting off a chair before sitting on it, holding a sandwich with his handkerchief because he didn't like to touch food with his fingers, then chewing every mouthful exactly twenty-five times before swallowing.

'Masticate, you have to masticate,' he said once.

'Yeah you're a fuckin' wanker all right,' replied Bluey innocently.

Don't get me wrong. Bluey really liked Tony, but his crazy habits were perfect targets for Bluey's twisted sense of humour and he simply couldn't help himself. Tony was always immaculate and I'm certainly not slighting him for it, but there was definitely something anal-retentive about his behaviour and it drove Bluey absolutely fucking crazy. We all found Tony's quirks and mannerisms hilarious at times, but if that's the way Tony was, that's the way he was. Except for Bluey, the rest of us laughed it off because at times it was genuinely funny to watch. Tony was well aware of his quirks and didn't take offence. The rest of us didn't care, but Bluey would rag Tony endlessly until he got a bite, and of course Tony always bit. Now when Tony got angry he would jump up and down in the one place and scream in this high-pitched Norfolk accent which at times made him impossible to understand.

So here we are having a break and they're at it.

'Ah you're a little Pommie poof,' yelled Bluey.

'Don't call me that, Bluey. You know how much I hate it!' Tony yelled back.

To hear Tony say the name Bluey was also hilarious, because he couldn't pronounce things correctly. Words like penguin for instance, Tony would pronounce as pengween.

No matter how many times he tried to say it, it always came out pengween.

'Ah you're a Pommie cunt all right,' goaded Bluey again, throwing a sly smirk at Col and me.

'Turn it up, Bluey,' said Col, who had a soft spot for Tony. He found him funny too and liked him a lot.

'Ah, get fucked,' said Bluey.

'No you get fucked,' came back Col.

'Get fucked . . . get fucked . . . get fucked,' they started at one another in their familiar routine.

'That's the only word you ever use, Bluey, you know that, don't you?' Tony interjected.

'What word?' said Bluey, knowing the hook was baited.

'Tha-haat word!' Tony replied. 'The one you're always using.'

'Which one?' goaded Bluey.

'*You know . . . you know* what I mean,' Tony said, falling right in.

'What fuckin' word?' Bluey asked again.

'That one! The one you just said,' replied Tony, falling even deeper.

'What word, you little Pommie cunt! Tell me the word, go on, say it.'

'I'm not saying it,' Tony said self-righteously. 'It's disgusting.'

'Aw say "fuck", Tony. C'mon, you'll love it once you get the hang of it. C'mon, say "fuck, shit, dick, balls, tits, arse and a big hairy twat" . . . you Pommie cunt.'

Well that did it. Tony went ballistic and started screaming something that sounded like obscenities, but none of us were really sure. He was jumping up and down on the spot like he was trying to put out a fire with both feet.

'Speak up, cunt, I can't understand ya! That doesn't sound right to me. What ya think, Thorpie? Sound like "fuck" to you?' Bluey asked me, grinning.

By this time we were all in hysterics, including Bluey, and I couldn't answer. Tony's still jumping up and down when who comes strolling through the door, resplendent in Kangol cap and brolly in hand? None other than Mulatto Mick. Now we're not the only ones who've noticed Tony's quirks. To the in-crowd and regulars they were becoming quite notorious. Some of the young girls loved them, of course, and thought Tony was the horniest, politest bloke they'd ever met. Which he probably was. But he wasn't interested in any of them, even though any one of them would have peeled his banana in a flash. You see, Tony was still a virgin at twenty-two and was saving himself for the woman he married. Definitely not a poof, just saving himself for the woman he loved.

So in waltzes Mulatto Mick, lunch in hand.

'G'day Thorpie, Vince, Blue, Col. What's Tony blueing about?' he asked, staring at Tony as he jumped up and down on the big marble theatre stairs.

'Ah somebody stole his fuckin' dummy,' laughed Bluey.

'Oh,' said Mick, like it was a perfectly normal reply.

'Listen, me old, I've gotta favour t' ask yous,' he said. 'Me 'n' Sal're gettin' 'ooked on Sundee arvo 'n' I wondered, er well, if yous'd be me guest groomsmen.' He went bright red with embarrassment and for a second looked like a little kid.

'We'd love to,' I replied, 'but we're working this Sunday. Maybe we could pop over between sets to the reception if you're having one.' I looked at Vince, Col and Bluey and they were as touched as I was. This street tough punter thought so much of us he wanted us to be grooms at his wedding, and we all realised what a mark of respect that was.

'Ah, mate, sorry,' said Col, 'but we'd love to come 'n' 'ave a beer with you and Sal. Wish you the best and all.'

'Fuckin' oath!' Bluey added. 'Congratulations, mate.'

'Yes, congratulations,' said Vince, shaking his hand and we all shook his hand, congratulating him. All except Tony, that is. He was still halfway up the stairs, fuming, and had missed all that was going on. Then he started at Bluey again.

'You're the rudest person I've ever met, Bluey,' he whined. 'You really are. You know that upsets me so why do you do it?'

''Cause you're a cunt!' said Bluey. 'So get fucked 'cause I'm talking to me mate Mick.' He winked at Mick and me to show us he was about to get Tony started again, and sure enough he did. Tony started jumping up and down again, cursing in his own language.

We were all standing in a sort of semicircle around Mick, about twenty-five feet from the stairs. I hadn't noticed before, but standing next to Tony was a large, green plastic garbage bin. The next second out of the corner of my eye I saw it come flying through the air towards Bluey.

'Look out!' I yelled.

Well of course nobody had any idea why I yelled and everybody sort of ducked a little, expecting a flying turd or something. Everybody, that is, except Mulatto Mick. He only ducks for semitrailers and low-flying aircraft. Then the garbage can sails straight over Col's head and hits Mick flush in the right eye, knocking him backwards off his feet. His Kangol flew in one direction, the brolly in another and

Mick's now sitting on the floor with his legs straight out in front of him, holding his eye.

'I'll get you next time, Bluey,' Tony yelled, 'you bloody sod!' and sat down proudly on the steps, oblivious to what he's done.

Mick's sitting on the floor with his hand over his eye, totally nonplussed at being hit because Mick doesn't feel pain. It just took him by surprise, that's all. It's when he took his hand off his eye and saw all our reactions that it started. He was cut right across the top of his right eyebrow. It looked like Tony had opened up an old war wound because blood was streaming down Mick's face and his eyeball was crimson red. The whole right side of his face was swelling purple and looked like somebody had backed a small car into it.

'Oh shit, Sal's gonna fuckin' kill me!' was the first thing Mick said as we helped him up. He waltzed over to the mirror to take a look at his eye.

'I promised 'er I wouldn't get in any stinks in case I get hit. She don't want me in no weddin' photos looking like I've been in a fuckin' blue and . . . Oh fuck,' he said as he saw the extent of the damage. 'She's gonna fuckin' haemorrhage when she sees this. I'll be fuckin' coated fer life! Oh shit . . . weddin's in three fuckin' days!'

He was freaked at the thought of what his ninety-eight pound bride-to-be was going to do to him when she saw him and I can understand why. He looked like he'd just gone twelve hard rounds with Floyd Patterson and got the serious end of the stick. During all this Tony hadn't said a word. We're all trying to console Mick and Col yells at Tony.

'Jesus, Tony, look what you've done. Mick's gettin'

married in three days and look what you've done to his face.'

'Well, he shouldn't have been in here in the first place, should he?' Tony replied. 'It's not my fault if he comes wandering in here during our meeting, is it?'

We all just stood there looking at one another in total disbelief. First, Tony's completely unapologetic about what's happened and, second, it hasn't dawned on him who it's happened to. Mick is a steel-hard street bloke and like all Crossies he's tremendously proud. Street pride, honour and face were of supreme importance to him and to lose them was unthinkable.

'Come on, Tony,' said Vince. 'Do the right thing. Come over and say sorry to Mick. Maybe we can speak to Sally and help him out.'

'Yeah. Good idea. Fuckin' oath,' we all eagerly agreed, trying to cool things.

'I'm not apologising to anybody! It wasn't my fault! If anyone's to blame it's Bluey! He's the one that started it, the bloody sod!'

Ooooh shiiittt! I heard my arse say as I realised the Aztecs' rhythm guitar player was about to die before we'd even released a record. Mick simply stood there, staring bullets at Tony. He didn't say a word, just stood there holding a cloth that Blue had given him over his eye, with blood streaming down his face and steam coming out of his ears.

'Come on, Tony,' I said. 'Do the right thing. You know Bluey was only ragging you. Apologise to Mick, mate, come on.'

'I won't!' said Tony defiantly. 'I'm the one who should be getting the apology.'

And then he said it!!

'Anyway, he's had his face cut before. He's been in so many fights people will only notice something wrong if he hasn't got a black eye!'

Ooooh shiiitt! said my arse again.

Well that was it. In the blink of an eye Mulatto Mick shot across the lobby, up the stairs and grabbed Tony by the throat.

'You little Pommie prick!' he screamed into his face. 'I'm gonna fuckin' kill ya. I'll kill ya. Apologise to me 'n' me missus or I'll break ya fuckin' poof neck, ya fuckin' mug. Ya hear?'

'I won't,' Tony half-garbled. 'I won't! I won't! I won't!'

None of us could believe what was happening. By this time we were all on the stairs trying to calm Mick down without pissing him off any more. In his rage he was ready to kill us all . . . then fuck us and eat us. Mick turned into a mad dog when he lost it. We all knew because we'd seen him nearly kill a couple of blokes in a fight one night. He was a maniac and you didn't fuck with maniacs. Mick was one of those blokes who became blinded by rage. He would kill and worry about hanging later. No thought for the consequences. Just kill, maim, obliterate and Tony was about to become a grease spot on the floor of life. Mick still had Tony by the throat with the four of us desperately trying to pull him off, but we couldn't budge him an inch. He was as strong as an ox. Tony was starting to turn purple and this was now a whole other situation.

'Don't put yer fuckin' hands on me! . . . Any of ya! I'll do the fuckin' lot of ya, ya hear?' Mick screamed at us. 'Now apologise, ya flamin' mug, or I'll do ya!'

He meant it and we knew it, and so must have Tony, but he either wouldn't or couldn't apologise. I'm thinking to myself, *Jesus I know we can get Mick off him, but what then? He's berserk and what are we going to do with him once we declare ourselves?* Mick's still choking away, with us hanging off him like flies on a turd.

'Oh shit, shit, shit! We gotta stop this,' yelled Vince. 'We'll all come round and see Sally before the show tonight,' he said in desperation. 'Tony too! Just let him go, for Christ sakes! You're killing him! You can't get married on Sunday if you're in gaol!'

Well 'can't get married' and 'in gaol' must have been the magic combination, because right after they hit the air, Mick dropped Tony, who slipped to the floor with a flop like a damp rag. He must have weighed all of 100 pounds soaking wet. What I hadn't realised was that all this time Mick had still been holding the cloth to his eye. He'd been strangling Tony with only one hand and even then four of us couldn't get him off.

'Yeah, we'll come around later,' I agreed.

'Me too,' said Col and Bluey.

In an instant Mick's rage subsided. 'Will yas?' he asked like a little kid again. His switch back to the other personality scared me as much as the raging bull. Mick was out there and we all saw it!

'Yeah, what's a good time?' Bluey asked.

'Aw, Sal gits 'ome frum work 'bout five-thirty. Can yous be there by six?'

'Sure! Yep! Yeah! Fuckin' oath!' we replied.

Mick turned and went down the stairs, picked up his Kangol and brolly, and walked out the door without a word.

'Wait a minute,' yelled Vince. 'What's the address?'

Mick waltzed back inside, scribbled the address on a

piece of paper, then turned and left, once again without a word. We all raced back to Tony who was still semiconscious on the stairs and just at that moment Ma Harrigan walked into the lobby. She saw us all around Tony's limp body.

'Oh boys, boys, what's happened? Is Tony all right? What happened?'

She pushed us out of the way and started administering CPR on Tony, who began to come around, moaning like an old cow. We sat him against the brass railing and he started to focus.

'What happened, boys? Who on earth did this?' Ma asked, bewildered.

We all started to talk at once.

'One at a time, please,' she pleaded and Vince told her the whole story.

'Oh, my, my, what a silly boy,' she said, looking at Tony. 'Why on earth didn't you apologise? You were in the wrong, you know. It would have been so easy. It's always easier to apologise than fight. Nobody wins when you fight. It's terrible . . . terrible!'

We all nodded our heads in agreement.

'So you're all going around to see his fiancée, eh?' Ma said. 'That's the right thing to do. What time?'

'I'm, er, not . . . going,' mumbled Tony.

'What do you mean?' I asked.

'I mean, I'm not apologising to, to anyone. It wasn't my fault, it was Bluey's. And that's all there is to it.'

'We should've let 'im kill the Pommy cuuu . . . Oh sorry, Ma,' said Bluey.

'Yes, well! What do you mean, Tony? You have to apologise or there's no telling where this thing may lead.

You know how proud some of those boys and girls are. Even if you were in the right, I'd apologise to save the consequences. Two words Tony, just two words. "I'm sorry".'

'I'm not going to apologise. If you all want to, OK, but I'm not and, and that's that.'

'Where would you like to be buried?' chuckled Bluey.

'Tony,' said Col, 'if Mick doesn't get an apology from you one way or another, sooner or later, 'e's going to pay back, and it won't be with a bunch of flowers. That's for bloody sure.'

'Yes,' I agreed. 'Mick's not going to lose face over this. God, he's getting married with an eye like a punch-drunk fighter and that's bad enough, the poor bugger. Can you imagine what the wedding photos will look like? I mean he's going to look like a Chinese bouncer in a suit anyway, but with that eye he's going to look hilarious, and Mulatto Mick definitely doesn't like being laughed at. He's a madman, Tony! For God's sake, you're turning this into something that's going to get very nasty if it's not stopped quick! This bloke's not one of your old school chums from Norfolk, raised on cucumber sandwiches. He's going to rip your head off!'

'I won't apologise. I won't,' Tony said defiantly.

'Ah, fuck him!' said Bluey storming off, mumbling obscenities to himself.

'He didn't mean any offence, Mrs Harrigan,' said Vince, like the gentleman he was. 'It was a real mess here and it upset Bluey as much as any of us. He's just upset, that's all.'

'I know, son,' she said appreciatively. 'Look, Tony, I'm going to ask you one more time for my sake. Please, son, do the right thing and go round with the boys and apologise. What you're doing isn't right. It's just not right, and these boys shouldn't be made to suffer any consequences that could come from this. You owe that boy and his fiancée an apology.'

'I'm not and that's final!' said Tony. 'Now if you'll excuse me I'm going to go home to lie down for a while. I don't feel very well, but I'll be all right to play tonight. I'm afraid I won't be doing much singing, though.'

His neck had a couple of big, blue bruises either side from Mick's death grip, but apart from that and the fact he was a little shaky on his feet, he seemed OK.

'Are you sure you don't want to go and see Doctor Jahil?' asked a concerned Ma Harrigan.

'No, no. I'll be fine. Just need a wee cup of tea and a lie-down and I'll be all right, thank you. Thank you all for trying to help me,' he said and walked down the stairs. 'Will someone pack up my guitars and put them in Mrs Harrigan's office where they'll be safe?'

With this he walked toward the front door. 'See you at eight forty-five sharp,' he said and left.

Well, that's how it all got started. None of us could believe it. Nothing like this had happened to the band before and we were completely lost on how to deal with Tony's ridiculous attitude and outright refusal to make it right. Mick was one of the Redfern boys and they were a tough tit-tie to suck. If this stupid incident got them all off-side we could be in for some real fun and games. We stood around talking about it for a while and then took off, having decided that, with or without Tony, the right thing to do was to go and see Sally and explain that it was an accident. She was a big fan of the band and a really nice girl. Our taking the time to go around would definitely take the edge off it a little. We agreed to meet at five-thirty, then get a cab out to Redfern.

I got back to Surf City at about five-fifteen and found Ma Harrigan sitting at a table in the lobby going through some photos of the band. We'd had some band jackets made about two weeks before and had our first band photos taken a few days ago. Bluey had constantly farted loudly during the session and it stunk bad. It broke everyone up and created some hilarious shots, but it totally embarrassed the photographer and his assistant who were both from the fashion business and very, very light in the loafers. To Bluey they were like a red rag to a bull. If farting hadn't offended them enough, I swear he'd have taken a dump right there on their studio floor just to get a rise out of them. He was a scream. The jackets were a copy of one that Jimmy Prescott had bought in London. We'd admired it so much that he let us take it to Pineapple Joe so that he could copy it for us. It was made from grey polished cotton with black buttons and piping all the way up the front and had no lapels. Sort of like a cool Guardsman's jacket.

'Oh, Billy, there you are,' Ma said. 'Mick's Sally just called and said there's no need to come over and that she understands. She realises it was all an accident. The only problem is that Mick's still fuming and demands a personal apology from Tony. She advises Tony to do the right thing because she can't control Mick when he gets like this.'

'Thank God for that,' I said, relieved at not having to go. 'Ma, I really don't think Tony's going to budge on this. You know how stubborn he can get. He has a weird sense of right and wrong. Sometimes he acts like he's from another planet.'

'I know, I know,' she sighed, 'but something's going to have to be done to change his mind. This thing's not going to go away. It's about honour. Now Sally said Mick doesn't hold any grudge against any of you boys and he said to say sorry for the way he acted to you all, but he has it in for Tony and he's not going to let it be from what Sally said.'

'OK,' I said. 'You tell the others when they get here. I'll pop in and see Tony and see if I can talk some sense into him.'

The early evening bustle of the Cross instantly took my mind away from what was going on. It always did. My fascination with the Cross, the characters and especially the night-shifters, never left me, and whenever I found myself walking its streets, its rich history and the excitement of my surroundings were a constant stimulant. As I crossed Darlinghurst Road the neon was just coming to life. The smell of the freshly cooked pizzas, barbie'd chicken and kebabs from the Kings Cross Bar-B-Que on the opposite corner hit my nose as the music of the street hit my ears. A light wind blew up from the harbour, jostling the hair and skirts of the pretty young girls walking past on their way home from work. Small willy-willies danced feverishly in circles like whirling dervishes, carrying little puffs of dust and litter along the footpath and street. The tiniest night-shifters, the sparrows, darted in flocks from rooftop to rooftop as the last hint of sunset put the final touches of deep red and blue on the ever-changing palette of the sky.

I made my way down Bayswater Road to the Hampton Court Hotel, climbed the stairs up to the third floor and knocked on Tony's door like a drum fill, but he didn't get it. There was no answer so I knocked again. Still no answer. Then it occurred to me that Tony could think I was Mick or one of his mates, so I yelled out to him through the old wood-panelled door.

'Tony, it's Billy, let me in. I need to talk to you.'

I heard rustling and grumbling inside and the sound of Tony coming to the door. He half opened it, looking warily left and right down the hall.

'It's OK, mate, it's only me. Listen, we've got to get this sorted out,' I said. 'Can I come in or are we going to have this conversation out here in the hallway?'

'Oh, sorry Billy,' he said with a gentle sigh. 'Come in, yes of course. Please come in.'

As I entered Tony's room I realised that this was the first time in all these months that I'd actually been inside. Outside of the band Tony was a very private person and kept very much to himself. He wasn't rude about it, he was simply a quiet loner and we all respected his privacy. The door wouldn't open all the way and when I squeezed around it I saw why. Tony's room was no more than twelve feet by eight and stacked floor to ceiling, on the top of the wardrobe, cupboards and sideboard, were comics. Hundreds and hundreds of them. They were under his bed, behind the door, in the sink, anywhere he could find to stash, heap or stuff them. Tony's room was jammed to the rafters with bloody comics.

'Holy shit!' I exclaimed. 'What's all this stuff, mate?'

'What stuff?' he replied as if it was perfectly normal living in a comic shop.

'What do you mean what stuff?' I picked up a comic from one of the piles behind the door. 'This stuff,' I said, waving it at him.

'Oh just a few comics,' he said. 'I like to read comics and I collect a few too. Oh be careful with that one. It's an original *Purple People Eater* with the Sheb Wooley record inside. That will be worth quite a lot one day.'

'Just a few! Jesus, there's hundreds,' I said, carefully putting the *Purple People Eater* back on its pile.

'Four thousand two hundred and fifty-three actually.'

'Four thousand! I, er, ah yes,' I said, mouth agape.

'Yes, I've read them all. Some of them a couple of times. I find them very stimulating and relaxing.'

Whatever turns you on, Tony my son I thought, smiling and nodding my head. *Christ, if Bluey ever finds out about this he'll never leave Tony alone. Well I'm sure as shit not going to be the one to open that can of worms.*

'Listen, Tony, we've got to get this thing sorted out.'

'What thing, Billy?' he inquired matter of factly.

'Don't give me that shit, Tony. You know what I'm talking about or did that strangling today deprive your peanut brain of so much oxygen you've got amnesia? Don't screw around with this. You may have a real problem here, mate. We've got to do something.'

'You can do what you like,' he said. 'I'm not doing anything! I'm certainly not apologising to that street thug and if he threatens me, or tries to do me any harm, I shall go to the police! I'll, I'll go to the authorities.'

'Listen, Tony, mate, Mulatto Mick doesn't give a shit about coppers. He eats two bloody coppers every morning with his rice bubbles. He's gonna top you if you don't do something. By his code you've insulted him and he wants satisfaction. It's that simple,' I said as convincingly as I could, but it didn't even make a dent. 'And by the way he's right.'

'What do you mean?' he said indignantly.

'Shit, where in the world did you learn to think like this? You lose your temper, throw a half-full garbage can across the lobby, hit some poor innocent mug who's just plucked up enough courage to ask us to be his groomsmen square in the eye, bust it wide open three days before his wedding, and you stand there and say "What do you mean?" What are you, fucking soft in the head or what? You're bloody wrong, Tony, and what you're doing, or more importantly not doing, is going to stuff us all up if you don't apologise. Christ, he deserves it! He may be just a street tough to you, Tony, but those street toughs as you call them pay their hard-earned money four and five nights a week to see our bloody band. Without them we'd be nowhere. They are good people and our biggest fans. They've fucking adopted us and consider us family . . . and you just spat in one of their faces and refuse to apologise. What are you, nuts or what?'

'No, I've just got my principles, that's all,' he replied.

'Principles! Princifuckingples! What the fuck are you mumbling about? Principles, my arse! Mate, if I were you I'd get your principles and your fucking seconds to start training hard, because this guy is going to take you apart and there won't be any pieces left to put back together when he's finished . . . because he'll have fucking eaten them all.'

'I don't care. I'm not being dictated to by anyone, and that's that! I had enough of that in England. That's why I'm here.'

'Look, Tony,' I said, making one last attempt to talk some sense into him, 'all Mick's mates in Redfern are going to know about this by now. He can't back down now, even if he wanted to. Don't you understand that? The longer you take, the harder he's going to hit you! Mate, you're starting something here that could get way out of hand.'

'Billy, I appreciate you coming here and I hear what you're saying,' Tony replied calmly, 'but you're not going to change my mind. So if you would excuse me I'd like to take a bath, get some fish and chips, have a cup of tea, and a little rest before the shows tonight.'

'OK, Tone old mate, if that's the way you want it, it's your neck and I hope not mine. But you better learn to swallow those fish and chips whole 'cause by this time tomorrow your teeth may be hangin around Mick's neck on a fucking string. See you at nine then.' I squeezed between the mounds of comics and the door and left.

As I walked down the hall I heard him sing out, 'Eight forty-five sharp, Billy. We start *playiiing* at nine.'

20
Mulatto Mick's Revenge

THE night of Tony and Mulatto Mick's little lunchtime saga proved uneventful. We did the gig and went home. Nothing unusual. Big Ivan sat backstage all night, bless his soul. Unfortunately if Mick and fifty Redfern boys had arrived, Ivan would have been about as much use as half a thimbleful of KY in a gay bathhouse, but the effort was at the least reassuring.

After the gig, Bluey, Vince and Col hopped into the '38 Hudson and took off for Hornsby, and Tony, Ivan and I headed down Bayswater Road. We saw Tony up to his comic shop and Ivan walked me home. Ivan never said that much because everything was hard for him to say, but halfway down the hill he asked me,

'Er, B-Billy, what's T-T-Tony g-going to do 'b-b-b-out this?'

'I don't think he'll do anything, Ivan. Why?'

'W-w-w-well, er, I know s-some of those R-R-Redfern

boys an' they're as t-tough as bricks. Some of them ha-have got g-guns, mer-mate. Tony's g-g-going to have to b-be c-c-careful, you know?'

'I know,' I answered. 'You just keep an eye on him and I'm sure he'll be OK. Goodnight, mate.'

'G-g-goodnight,' he said and lumbered back up Bayswater Road.

The next day the band decided not to rehearse. Pepper and I went to Camp Cove, which is one of the most beautiful little harbour beaches in Sydney. It was a gorgeous day, the water was warm, refreshing and relaxing and the sun burnt hot in a cloudless blue sky. A mate of mine, Jimmy Errol, always arrived at the beach in his speedboat and that day, after tying up to a buoy about a hundred yards from the shore, he and his girlfriend Paula swam ashore dragging a small punt which was loaded with fresh seafood he'd bought at Watsons Bay. We ate a fresh crayfish and prawn lunch on the beach, watching huge liners and sailing boats going to and fro between Sydney heads and the harbour. An afternoon on an Aussie beach, looking at someone like Pepper in a string bikini, can make you forget just about anything. The water in front of us must have been particularly warm and refreshing, because lots of blokes seemed to end up swimming there. I hadn't thought that much about Tony and Mick all day and it wasn't until I got to the dressing-room at Surf City that it really came back. Bluey, Col and Vince were already there and by the excited chatter I heard as I walked down the stairs, I knew all was not well in Rock'n'Rollville.

As I walked in the door they were all huddled talking to Stan the Shine. Stan had a shoe-shine stand in a little basement alcove under the Hampton Court which also contained a barber's and the Kings Cross dry cleaners. You could go into that alcove looking like a bum, get a haircut and a shave, sit in a booth in your underclothes while they pressed your clothes and Stan put a mirror shine on your shoes, and walk out looking like a million quid.

Spit-polished shoes were all the fashion and Stan was a wizard with a can of boot polish, some water and his rags. There was none better. He was an artist. Everybody kept their shoes immaculately clean and spit-polished, especially the Crossies. It was *de rigeur* and the key to being well dressed. In those days you could tell a lot about someone by the state of their shoes and to step on somebody's mirror shine was to provoke an instant altercation. Anyone who didn't bother to take care of their shoes or had grotty clothes was regarded as a 'chat', and to be called a chat was a low insult. The two best known shines in Sydney were Stan and the stand at Edward Mellor's shoe store in the city where, amongst others, Bobby Stutters worked. Bobby was a Brisbane knockabout I knew who got his stutter after being knifed in a fight.

The shine stands sometimes doubled as SP betting shops and if you needed something like a radio or TV at the right price and didn't mind having to put on asbestos gloves to turn it on, the stand was the place to find out where to get it. They also acted as the information centre for the grapevine. The 'drum', which is street slang for whatever was happening, or rumours of anything that was about to go down on the streets, came through the shines. They were the ears of the street and the drum was generally reliable.

As I walked into the dressing-room Col saw me and said, 'The drum's on the street that Mulatto Mick's going to do Tony this weekend.'

'What?' I said.

'Yeah, 'e's gunna fuckin' giv'im the 'idin'v 'is life,' said Stan, who spoke by running all his words together. 'Mick's putout th'drum 'n' its ferfuckinreal, me old. Tony's fuckin' coated fersure.' He shook the lapel of his jacket with his forefinger and thumb.

To be 'coated' or 'put on the coat' was street slang for hung out to dry. If someone was coated it could mean they would get a hiding or everybody should 'drop off' them, which was like being sent to Coventry. Or a bloke might say, 'me missus has given me the coat', which meant she'd split. It all depended on context. The street signal for someone being on the coat was a shake of the lapel, and Tony had been coated. I knew Stan well enough to know that if this had come through him it was real. In 1964 there was no better shine and, except for old Dulcie, no better pair of ears in the city. Stan got the real drum on everything.

'Now yous dunafta wurry,' Stan continued. 'Drum's that yous ersweet! It's Tony'scoated, not yous. Yerserall sweet. Now gotta 'sorf. Sweet?' he said, touching the tip of his nose with his forefinger in the old street sign.

'Sweet as a nut, Stan,' I replied, touching mine. 'Any idea of when?'

'Drum sez Saterdee, me'old. Now I gotta hit the toe. See yous.'

'Bye mate and thanks again,' we replied. 'Yeah thanks. Thanks Stan. Fuckin' oath.'

Tony arrived right on eight forty-five as usual and we played two sets to about a thousand punters. It's weird how you don't see something until it's not there and what I saw was that the make-up of the crowd was different. A lot of the regulars were missing. The drum was out all right, and

Tony was in the shit! Before he arrived we had decided, along with Ma Harrigan, not to say anything to Tony about Stan's little visit. There was no way to know how Tony would handle it. He was likely to get on the microphone, start jumping up and down, tell the whole bloody city what had gone down and make things even worse. We decided to handle it our own way, with a little help from Ivan. Ivan had offered to act as Tony's bodyguard and sit outside his room on a chair for a few nights, just keep an eye on him and escort him to and from the gig. John Harrigan organised some extra security for the next two nights and we all waited to see what would happen. Friday night was uneventful and come Saturday night Surf City was packed with about 2000 dancing punters. As usual I walked in through the crowd and said hello to some of them. At least half the crowd were Crossies. They were all there. Paddo, Glebe, Maroubra, Bronte, Coogee, even guys I'd only seen once or twice from Parramatta, Bankstown and Dee Why. What I didn't see was Redfern.

Christ, what's going on here? I thought as I walked through the crowd, shaking hands to choruses of 'What's doing, me' old?' and 'G'day, Thorpie.'

I went backstage to the dressing-room. Tony and Ivan were already there. Tony looked immaculate as usual, but poor old Ivan looked the bit worse for wear from having spent the last two nights asleep in a chair outside Tony's door.

'Jesus, Ivan,' I said, 'you look a bit buggered tonight, mate.'

'N-n-not m-m-m-much sleep,' he mumbled.

'Listen,' I said. 'Tony's fine down here for the moment. Why don't you slip out for a coffee and take a break. We don't go on for another half hour. You'll have plenty of time.'

'M-M-Mrs Harrigan s-s-said n-not to l-leave Tony alone,' he replied.

'Mate, he'll be fine here,' I told him. 'I'll sweeten it for you if she spits the dummy. Go and relax for half an hour.'

'O-O-OK,' he said and off he ambled, the whole dressing-room shaking as he went up the stairs.

'So how are you, Tony? Feeling all right?' I asked. 'You get some sleep?'

'I'm fine, thank you, Billy. Don't worry about this silly rumour. I'll be fine. It will all blow over.'

'What rumour?' I asked innocently.

'Come on, Billy, I live in Kings Cross too, you know. I know what that brute is threatening to do and I don't believe a word of it. It will all blow over soon and I'll talk to Mick then.'

'What!' I exclaimed. 'You'll talk to Mick after its blown over, but not in time to blow it over. What the fuck is wrong with you, son? Have you lost it completely or what?'

'I've got my pride too,' he said pathetically. 'I won't be told how to act. *I won't!* I'll do things in my own way, when *I'm* ready!'

Even though his pride was causing a bloody awful stink, in a way I couldn't help but admire him. He'd just admitted he was wrong by saying he'd talk to Mick, but he was sticking to his guns no matter what. I had to respect that, even though I thought he was a mug for letting it get this far.

'Get fucked! No you get fucked! Aw go and get fucked!' No mistaking that old refrain. The rest of the band had arrived. They all came rumbling in together and we all said g'day.

After we'd changed, Col pulled me aside. 'Billy I've brought a few mates down from Hornsby,' he said, 'just in case we need 'em. There's about a dozen of 'em and they're all tough bludgers. These boys go off like a fuckin' charity moll at a poorhouse picnic. They're gonna 'ang 'round near the front of the stage 'n' keep an eye on things. They'll stick round after and 'ave a few beers to make sure everything's OK, so don't worry, my son. Between Ivan, fifteen bouncers and these blokes we can handle the fuckin' St George football team. Sweet?'

'Sweet as a nut, mate,' I replied, shaking his hand.

We went on and played the first set which was a bit tense but went over like gangbusters.

The crowd was fantastic and reacted strongly to everything we played, especially to a couple of new songs we'd learnt that week called 'Poison Ivy' and 'Sick 'n' Tired'. Jimmy Prescott had given us the original recordings on his last visit. The dance floor was packed as usual with different combinations of Crossies and Surfies and the joint was rocking hard! All through the set I kept looking around the packed room and up in the balcony for any signs of trouble, but everything was normal. Col's mates all hung around the front of the stage, and some sat at the foot of the stairs. Ivan had placed bouncers at crucial spots all around the room, their white shirts glowing like neon in the black light that gave Surf City such a magic atmosphere. From where they were standing they could quickly get to the stage or dressing-room at any sign of trouble. Ivan sat on a chair behind the main stage curtain to our right, just out of sight of the crowd. Throughout the set all of us on stage glanced at one another giving 'everything seems OK' signs, and everything did indeed seem to be sweet. It looked like the threat was just that and nothing more.

The first set ended to applause and cheering and when I

announced we'd be back in thirty minutes another cheer went up. 'My Boyfriend's Back' hit the PA system and the dance floor filled up with about 300 Crossie girls who immediately formed up in lines of pairs, cutting straight into the Wellington, much to the delight of the crowd.

Business as usual, I thought as I left the stage. I caught Col and Bluey checking out the happenings on the floor below. They both looked over at me and from their smiling faces I could see they were thinking the same. *It's all sweet!*

We took our break and everybody was happy. John Harrigan came down to see how things were going and have a beer with us. We relaxed with John and some friends who'd popped in and, before we knew it, it was show time again and we went back on stage for the next ninety-minute set. Everything started off normally, with punters shouting out requests as we plugged in.

'Do "Poison Ivy" again,' a girl's voice shouted from the crowd. 'And "Sick 'n' Tired",' another shouted. 'Blue Day', 'Shout', 'Walkin' the Dog' came more requests as I counted in 'Poison Ivy'.

We were about halfway through the set when a fight started at the back right-hand side of the theatre and it looked like a beauty. The nearby crowd all shot to the other side of the room and although we were a hundred-odd feet away, and it was dark back there, I could see at least a dozen blokes going at it big time. As usual, as soon as someone went down others came out of the crowd to put the boot in, then melted back. Then someone would whack one of the anonymous kickers and more guys got stuck in. That's the way they all seemed to develop. There weren't that many big fights in Surf City, but when there were they were usually beauties. Straight away, all the bouncers shot back to get into the action and I could see gleaming white shirts throwing punches, dragging people off one another and carrying them across the room to the door at the rear of the room. Although I couldn't see it, I knew their next destination, via mid air, was down a flight of stairs, through the double fire doors, and out onto the Victoria Street footpath. Kaathwack!

When fights start at gigs, most times the worst thing the band can do is to stop playing. This just draws attention to the trouble and everybody gets involved. Particularly in a place as large as Surf City. Most of the time the punters not in the immediate vicinity are either unaware or not affected by the trouble. So we kept rocking and most of the crowd kept rocking right along with us. As usual the tough, well-organised Surf City bouncers seemed to be getting things under control and I casually looked around to see what Ivan was doing during all this.

Ivan was gone!

Turning back to the audience I looked up into the balcony. Thirty seconds earlier it had been full of punters. Now they were gone too! In their place stood about twenty-five Redfern boys and, held firmly in their grip, stood a helpless Ivan.

Oh Christ, it's on!

I turned to see if Tony had noticed Ivan on the balcony and freaked!

There, standing on the stage right next to him was Mulatto Mick, dressed in his usual outfit, his swollen black eye glowing in the stage lights. He was on Tony's right, slightly behind him, and Tony hadn't seen him yet. Tony was just smiling at me and playing along. I think the rest of us saw Mick at the same time. Before anybody could move, in front of 2,000 people, Mick spun Tony around, tore his guitar off and threw it into the crowd, then fired a massive right into his gut.

Oooossh! was the only sound Tony made as the air shot out of his lungs.

As Tony doubled over Mick stepped back and, putting all his weight behind it, hit him with a sledgehammer right uppercut to the chin. Tony shot straight up in the air and about two feet off the stage floor, went into a backward arc and sailed off the front of the stage like an Olympic high diver, down into the crowd fifteen feet below. I expected to see people holding cards up with 10 on them, it was so graceful. The crowd parted and Tony hit the floor like sixteen tons of wet shit. He was out cold before he even got into the air, so he didn't feel a thing when he landed.

In a split second people, some of them female, came from everywhere and started to put the boot into him bad. Some of Col's mates jumped in and started firing punches in all directions. Bluey, Col, Vince and I all jumped off the stage at the same time, flattening about a dozen people as we landed. Then we all got stuck in as well. Tony was lying on his back like a rag doll with one of his legs twisted under him. His face was a bloody mess and he looked seriously hurt. Col's mates were managing to keep people from getting to him and, realising the fight up the back was a diversion, the bouncers had come down and were now in the thick of the fray. Some of our other Crossie fans and their girlfriends joined in to give us a hand, which was fantastic, except this got a lot more people going who didn't like seeing a mate get hit. Before I knew it the whole place went off like a fucking atom bomb!

I got knocked down from a punch in the mouth as soon

as I hit the floor. And I saw Bluey and Col both go down as well. I got straight up thinking *fuck this!* and got knocked flat on my arse again. This time when I got up I hit anything, male or female, that looked like they wanted to have a go. Within thirty seconds my suit was in shreds and I was covered in blood, fortunately a lot of it other people's.

Now I'm only five feet eight and a half . . . believe me that half is very important! Anyhow, I'm only five eight and a half, but as far as I could see in every direction was one massive brawl. There must have been 300 or more people going at it big time! The screaming became hysterical as more and more people got sucked in. Waves of them were being pushed on top of one another by unlucky punters trying to get out of the way as new hot spots flared around them, and the brawl became even more intense.

The main house lights were still out and in the eerie black light it was impossible to tell who was who. All we knew was that Tony was still lying unconscious, with us all around him either trying to keep Mick's boys from giving him a kicking or just keeping the fight in general from trampling him. Some big rough tart about twice my size had me off the ground by my hair and was giving me a terrible hiding, when a microphone stand hit the floor beside me, followed by another, then a third landed right on top of her ugly fucking head with a hollow sounding doiiing! She gave me a 'where the fuck did that come from?' look and dropped out cold, dropping me on my head as she fell.

I looked up and saw Bluey frantically tossing the stands from the stage. He let out a rebel yell and, mike stand in hand, jumped back into the fight feet-first. Loved a stink, did Bluey! Col and I grabbed stands and started swinging them. Two of Col's mates did the same and it started to clear a path. People were going down left and right like bowling pins. I had no idea who I was hitting, I just heard the splat and felt the shock wave run up the stand every time it connected. This was no time to be discriminating. We had to get Tony out of there.

A big, handsome bouncer mate of mine by the name of Reg Delaney picked Tony up off the floor, put him on his shoulder in a fireman's carry and started for the side emergency exit which was on the opposite side of the bloody room. A mixture of punters, bouncers and Col's mates got in front of Reg and a similar group, including the band, got behind him and to his left, and together we started clearing a way through the brawl. We had the edge of the main stage to our right so we didn't have to worry too much about that side. Reg was in the centre of us, carrying Tony, and was pretty well protected on all sides. Tony hung unconscious over Reg's shoulder with his upper body and head dangling lifelessly down Reg's back.

As hard as we tried, we couldn't stop some mugs from getting at him. Every few feet a fist or foot came out of the surrounding melee and hit Tony on the side of his face or back of the head and he just flopped around like a human punching bag. By the time we made it to the exit Tony must have taken at least six more solid hits to the head and a dozen hard blows to his upper body. I thought he was dead.

'Someone get up over the main stage and open the fuckin' emergency exit,' Reg screamed. '*Quick!!*' Bluey and I clambered up together, ran down the backstage stairs and opened the big fire doors. Just as we got them open Reg ran around the corner of Victoria Street with Tony still over his shoulder. He had Col, Vince and about a dozen of our helpers with him but no one else, thank God. He carried Tony inside, taking him straight into the dressing-room. All we could hear from upstairs was what sounded like roaring, stampeding elephants as the fight continued.

Reg laid Tony on the couch. One of the helpers ran out to call an ambulance, and the full extent of Tony's damage became obvious. His head was swollen up to the size of a small watermelon, his face an unrecognisable mess of blood and dirt. I listened to his heart and it was beating erratically but fairly strongly. Reg grabbed a towel and soaked it in an ice tub and started cleaning the blood from Tony's face. Because the face bleeds so much when it's cut, it's impossible to assess the damage until it's cleaned. From the position of his jaw it was easy to see that it was badly broken. Both his eyes were blue and swollen shut, blood trickled from his mouth and his lips were split and swollen like two over-ripe Chiquita bananas. Both his cheeks were cut open, he had a gash running from the middle of his forehead down to the corner of his right eye, and several egg-sized bumps on his head. He also had patches of hair missing all over his scalp. In its place were large scratches and abrasions where the triple-D point kickers had peeled it off. Opening his mouth to see where the blood was coming from, I could see his gums were bruised and bleeding, but his teeth were all still there and intact. Tony would have liked that because he brushed the bastards a dozen times a day. Just then John and Ma Harrigan came in. She burst into tears at the sight of Tony's face.

'Oh Mother of God,' she screamed and rushed over to him. 'Tony! Tony! Are you all right, son?' she sobbed, but Tony couldn't have moved his mouth for a million quid.

She instantly composed herself and took charge. 'Put

some ice in that towel and hold it to his face. Let him breathe! Give him air!' she ordered. 'Somebody fan him with a towel. Now let's check his body.'

She asked me and John to take Tony's shirt off.

'Carefully! Be careful,' she instructed as we removed what was left of his shirt. His jacket was gone, along with his socks and shoes, and so was most of the right leg of his pants. His shredded shirt came off like wet, red tissue paper. As dirty as he was, it was easy to see that Tony's upper body had no actual cuts, but it was badly bruised and scraped from the kicking he'd taken, and from being dragged around the floor.

'Reg, soak another towel so I can clean his back,' Ma shouted. 'Quickly!'

While Reg got the towel she asked the rest of us if we were all right.

'We're all standin' here, ain't we?' said Bluey, sucking on a cold one.

'We'll be fine,' Vince said, 'just worry about Tony.' Col was standing nursing his head but he nodded he was OK.

Ma Harrigan began to clean Tony up. He had bruises and scrapes all over his upper body, front and back. She examined his ribs, collarbone, arms and hands and said nothing appeared to be broken. She thoroughly examined his legs, hips and groin and said there were no breaks, but his groin was badly swollen. She checked his jaw and confirmed it was snapped clean. I heard the sound of an ambulance outside. In a flash two St John's Ambulance men were working on Tony and insisting that everybody leave. Ma Harrigan said she wanted John and the band to stay. Everybody else shuffled out.

There had been about ten other people in the

dressing-room with us but none of us had really noticed. They were mainly Col's mates, a few regulars who'd joined in to help, a couple of the bouncers and some old drunk off Victoria Street who had wandered in and had been quietly sucking our beer down without anyone noticing.

We all shouted our thanks as they left. 'Come back and 'ave a beer after they've seen to Tony,' shouted Col.

'Shweet asafuggin' nutmaaaate,' mumbled the drunk as he fell out the door. The others followed.

The medics had an oxygen mask on Tony's face and some sort of drip in his arm. Ma Harrigan began giving them a detailed description, using medical terms, and it occurred to me by the way she'd handled things and the way she was now talking that she must have been a nurse at some stage.

What a bloody amazing lady you are, I thought as I watched her. *Just amazing!*

'Well, you're right, Mrs Harrigan,' I heard one of the medics say. 'There don't appear to be any breaks except for the jaw.'

'How bad *is* that?' she asked.

'Oh, snapped in two places, I'm afraid, but they're clean breaks. Should be good as gold in about six weeks, maybe less. Course I can't be a 100 per cent sure until we X-ray him. We need to X-ray his skull too, but everything seems to be in place. There's no sign of any internal bleeding or any bleeding from the brain. The eyes are dilated but fairly normal for this kind of shock. He's breathing pretty well on the oxygen and his lungs sound fine. No blood in there by the sound of it. He seems to have taken it pretty well. Don't be too alarmed at the head swelling, it's normal with this kind of trauma. I've seen a lot, lot worse! He's in shock of course and probably has a concussion. We'll take him to St Vincent's for a thorough examination. You're welcome to come if you wish, but just you, please, Mrs Harrigan. Have the police been called yet because we'll have to report this, of course.'

'Oh yes, of course,' she replied.

'Good,' he said, 'then as soon as we get a stretcher in here we'll be on our way.'

'Very good,' she replied, 'and thank you.'

'You're welcome,' he said. 'Anyone else in here think they might need some attention?' he asked to the room in general.

Nobody answered.

'Very well,' he said, 'but if any of you change your mind, come straight down to St Vincent's at once. Don't dilly-dally if you're hurt. OK?'

'OK,' we all replied.

While we were waiting for the stretcher, Ma Harrigan came over and asked again if we were really all right. I don't think any of us had given it any real thought until then. When we looked at each other and saw the state we were in, we burst into laughter and stood there shaking our heads.

'Oh boys, that's good. That is good news,' she said.

The stretcher arrived and they carefully moved Tony onto it.

'I better go with Tony,' Ma said. 'Don't worry, I'll stay with him until all the tests are done and I'll let you know as soon as I hear. Now, you boys get yourselves cleaned up and relax. It's been a big night and I pray that all this silly business is over. So stupid, so very, very stupid.'

As soon as she left we started examining ourselves for

injuries. None of us had any clothing left from the waist up, and we were all covered in blood and dirt.

'Aw I lost a fuckin' tooth. No, two!' said Bluey. 'Jesus my fuckin' face 'urts. Fuck!'

'Mine too,' said Col. 'I've lost a bloody tooth as well. Fuck it.'

My lips and tongue were swollen numb and I hadn't thought to check my teeth. Fuck me if one of them wasn't gone.

We all looked at Vince and he smiled a perfect set through his bloody face. The bludger! We looked at each other and fell into each other's arms, laughing.

'Fuckin' good blue though, eh?' said Bluey. 'What about that fat bludger I hit with me mike stand? I thought I'd killed the bastard.'

'What about the big sheila that jumped on ya back!' Col added excitedly. 'She was screaming and kickin' like a fuckin' mad woman, so I hit 'er on the chin and then some mug hit me on the head with a fuckin' bottle. I hit him in the nuts with me mike stand and 'e went down like a fuckin' turd down a toilet.'

'Yeah, she scratched the shit outta me back! Look at the bastard.' Bluey turned to show us the eight parallel scratches running across both sides of his back.

'That looks bad,' said Vince.

'I'll live. Only bloody scratches. I've 'ad plenty there before,' Bluey winked and laughed.

'Did anyone see who knocked me down?' I asked.

'Which fuckin' time?' laughed Bluey.

'The first time. You know, when we all jumped off the stage.'

'It was a sheila,' Col said, laughing.

'Ah bullshit!'

'It was. It was that big, tall, fat sheila from Darlinghurst. You know, always comes in with that ugly redheaded girlfriend of 'ers. Bluey calls 'em the Von Ugly sisters. You know her, Thorpie.'

'What, big Helen?' I said in disbelief. 'Why the fuck would big Helen hit me? She loves me.'

''Cause you landed right on top of 'er and 'er ugly fuckin' girlfriend,' Bluey informed me. 'You knocked her dopey girlfriend out cold. That's why, you silly little prick!'

'No I didn't . . . did I?'

'Yes you did!' They all laughed together. I just stood there with an 'Oh shit!' look on my face.

'What about that bloke that come sailin' off the balcony onto the fuckin' crowd?' said Bluey. 'You see that?'

I nodded.

'Me too,' said Col. 'Fuckin' amazing!'

'There was more than one,' I said. 'There were a few blokes fighting upstairs and every now and then they tossed someone into the crowd below. Christ, that's got to be twenty-five feet or more! It was like a bloody John Wayne movie.'

'Only better!' laughed Bluey. 'Now we're a fuckin' band. Let's have a bloody beer on it, come on.'

Bluey went and got us a beer each and proposed a toast. 'To Billy Thorpe and the Aztecs,' he said. 'If we can survive that we can survive any bloody thing!'

'To Billy Thorpe and the Aztecs,' we all answered and skolled the beers.

'Now its a fuckin' band,' Bluey repeated proudly.

We drank another beer and got cleaned up, washing ourselves as best we could in the dressing-room sinks. Every now and then someone would say, 'Look at this' or 'Jesus, will ya take a look at this' as we discovered new battle wounds. In general everybody was in pretty good shape, considering. Apart from a lost tooth, black eye, swollen mouth and jaw, bleeding gums, lots of scratches, very tender nuts, some missing hair and a bruised head, I was OK. If you're lucky you generally don't really feel the extent of being hit until the next day. It's like football injuries. I'd been hit and kicked plenty of times and I remember going down at least five times, but I was OK. One of the advantages of being small in a fight amongst so many people is that you don't stand out. If you're hard to see you're hard to hit. My adrenalin was pumping so bloody hard at one stage, and my little arse was moving so fast, you could only see where I'd been!

Anyway, I felt good, all things considered. Fights prove nothing and they're bloody insanity, but we had no choice. We were just four little guys from a rock band trying to help rescue our 100-pound mate from some very tough nutters who were kicking the shit out of him. We had more than held our own in that brawl and we all shared the pride in it. The only effect it would have on us was to make us stronger and closer. It had done already. As Bluey so aptly put it, 'Now we're a band.'

At some stage, I heard 'Mr Postman' blasting from the PA upstairs and the sound of the fight had died down. None of us had given any particular thought to what was happening upstairs or to how in hell Mulatto Mick and his boys had pulled the whole thing off. We were talking about it when John Harrigan walked in the dressing-room to see how we were doing. That's when we found out what had really taken place. It seems that Mick and his boys had inside help in getting him on stage. And the Darlingston coppers had been sent on some wild goose chase to a fictitious gang fight to get them out of the vicinity. These boys had been organised!

'What happened to Ivan?' I asked. 'Is he all right or what?'

'He's OK,' said John. 'He's got a broken jaw and nose. He's up at St Vincent's getting fixed up now. You know Ivan, he wouldn't even feel it.'

'How did they get him up in the balcony?' I asked.

'Well, it seems that someone came running backstage and told him there was a guy in the balcony with a gun and he was going to take a shot at Tony. Ivan raced up there and about twenty guys jumped him.'

'Was there a gun?' Vince asked.

'No. It was just a rort to get him away from the stage.'

'And it worked like a fuckin' beauty, didn't it?' Col responded.

'Jesus, what about the balls of those blokes?' I said.

'What about Mick? Has he got a serious set of nuts or what?' Bluey asked, laughing.

'Yeah.' I had to agree. 'Whether it was a shit act or not, it took some balls to get up there in front of two thousand punters and belt Tony like that. What a maniac!'

'Was anybody badly hurt?' Vince asked.

'Yeah, I think I crippled some poor bludger for life with me mike stand,' Col said.

'Well, there were quite a few busted heads and lost teeth, things like that, but no-one was hurt badly enough to require an ambulance,' said John. 'And a lot of those involved would never ask us for any help. They'll take care of their own in their own way.'

'What about the coppers?' Bluey asked John. 'Is anybody going to be charged or what?'

'Well, I called the police as soon as we realised what was happening. They don't care too much about this kind of trouble and are usually pretty slow to respond anyway. It's just bloody rock'n'roll larrikins fighting as far as they're concerned. Anyway, they were all down at Broadway trying to find some gang fight that had been called in by a number of people. By the time they got here all the heavies had left.'

'What about the punters?' Col asked. 'Did any of them want to press charges or anything?'

'No. Most of the ones who got badly hurt were involved and there's no way any of them would want to be talking to the police. What about you fellows and Tony? Do you want to do anything about this?'

'Like what?' I asked.

'Like press assault charges against Mick and his mates. I'm sure we can find plenty of witnesses.'

We all looked at one another.

'Press charges against them? You're kidding, aren't you, John?' I said. 'Leave it alone! It wouldn't surprise me to see them all come waltzing in the next time the band plays like nothing's happened. It's over.'

Everyone agreed with me.

'Good,' said John. 'I agree we should let it go. I already told the police that it was some drunken gang who weren't regulars, and I didn't think we could identify them anyway.'

'You shifty bastard,' said Bluey.

'That's why you hired me as your manager,' John laughed and we all laughed with him. 'But what about Tony?' he asked. 'Do you think he'll want to press charges?'

'I'll personally put me boot right up 'is Pommy arsehole if he does,' shouted Bluey.

'No, John,' said Vince. 'I think we can handle Tony. Right, boys?'

'Right!'

'Yeah, I think this has straightened a few things out in old Tony's head,' I added.

'And his trousers,' laughed Bluey and we all joined him.

'Great,' said John. 'My mother will be at the hospital for a while. Evidently Tony came around for a bit but he's under sedation now and we won't know any more until the morning. She said there's no point in you boys going up there. There's nothing you can do. You can call in the morning to see how he is. Now I've got to get back upstairs. We can talk on Monday about what we're going to do while Tony recovers. I'll be here for a while so stay as long as you like. Is there anything you need?'

'All right if I have a few of me mates come down and 'ave a beer?' Col asked. 'They really helped us out.'

'On me, Colin,' said John. 'Will six dozen Tooheys do?'

'Sounds 'bout right for a start!' Bluey suggested.

'I'll get someone to organise it. See you all on Monday. Maybe you should think about whether or not you want to play a few nights without Tony. You did it for quite a while, you know. I don't need an answer right away and it's your decision.'

'OK,' everybody replied.

Not long after he left we all went upstairs to see the battle-ground and to our amazement found there were still about fifteen hundred people dancing and laughing to the music as if nothing had happened. As we walked from behind the curtain and down the stairs to the floor, a cheer went up.

'What's happening?' Vince said to no one in particular.

As soon as we got down on the main floor groups of people came up to us and started shaking our hands and patting us on the back with 'Bloody good on yas', 'Yous were grouse!' 'Fuckin' oath!' and the like. Apparently we were bloody heroes. Many people asked about Tony and groups of young girls came up to us in tears over what had happened to him, wanting to know where he was so they could visit and send cards. Some of them were gorgeous. I caught Bluey ogling them.

'Jesus, mate, look at some of these fuckin' sheilas, will ya,' he whispered to me. 'That little Pommy cunt! Listen, take me up on the stage and bash me senseless with me fuckin' bass, will ya? I can 'andle some of this bloody sympathy.'

Vince and Col heard it too and we all started laughing. What was happening was really amazing and something told me to take advantage of it. I went back up on the stage and signalled the lighting man to give me a spot. The music died and as the spot hit me a cheer went up. Then absolute silence.

'I'm sorry for all the trouble tonight,' I began. 'As most of you know, shit like this doesn't happen here that often because we come here to have a good time, not to fight each other, right?'

'Right!' yelled the crowd.

'Right!' I yelled back. 'People are asking about Tony. For any of you that are interested, he's up at Saint Vincent's. The doctors seem to think he'll be OK!'

Another cheer.

'Obviously we won't be playing for a while but we've just finished our first record and it will be out in about a month, so go out and buy it. And if you like it tell your friends about it.'

'Yeah!' went the crowd.

'Tony, Bluey, Col, Vince and I want to thank you for giving us a hand and we'll see you as soon as Tony gets better. OK?'

'OK!' the crowd responded.

'All right. Now enjoy the rest of the night and we'll see you all soon.'

'Sherry, Sherry Baby' blasted out of the PA and the crowd got straight back into it.

About a week after the brawl I had a visit from Stan the Shine who told me that Mulatto Mick wanted to meet and could he set it up. I agreed and Mick and I had a coffee at the Spaghetti Bar. I told Angelo what it was all about and he put me in a booth at the back, out of view of the street. Mick arrived dressed as always with his Kangol and brolly.

'It's all sweet, me old,' he said. 'Tony's off the coat. No bad vibes. Sweet?'

'Sweet as a nut, Mick,' I replied.

He asked me to sweeten it with the Harrigans to get back into Surf City, and I did. They both agreed with me that it would be much better to have them all on side again, rather than create more friction by barring them. Apart from the fight, they'd been good to us and some of our staunchest supporters. I wanted them back. They had been there since the beginning. Regardless of how far he took it, Mulatto Mick had been legitimately provoked and I didn't foresee any future problems because he'd sworn to me there wouldn't be any. Big Ivan hated the idea but reluctantly went along with it. So it was sweetened.

That night was a major turning point for the band. What at first seemed to be a totally negative situation turned out to be one of the most positive things that could ever have happened to us. Miraculously, Tony didn't have any permanent damage and recovered fully. While in hospital he received hundreds of cards from people, mainly young girls. The hard-core fans became even more loyal and as word went out about the fight, the band's actions took on legendary proportions that had us single-handedly battling 500 mugs with nothing but our bare hands. As a result, other people became interested in us and our following got even stronger. It created an image for the band as ordinary blokes. Just average Aussie battlers who weren't afraid to get down amongst it when the shit hit the fan. It made us one of them and the events of that night were worth their weight in gold.

When our first single came out, I swear everyone in that crowd and their friends must have rushed out to buy it the same morning because the stores ran out. It created an incredible demand for the record and as a result people called radio stations like 2SM and 2UW requesting it. The stations played it a lot and this caused an even greater demand. Overnight we had our first hit with the song that Tony had written for us—'Blue Day'.

Life's weirder than shit, ain't it?

21
A Face at the Window

TONY was much better, so we started to play Friday and Saturday nights again and it was great to be back. After a week's rehearsal the band sounded better than ever and on our first night back 3000 fans crammed into Surf City and gave us a royal welcome. Mulatto Mick and some of his crew came in one night and he sent me a message that he wanted to speak to Tony. We agreed. Ivan reluctantly brought Mick backstage during a break and Tony was very nervous about it too, but when he saw Mick's smiling face he knew it was sweet.

To our surprise, Tony said 'I deserved it' and they shook hands.

It was all over and life went back to normal. 'Blue Day' had come out and was selling well and getting a lot of airplay. We were no longer under-bubblers. We were now contenders and a music business that had treated our success to date with complete indifference was now forced to take notice.

The music revolution was gaining pace. The Beatles had conquered the world in seven short months and by February 1964 they'd had four massive hits and Beatlemania had already spread as far as Australia. As I mentioned earlier, this new youth culture emerged worldwide in 1963, and for the same reasons everywhere. And we were part of this revolution and not—as so many people have been incorrectly informed since—a consequence. Of course the 'English Invasion' was a great benefit to us, but we had already put our roots down way before it hit big time.

Bands like the Beatles, Rolling Stones, Brian Poole and the Tremeloes, Johnny Kidd and the Pirates, the Searchers and Gerry and the Pacemakers were all becoming popular in Australia and our audiences, and some of the media, started to see us as the first Australian contribution to this phenomenon. For the first time since the glory days of Australian rock in the '50s and heroes like Johnny O'Keefe and Col Joye, Australia started to take its own musicians seriously again and, along with the excitement, a definite pride surrounded the local scene.

Although we were aware of other new young Aussie bands around Sydney, nobody significant had emerged as yet but it was undeniable that something very special was happening in the local scene. It became obvious from the offers we were receiving that we would be performing more and more outside of Surf City. John Harrigan became concerned that his crowds would dwindle when we weren't there, so he began auditioning bands with an eye to filling the spot in our absence. Dozens of young hopefuls tried out until John saw something that he felt showed promise. They were called Ray Brown and the Whispers and they had played at Surf City with us during weekend afternoons a number of times. Each time they came back they sounded and looked more like us, but that's the biz. Everybody cops somebody at the start. Like us, they built up a following and eventually went on to have national success with a number of hit singles, the biggest being 'Fool Fool Fool'.

We did an impromptu acoustic performance as a promotional stunt in the middle of George Street, in the heart of Sydney, one lunchtime, and some of the newspapers turned up to see why hundreds of kids were blocking traffic in the centre of town. That was the first time we had our photographs in the paper. Some radio stations picked up on it and as a result we did our first ever radio interviews, receiving dozens of calls on the air. By the things the callers were saying, I could tell they were all the Surf City crowd.

Pepper had not had any real time off from the Pussycat the whole time she'd worked there, so she asked Sir Wayne and Last Card if she could take a holiday and they agreed. She was a hard worker and they assured her her gig would be there when she wanted it. They even dropped fifty quid in her kick as a belated Christmas present. You know, people that run joints aren't always the scumbags most straights tend to think they are, and Last Card and Wayne were good people.

It was a Wednesday night, the *Maracosa* was back in port, and Natalie, Pepper and I took Candy and Jimmy down to Checkers as a treat to see the legendary black American Hammond player and singer, Earl Grant. Apart from the Silver Spade and Andre's, Checkers was the other elegant, happening room in Sydney and was set up like New York's famous Copacabana. It was owned by the wealthy Chinese businessman Dennis Wong, who was infamously tight. I was told that one night he booked the popular Sydney vocal group the Delltones and became famous in the industry when he tried to cut costs by trying to fire Pee Wee Wilson because he felt Pee Wee's low bass voice sounded like the bass guitar. He thought he could get the group cheaper for the night with one less singer. John Harrigan and Dennis had just started doing business together and I was always guaranteed a front row table, where I would be seated ceremoniously by one of Sydney's most famous maitre d's, Casim—or Casey to those who knew him. Casey made a big fuss of Pepper, Natalie and me that night, shouting us a bottle of Dom. I got invited to sing with Earl Grant and it turned into a fantastic night. The *Maracosa* boys had a ball and after a 1 a.m. nightcap listening to Sammy, who came in to sing for the late show, we said goodnight and got a cab home.

As soon as we were in the cab Pepper and Natalie started letching at me, wiggled out of their undies and threw them out the window . . . to the amazement of the old cabbie who couldn't believe his eyes at what was going on in the back seat. Both the girls had worn evening coats over their dresses and by the time we hit the Cross they'd both slithered out of their dresses and were naked under their coats except for suspenders and stockings. Out of the blue Natalie asked the driver to take us to Camp Cove.

'What?' he said in surprise, still trying to handle the only boner he'd had in twenty years.

'Camp Cove,' said Pepper. 'Down in Watsons Bay.'

'OK.' We saw him laughing in the rear-view mirror. 'Watsons Bay it is.'

By the time we got to Double Bay the girls had my pants down and were fondling and teasing me, and I was ready. Pepper climbed on my lap facing me and put me inside her, rocking slowly back and forth with the motion of the cab while Natalie kissed me and stroked Pepper's breasts. I was so aroused I thought I was going to faint and nearly did a couple of times when the cabbie practically killed us all trying to negotiate the turns on New South Head Road in Vaucluse while craning his neck to get a perve at the two most beautiful bodies he'd ever seen. The old fella must have been near seventy and any minute I expected him to come in his pants, have the big one at the same time, and run off the road and kill us all. Jesus, what a headline that would have been!

Pepper was riding me hard now and starting to lose control. From the combination of the eroticism of the situation in the cab, and Natalie's caresses, she quickly reached the edge. She stiffened and began to tremble and I knew she was about to explode. She leant forward, kissed me, trembling from head to toe, and came with such a scream the cabby stuck his foot on the brakes and we all shot onto the floor.

'Come on, mate,' said Natalie. 'We're not there yet.'

'I am!' said Pepper and we all broke up and clambered back up on the back seat.

I expected the cabby to toss us straight out but he was into it and amazingly he just drove off obediently. Pepper and Natalie swapped places and now Natalie was sitting facing me, screwing me slowly to the motion of the cab. Natalie always liked to be kissed when she made love and she smothered me with her lips, softly whispering 'Oh that's good, that feels so good' as she moved up and down on me.

Although they were very different sexually, at times they felt very much alike. I mean their sexual styles and movements. Sometimes I'd wake up in the middle of the night with one of them on top of me screwing me gently in my sleep, and it was hard for me to tell which one it was. It was always so great it didn't really matter.

Natalie leant over, kissing Pepper passionately as she rode me. The sight of those two beauties touching and caressing each other was the ultimate turn-on for me and they knew it. They never made it together without me and that's what always made it special when we made love as a threesome. Pepper always trembled silently in her climax but Natalie always moaned loudly when she was about to come.

'Fuck meeee . . . Oh fuuuuck,' said Natalie and we both came.

The cabbie slammed on the brakes and we all shot on the floor again. 'That's it,' he said. 'Out! We're here.'

I got my pants on and paid him, putting the money in his shaking hand as the girls gathered up their things. The cabbie then tore off, probably to find a quiet spot to practise the five-finger boogie, the poor old bugger. Pepper and Natalie were still naked under their coats and carried their dresses. I followed them like an adoring puppy and we walked along the concrete walkway and down the steps to the beach. Both of them took off ahead of me, slipped out of their stockings and garter belts, and were in the water before my feet hit the warm Camp Cove sand. It was a beautiful moonlit night and, apart from a group of people sitting around a small fire way off at the far end of the beach, we were alone. Although it was no big deal to see people swimming naked at night on Sydney beaches, I waved to the girls to swim towards the heads, away from the people. I picked up their things and walked along the beach and they swam parallel to me until we found our own private spot. I broke the world record for getting undressed and dived into the warm, refreshing, clean water. When I came up between them they immediately began rubbing their bodies against me and touching me.

I could die tonight, I thought.

Who cares? said my dick.

The three of us held each other and kissed, moving from one set of lips to another and back again and again as the sound of the warm waves lapping on the beach mingled with the sound of our hot breath. I was so hard there mustn't have been a drop of blood left anywhere else in my body. I loved being with them. It always felt right. Never anything lurid or dirty about our threesomes. It was always erotic and sensuous and the most intense and satisfying physical pleasure I've ever known.

Pepper and Natalie took me by my hands and walked me out of the water behind some rocks.

Spreading our their evening coats on the sand they lay down together and began to kiss and fondle each other. I went to join in and they both said in unison, 'Oh no you don't.'

'You just sit there for a while and watch like a good little boy,' Natalie whispered seductively.

'O-OK,' I managed to reply.

Natalie slid on top of Pepper's wet body and pretended to screw her like a man. 'Does this make you hot, Bill?' she whispered to me.

I couldn't speak. What was I going to say? 'No'? In the moonlight the two naked, wet, milk-white nymphs looked like Rodin sculptures and I sat there transfixed by their beauty and the erotic scene taking place a foot away.

Natalie kissed Pepper on the lips and neck, slowly working her way down to her breasts, kissing them and gently nibbling and caressing her erect nipples. All this time Pepper stared at me in the moonlight. Her eyes never left mine as Natalie kissed her way down over her stomach, down her thighs, calves and ankles to her feet and toes, which she nibbled and kissed. Pepper's eyes closed gently from time to time as the pleasure took her, only to open again and meet mine with the same sensuous gaze. It was driving me crazy and I couldn't just watch much longer. There was no blood left in my brain. Natalie gently slid her head between Pepper's legs and began to stroke and kiss her. Pepper had this glazed look in her eyes and put her arms out to me, beckoning me over, and I went and lay beside her. She put her arms around my neck and we kissed as Natalie stimulated her with her tongue and fingers. All the while Pepper made the gentle mmmmm-ing sound that she always made when she was aroused.

Natalie rolled onto her stomach between us and continued stimulating Pepper. I lay on top of Natalie and entered her. She was soaking wet and the three of us went into a shared state of aroused bliss as the electricity coursed through our bodies in waves. As I moved gently in and out of Natalie, she moaned softly with every stroke, her gorgeous arse rising to meet me in perfect unison. Pepper reached out and held my hand and we all became high from the shared pleasure.

I could feel they were both close to the edge and so was I. Natalie began contracting involuntarily around me and she started to quiver uncontrollably. Suddenly Pepper's hand squeezed mine like a vice and her body began to tremble. Natalie sighed 'Fuuuuuck!' and we all rocked and shuddered in an enormous shivering climax. We lay there for a while holding each other like lovers do, just enjoying that private, satisfying, almost meditative silence that always follows great sex. It hadn't been an epic session of lovemaking, but regardless of the time and effort consumed, the intensity of our ménage à trois was always exhausting, seeming to drain every ounce of adrenalin and energy from our bodies. We didn't speak, just lay there holding each other, sharing the magic. It was Natalie who spoke first, and when she did I noticed a silver tear trickle down her face in the moonlight.

'Oh I love you both so very much,' she choked. 'You've both been so great to me. How can I ever repay you?'

She put her arms around us and held on like a lost child who'd just found its parents. There was nothing to say. We were family and ridiculously close. Moments like this made us all realise how much we meant to each other. Words like love, trust and close just didn't come close to how we felt. There was no doubt we were all in love, but there was something else that was indefinable, something extra special, a magic we would carry with us all our lives.

'We'd better get going. It'll be light soon,' I said breaking the silence.

'Let's have a quick swim before we go,' said Pepper and raced into the water.

Natalie and I jumped up and, holding hands, we dived in after her. We swam for about ten minutes, occasionally hugging and kissing, not sexually, just tenderly, until it was time to leave. We dried ourselves on their coats, got dressed, walked around to Watsons Bay and called a cab from a phone booth near the shops. The three of us were crammed into the booth as I made the call and the letching started again.

'Ooh I've never done it in a phone booth,' said Natalie.

'Me eiver,' giggled Pepper.

Nor me, said my dick. I swear we couldn't help ourselves. Luckily the cab arrived just in time to save my life and we headed dreamily home to bed.

Like I said earlier, Where did I go right?

It was about 11.30 p.m. on the following night and I was bored stiff. Even though I knew we would be playing the next night, the nights seemed to drag when the band didn't play. I'd become so used to the regimen of rehearsal and work that nights off made me edgy. After Checkers and Camp Cove we'd slept till the late afternoon. We ate dinner at home that night, then Natalie went out to see some friends and Pepper crashed early. I wasn't tired so I sat up for a while twiddling my thumbs and had a couple of beers. I was standing by the window looking out across Bayswater Road when at the eighth-floor window of Bayswater Courts, I saw that face again, peering at the Pagoda.

Bingo! What a dumb fuck I am! That's a perve getting his rocks off! It also occurred to me for the first time that I lived with two beautiful girls who had a habit of walking around a lot half-naked. Our apartment must be a perve's paradise!

That low prick, I thought. *I hate perves. They're scumbags! Voyeurs, gentlemen of refined taste all, but perves are low lifes*.

The next morning I told the girls what I thought and they hit the roof.

'The low-life fuck,' said Natalie. 'I'll go over there and castrate the greasy bastard.'

'Easy, mate,' I warned.

'Oh Christ, perves give me the willies,' said Pepper.

'I've got an idea how to fix this bludger,' I told them. 'I'll speak to Jean-Pierre later and see if he'll give me a hand. But I'm going to need your help.'

'How, mate?' Pepper asked.

'Look, both times I've seen this bloke . . . '

'Both times!' they yelled.

'Yes, well the first time I thought it was just somebody looking out their window and I waved like a stupid prick.'

'You mean this bastard's been at it for a while?' asked Natalie. 'How long?'

'Well, if I'm right, a few months at least,' I said.

They both shuddered.

'OK, as I said, both times I've seen him it's been around eleven-thirty to midnight. I guess that's the perving hour 'cause a lot of people are getting undressed for bed and wandering around.'

'All right, what do you want us to do?' asked Pepper.

We did nothing that day. Natalie went into the city for something and I just sat watching TV and strumming on my guitar while Pepper tried on different outfits. It was getting harder and harder to concentrate, so we both stopped and spent the rest of the afternoon in bed. Natalie came home and didn't disturb us. We must have fallen asleep because she woke us up shouting, 'Dinner's ready.'

That was another great thing about them. They loved to cook. They were both country girls at heart and loved to get into the kitchen and mess around with recipes. They baked and cooked all kinds of delicious things and I loved to eat them, so it was a magic combination. Natalie had made some chicken schnitzels, vegetables and an apple pie for dessert. We cracked a bottle of red and dug in. The rest of the evening was as lazy as the day and it soon came to be around ten-thirty. Funny how time flies sipping wine and watching TV with two ripping sorts wearing next to nothing. It was still hot out, but we'd kept the curtains closed. I walked up the Cross to see Jean-Pierre and asked him if he would help us out and he agreed. We organised to meet at the apartment at around eleven and I went back and waited.

'OK, Jean-Pierre, here's the story,' I said when he arrived. 'The perve's on the eighth floor of Bayswater Courts over there. Wait for me downstairs and when I come down we're going to get this bastard.'

'OK, Beel, vot yu vant me to do?'

'Just wait for me and we'll play it by ear.'

'Oui, bon.' He smiled and left.

I was still taking the odd savate lesson from Jean-Pierre whenever I could and I saw him every week when I went over for a graze at the Hasty Tasty. He had known both the girls long before me and when Natalie was in hospital he went to see her a lot, taking her flowers, books and small gifts to cheer her up. He hated Joey for what he'd done to her outside the Hasty Tasty and cursed him openly when he found out. He also put the drum out that both Pepper and Natalie were hands-off or die.

'OK, girls, you ready?' I asked.

'*Ready!*' they giggled and came waltzing out of the bedroom, both dressed in the horniest lingerie they had. Natalie was in all black as usual and Pepper in all white.

'Screw the perve!' I laughed. 'I'm not wasting this!'

They both giggled like little kids playing a game, except perves are not a game.

'Now here's what we're going to do,' I said. 'When I open the curtains, you two start slow dancing and smooching together and I'll see if this turd is at it.'

Natalie put on a record. She and Pepper started doing their thing and I opened the curtains.

'Oh you wouldn't rub some oil on my boobs, would you, Pepper?' giggled Natalie.

'Only if you rub some on mine first,' Pepper giggled back.

'Ah knock it off, you two,' I said. 'I'm getting a hard on.'

I looked out the edge of the window and, sure enough, there was our perve. His pants must have been popping at the show he was getting from across the street. Suddenly I caught the glint of light off something and realised he had binoculars.

'OK girls, keep it up until I whistle. I'm going to slip out and we'll bust this fuck, dick in hand.'

'Hurry back,' said Pepper, 'this is making me horny!'

'What do you mean making,' Natalie letched. They both moaned enticingly for my benefit as I left.

Jean-Pierre was waiting for me in the lobby. We sprinted across the road in the dark, climbed the security fence at the back of Bayswater Courts, took the stairs to the eighth floor and crept along, counting the apartments until we got to the right one. When we were outside the perve's door Jean-Pierre took one step back and bamm! with one straight kick took the door off its hinges. The perve was so taken by surprise he was still staring out the window as we ran in. He had no pants on and instead of binoculars had a camera with a zoom lens in his hand. Jean-Pierre grabbed him with one hand and backhanded him with the other. The guy shot across the room like shit out of a shanghai and hit the wall. All the lights were out in the room and it wasn't until I switched one on that I saw who it was. Manny the Man! I didn't know Manny, I didn't want to

319

know him, but Natalie had told me all about him and pointed him out a couple of times on the street.

'Aw maaan, fuck. Whydya do that for, maaan! You busted me fuckin' cameraaaa,' he whined. The camera was in pieces on the floor.

'You rotten fucking perve. You fucking low life prick!' I yelled at him.

'Aw maaan, just havin' some fun. Cool down, maaan. Be cooool.'

I went to the window and whistled to the girls. It was then the full impact of the room hit me! The walls were plastered with perve shots and photographs of nude girls. There were a lot of our flat and of Pepper and Natalie in various stages of undress. There was a whole row of photos of them.

'You fucking mongrel,' I screamed at Manny and lunged, catching him with a kick to his nuts.

His feet left the floor, he shot back and hit the wall again . . . out cold. I was so pissed off I started to practise my Fred Astaire on his ribs when Jean-Pierre pulled me off him.

'You'll keel 'im, Beel,' he said. ''Eez out cold.'

'That's the fucking idea, Jean-Pierre,' I said and sunk the boot in again.

'No, no, sat eez enurf, Beel,' he said, grabbing me and holding me so I couldn't move.

'OK, OK mate, it's over. Over! Let me go,' I said. He let me go and I sunk one more in for luck. 'Jesus, look at this room.'

Manny had spent a lot of time at this because all the pictures were well focused and professionally developed. Some had obviously been taken using high-speed film and some were even cropped. If these were the ones he'd chosen, he must have shot hundreds.

'Jean-Pierre, go around and look for any more pictures, will you, and tear them down.' I found some more of our apartment taken before Natalie had moved in and some just after. He had been at it a while, the low bludger.

'Jeeezuz, ju 'ave a nize arze, Beel,' Jean-Pierre laughed, looking at one of the photos.

'Show me that,' I said, grabbing it out of his hand. Sure enough there it was in all its finery, leaping off the couch at a half-naked Pepper.

I called the girls, 'Oh yes, we got him all right, and guess what?'

When I told them who it was and about the photos, I heard their scream pierce the midnight air and ricochet across Bayswater Road into Manny the Man's window.

I spent about the next five minutes rearranging Manny's flat and did a little redecorating using mayonnaise, soft drinks, butter, toothpaste and tomato sauce, topping it off with liberal handfuls of cornflakes which stuck to the gooey walls like shit to a blanket. When Manny came to he was in for a full night of cleaning. The prick! We went through the cupboards and drawers and found boxes of negatives and undeveloped rolls of film which we exposed, then dumped in the shower and turned on the hot water. For the *coup de grâce* Jean-Pierre and I pissed on the still unconscious Manny.

Jean-Pierre then went back to work and I went home to get some sleep. The girls were beside themselves, wanting the details. They both freaked out when I told them the whole story and when I showed them some of the photos they went orbital. Natalie grabbed them and went over to the stove and burnt them one by one on the element, dropping the burning ashes into the sink and drowning them down the plughole. It was then that she told me the story about finding out about Manny perving at her at the Hampton Court. Evidently the management had got wise to his game and he'd been barred from the place. They asked her if she wanted to press charges but she couldn't be bothered. Not long after that she had moved in with us and she put it behind her like all the other shit from her former life. We talked for a while, then the girls went to bed. I sat there and fumed about Manny the Perve, and the more I thought the more I fumed.

I knew it would go nowhere to report it to the police, and we'd assaulted him, so I just kind of hoped he would disappear and that he would get his some day. Little did I realise how quickly it would come. A few days later Stan the Shine told me Sergeant O'Malley had busted Manny for smack dealing and Manny the Maaan was in some serious shit! None of us had mentioned the events of the perve night to anyone else and when I asked Jean-Pierre he said he hadn't told anyone either. It was a coincidence, but how fitting!

'Instant Karma's gonna get you.' John Lennon never wrote a truer lyric.

22
A Question of Who

ABOUT midday the day after I'd heard Manny had been busted the phone woke me from my blissful slumber between Pepper and Natalie.

'Billy, it's Sergeant Brian O'Malley here. Sorry to wake you, son, but I need to talk to you urgently.'

'That's OK, Sarge. Where and what time?'

'How about in Rushcutters Bay park? On the bowling alley side down by the water in about, oh, half an hour.'

'Why the park?' I asked, confused.

'I'll explain when I see you.'

'OK, Sarge, I'll see you there in half an hour.' *The park?* I thought to myself.

'Oh and Billy,' he said. 'Tell Pepper and Natalie where you're going and tell them not to leave the apartment, and come alone. Keep your eyes open and make sure you're not followed.'

'What's all the secrecy, Sarge?'

'I'll explain when I see you, son. Just trust me, OK?'

'All right, Sarge, see you soon.'

Pepper and Natalie were still asleep. I woke them up, told them about the Sarg's call, got dressed and left for my mysterious rendezvous. I hailed a cab in Bayswater Road and told the driver I had to pick something up at the Chevron, then we'd be going into the city.

'No worries,' he replied cheerfully. 'Hey, aren't you in that bloody band that plays up at Surf City? My young sister's done her tits over you. She's there every bloody night. Can't keep 'er away from the fuckin' joint.'

'Yeah, that's me,' I said, and we drove in silence through the Cross to the Chevron Hotel.

I walked in the front door and straight out the back, cut down Tusculum Lane and hailed another cab. Rushcutters Bay is about a ten-minute walk down Bayswater Road from the Pagoda. The most prominent feature in the tiny bay is the marina where millions of dollars worth of floating luxury languish in sad lament that their future is one of ploughing the harbour on weekends under the captaincy of some half-pissed would-be, out-to-impress his latest piece of slash into getting her gear off below decks.

I felt sorry for the cabbie I'd left sitting out the front of the Chevron. It may have been a bit Mickey Spillane, but it's the first thing that came into my head so I just went with it. I got the second cabbie to drop me at the entrance to the marina on New Street, then cut behind the boat sheds to the spot the Sarge had nominated. I could see him standing in a clump of trees down near the wall overlooking the bay. He was out of uniform and had some young guy with him who looked vaguely familiar.

'What's all the mystery, Sarge?' I asked as I walked up.

He gestured with his head for me to follow him and the other guy behind the trees.

'This is Constable Hicks. You remember him, don't you?' The Sarge nodded to his companion. The young constable gave me a 'fuck you' with his eyes and I remembered. He was the young copper I'd thrown halfway across the lobby at the Canberra Oriental the night of Nurse Pepper and Jackie Marsh. He was out of uniform too.

'Look, son,' O'Malley said, 'someone at Darlingston is a grass. I've got an idea who it is, but I've got no real proof yet so I'm playing safe. I'm sticking my bloody neck way out here but you may be involved without knowing it and I need all the help I can get. I do know we can trust young Hicks here though. OK?'

'OK, Sarge, but . . .'

'Don't talk, son. Just listen. Now here it is in a nutshell. The reason I'm telling you is I think Natalie may be in danger.'

'What? How is . . .?'

'Just listen. All right?'

I nodded.

O'Malley then proceeded to tell me the whole story about busting Manny. I couldn't work out why the fuck he would be telling me but after the reference to Natalie, and knowing my ears work better when my mouth is shut, I listened. It seems that after he'd taken Manny the Man to Darlingston station, he'd questioned him until around six that morning. During the interrogation Manny had started to come down off the smack. He became more nervous as the time for his next hit ticked closer and the prospect of a cold turkey in the slot was really freaking Manny boy right out. The Sarge had planned on this and as Manny's smack buzz wore off about four in the morning he got more agitated and started to volunteer information about himself and his smack connections. He ended up giving up everybody but his grandmother.

The Sarge's description was both visual and detailed and his words conjured images in my brain. As my mind's eye visualised a strung out, cold-sweat, terrified Manny undergoing a vigorous questioning by this tough, seasoned old copper, my imagination painted a vivid picture of the interrogation.

'Oh maaan!' scratch scratch, sniff. 'I'm sick. I'm fuckin' sick, maaan,' Manny moaned. 'I gotta get out of here. Please I dunno anything, maaan! Honest I don't.'

Whack! 'Watch yer fuckin' mouth, yer bludger,' the Sarge yelled. 'You call me sir, you mug! Call me maaan one more time and I'll fuckin' belt yer again, you understand, you piece of shit!'

'Owww maaan,' sniff, 'er, I mean sir. Don't hit me! I didn't do nothing! I just deal a little bit to a few friends and the molls from time ta time, maa . . . er, sir.' Scratch scratch.

'What molls?' the Sarge pressed. 'Who they working for? Come on. Who's the bloody hoon?'

'Aw I'm not a grass, er, sir,' Manny blurted. 'I'm not gonna give . . . give no one up. I'll get done.'

'I'll fucking do you myself, you bludger,' the Sarge yelled. 'Come on, what molls?'

'Aw, just molls. I ain't seen a couple of 'em in a while. They just took off, you know, disappeared.' Manny knew he was in some deep shit now. 'Dunno where they are, Sarge. Most of 'em get their gear from their hoons now. I don't deal to 'em anymore. Honest!'

A bell rang in the Sarge's brain and he shot out of the room, returning a minute later with something in his hand which he thrust into Manny's sweating face.

'Come on, you lying turd, take a look at these. Come on! I want the bloody truth. Look at them, you shit.'

The Sarge forced Manny to look at photos of three dead girls. The same photos I'd seen months before. Manny stared at them, a terrified look on his face, eyes wide as saucers . . .

I just stood there with my mouth open, listening to the Sarge describe it all. Transfixed but still wondering what the fuck all this had to do with me. The Sarge continued and the images of Manny at Darlingston returned.

'Aw fuck, maaan! I don't know nothing about them, honest. What's this got to do with me, maaa . . . sir?'

'Do you know them?' the Sarge yelled.

'No! Not me, maaan, sir! I didn't kill nobody!' Manny shivered through his come-down cold sweat.

'Who said anything about them being murdered, eh?' the Sarge shot at him. 'You know them, don't you? Come on! Now who are they and what's your connection, you bludger?'

O'Malley's ear itched, telling him he was on to something.

'OK! OK, maaan.' Whack! 'Owww maaan, I mean sir.' Sniff. 'Look, I knew them. All right? But I didn't kill 'em 'n' I dunno who did! Scratch, sniff. 'Honest. They was just molls, you know?'

'No, I don't know, you bludger! Now tell me what the fuck is going on here, or you're gone.' The Sarge was screaming at him now. 'Where'd you meet them? Up the Cross or what?'

'No sir. Joey Szaso.' Sniff! 'They was all workin' for 'im.'

'What's that bludger got to do with it?' the Sarge asked, his mind ticking.

'Joey's me connection. He was dealin' before 'e became an 'oon. That's 'oo I, er, I get me stuff from.' Scratch, sniff. 'He wuz their 'oon! They was 'is molls. They was on the game an' inta the hammer 'n' tac long before they worked for Joey,' he cried. 'After he got 'em they stopped buying from me. Honest!'

From the way the Sarge was describing it, Manny the Man was now completely unstuck, sweating cold and blubbering.

'Joey had 'em by the tits. They was all hitters, I ain't seen 'em in ages!' Sniff. 'Honest! Never had anything ta do with 'em after Joey. He'd of done me for sure. You gotta believe mee-heee,' he blubbered.

'How long have you been in business with that turd?' asked the Sarge.

'Oh what?' Scratch, sniiiff, shiver. 'Just a couple a years. He gets real good shit, regular like, every few months. Started getting it fer 'is molls, then started movin' a bit through me.' Shiver, sniiiff. 'I didn't do nothing to them molls, 'cept deal to 'em early on! Honest I didn't. Oh Jeez, I gotta get out of 'ere,' he screamed. 'I'm fuckin' dyin'.'

The Sarge went on to tell me a few other details, saying that Manny had agreed to testify against Joey. The Sarge had booked him, then let him go. Seems Manny could raise the scratch to post bail anyway. Although he'd confessed to being a dope dealer and the Sarge had him dead to rights, he'd only found a small stash in Manny's flat. He was after bigger fish and would rather have Manny in his pocket out on the street to see what panned out with Joey boy. As far as anybody else at Darlingston station was concerned, the Sarge was questioning a dope dealer and at this moment only he, Constable Hicks and I knew of Manny's connection to the dead girls.

'So I let the bludger go and told him to report to me this arvo,' O'Malley said. 'I've put a man on him to make sure he doesn't scarper.'

'Sarge,' I said. 'I busted Manny perving the other night and gave him a bit of a hiding.'

The Sarge listened in disbelief as I told him the story.

'Is that why I'm here?' I asked. 'I still don't understand all this secrecy. Why are we here in the park? Why are you both out of uniform? What the fuck is going on?'

'Look, son,' he replied. 'I'm with vice and robbery. I'm not supposed to have anything to do with murders. When I went to homicide and told 'em my theory about the dead girls, they laughed . . . told me to keep my bloody nose out of it, which I've been pretending to do ever since. But I bloody know I'm right and if it costs me my bloody pension to prove it, so be it! There's a mongrel out there murdering young girls and I want his fuckin' arse! I know all about bloody Joey the Hoon and his molls, but he's only small time. I didn't make the connection to the murdered girls. None of my other constables did either.

'As soon as I heard Manny's tale my bloody ear started itching and I smelt a grass. Someone's on the bloody take up there, but I know I can trust both you blokes and I need your help. Now Constable Hicks, I know you're still dirty on Bill but I want you to sweeten it right here and now, you understand? Bill's all right, so shake bloody hands 'cause we've got more important things to sort out.'

We both put our hands out and it was sweetened.

'Now Bill, as you've probably guessed by now, there's another element here, ain't there?' the Sarge asked.

'Yes,' I said. 'Natalie. She used to work for Joey, but that's all long gone, Sarge.'

'I know that. Don't worry, I know she's straightened out, but she may be in trouble just like Joey's other girls. If he's a murderer, then one of his girls must know something and can make the connection. So as of now they're all in danger. But I can't go and round up all of Joey's molls for questioning right away. As soon as we picked one up the rest would scarper and we'd tip Joey off. So I sent a couple of mates looking for him but it looks like he's gone to ground, which confirms my suspicions even more. Someone at the station must have tipped him off, otherwise how would he bloody well know?' He was making a statement and asking himself the question at the same time.

I nodded my head, taking it all in. Natalie had lived with Joey for the best part of a year. Even if she didn't realise what she knew, if Joey was a murderer then Natalie was probably in deep shit!

'Where's Natalie now?' the Sarge asked.

'She's at the apartment,' I replied. 'Why? What do you want me to do?'

'I've already got someone into Bayswater Courts to keep an eye on Manny and watch your place. I want you to go home, tell Natalie the whole thing and get her up to my flat in Bondi. I want her to take a look at those dead girls. I'll be back at Darlingston in about an hour so if you hear anything, call me, but I don't want her to go anywhere near the station.' He handed me a card with his home address. 'And you and Pepper be careful.'

'Why Pepper? She doesn't know anything about any of this.'

'Joey doesn't know that, son! She and Natalie have been best mates for years and as far as Joey's concerned she may know everything. You too for that matter.'

'What?'

'Listen, he'd be well aware that you three have been sharing a joint, so put it together yourself, son.'

'OK, Sarge, I'm gone! I'll have them at your place within an hour.'

'Now you watch your arse. I'm not sure who's grassing, so I can't put many blokes on this. I have to handle it with just the ones I trust, which including you and Constable Hicks makes five of us. If this bastard is the murderer he'll be desperate. Even if he's not he knows he's going to be looking at twenty-five years for heroin, so either way he's still bloody dangerous. If he hasn't hit the toe he's desperate, so keep your eyes open, eh? You know what I mean?'

I knew exactly what he meant. *Now I'm a rock'n'roll singing, cop-spying, potential fucking murder victim!* That's what he means. *Mummy!*

When I got back to the apartment Pepper was up and dressed but Natalie was nowhere in sight.

'What's the matter, mate?' Pepper asked when I walked in.

'Where's Natalie?'

'She's gone into the city for somefing. Someone phoned her while you were out and she shot out straight after it. Said she had somefing important to do. She was humming like a kid when she left. Why? You look awful, mate. What's wrong?'

'I told you both not to leave the fucking apartment,' I yelled at her. 'What the fuck is wrong with Natalie? Chariist!'

'It's not my fault,' Pepper said. 'I tried to stop her, but she got excited after the call and just took off. I couldn't stop her.'

'I'm sorry. I didn't mean to shout, but this is really serious! Did you answer the phone or did Natalie?'

'Natalie, why?' she asked nervously. 'What's going on?'

'Sit down,' I said. 'This is real important!'

She settled into an armchair and I told her all about the meeting in the park. Pepper sat there with eyes wide, not saying a word.

'Fuuuck!' she said when I finished.

'Fuck's dead right, mate,' I said. 'Now do you have any idea where Natalie might be? Think! Did she say anything at all before she left? Anything?'

'Nuffing much. After she got the call she got real excited and gave me a big hug. Only fing she said was . . . "I've got it!"'

'Got what?'

'I asked her that,' she said. 'Natalie got real mysterious and just laughed.'

'The Sarge seems to think that we might be in trouble too,' I told Pepper, 'and I think it might be a good idea for you to go to his place as well.'

'Why?'

'Well, he reckons Joey might think that Natalie has told us something that can incriminate him and . . .'

'I'm not going anywhere, Bill! There's a copper over the road and I want to stay here in case Natalie comes home or calls. If I hear from her I'll get her straight to the Sarge's, I promise, but I'm not going to let that greasy fuck scare me out of my own home. If Joey comes round here I'll bust his balls again.'

'OK, let's concentrate on where she could have gone. Is there anyone we can call?'

'You know as many of her friends as me. Jesus, she could be anywhere.'

'What about her parents? Do you think it's worth giving them a call?'

'Might as well, mate. Anyhow I can tell Vlad and Sergei about this. Maybe they can help. What do you fink, mate?' she said.

'Good idea! I know the Sarge wants to keep this quiet but they're her brothers. There's no way they're going to blow it. It gives us a coupla more heads as well.'

Pepper called Natalie's parents. Her brother Sergei answered and Pepper told him everything. She laughed when she'd hung up.

'What's funny?' I asked.

'He said he and Vlad would come into the city and sniff around for Joey. Said they'd break arms and legs if they had to. They'll call when they get here.'

'Great,' I said. 'And I know someone else who might be able to help.'

'Who?'

'Dulcie. If anyone has any idea about Joey it's Dulce. I'll go around and see her.'

I called the Sarge and told him about Natalie taking off. He was furious, but realised it was nobody's fault but hers.

'Listen, Sarge. I need those photos for about an hour. Is that OK?'

'What bloody for?'

'Well, if anyone's likely to know anything about Joey's whereabouts it's old Dulcie. You know her, don't you?'

'Dulcie Maysberry?' he asked. 'What's she got to do with this?'

'Sarge, if someone farts in a restaurant in the Cross, Dulcie hears it before the bloke at the next table smells it! It's worth a try. Now can I get the photos or not?'

'OK,' he said, 'but I don't want you around the station. I'll meet you out the back of the fire station in ten minutes.'

'I'll be there.'

I told Pepper what I was going to do, asked her to keep the place bolted shut and told her not to leave before speaking to either me or the Sarge. She reluctantly agreed. Ten minutes later I was standing behind the Kings Cross fire station and O'Malley pulled up in an unmarked car.

'Get in,' he said, 'I'll take you to Dulcie's. In fact I'll come in with you.'

'Not if you want the real drum you won't.'

'What?' he asked.

'Well, Dulcie isn't too fond of coppers. If she sees you coming she'll clam up tighter than a crab's arse. Just drop me down on the corner of Forbes and Cathedral and I'll walk from there.'

The Sarge gave me the photos and dropped me where I asked. I walked round to Dulcie's and knocked on her door.

''Oo's bloody there?' came the stern voice from inside.

'It's me, Dulcie, Billy Thorpe. Let me in, mate, I need to talk to you.'

'OK, darl,' she said, her voice now bright and chirpy. I heard her unlock about fifteen dead bolts. 'Billy, darl, come in. Come in.'

She took me into her little drawing room and once again I found myself staring at the nude portrait of young Dulcie hanging above the fireplace.

'Now wot d'ya want, darl, that brings you round 'ere panting at a painting of me young naked arse?'

'What? Well, Dulce, it's like this . . .' I told her the whole story. She didn't say a word, just sat there shaking or nodding her head as the facts took her.

'Have you seen or heard anything of Joey Szaso?' I asked at last.

'Yeah,' she said. 'Saw 'im late last night on Victoria Street and 'e was with an 'ole friend of yorn.'

'Who, Dulce? Tell me, mate, don't play games,' I scolded her. 'This is serious.'

'So is this, mate,' she laughed. ''E was with Jackie bloody Marsh! They 'ad a good 'ole mag. I was gonna call yer and tell yer.'

'What!' I exclaimed. 'You sure?'

'Darl, it's Dulcie! It's the drum, swear it. You know me.'

'Where on Victoria Street and what were they doing?'

''Bout an 'undred yards down from the back o' Surf City. I was jist comin' outta Springfield Lane when I spotted 'em. They din't see me so I 'id in a doorway till they left. They magged fer about five minutes then took orf, separate like.'

'Did you manage to hear anything?'

'No, darl, I was too far away.'

'Dulcie, can I ask you to look at some photos for me?' I asked. 'They're not real pleasant but you might be able to help.'

'Sure,' she said. 'Let's 'ave a squiz.'

I showed her the photos and she didn't bat an eye. All she said was, 'Did that bastard Joey do this ta these poor sheilas or what?'

'Could be,' I said. 'Do you know any of them?'

Bugger me if she didn't recognise them all.

'Yeah that 'un's name's Sophie. 'N' that un's Charlene. Let me see, darl, that 'un's Brenda, I think, or somethin' like that. They was all on the game,' she said matter of factly.

'You knew them all?' I asked in disbelief.

She shook her head. 'Jus' saw 'em round from time ta time. They din't work the streets. Mainly out of the Canberra Oriental and the Mayfair. Saw 'em all with Joey one time or another, though . . . The low prick that 'e is!'

'Are you sure?' I asked.

''Course I'm bloody sure,' she said indignantly.

'Listen, Dulce, I know you hate coppers but . . .'

'No bloody Jacks!' she said. 'I ain't talkin' to no bloody Jacks.'

'Brian O'Malley's been onto this thing for over a year and between crooked coppers and mug detectives he hasn't got anywhere until now. He's a bloody good bloke and can be trusted. He did the right thing with Pepper and me that time with Jackie Marsh.'

'Yeah, I know 'im. 'E's all right, I s'pose. Give me a few bob from time ta time.'

'Dulcie, there's a bloody maniac loose around the Cross and it could be you next! You never know! I need you to talk to him right away and tell him what you've just told me. Will you please do that?' I pleaded with her. 'It's not for me, mate, it's for Natalie and Pepper.'

'Struth,' she said. 'I hates bloody coppers, swear I does. But fer Natalie and Pepper I'd chew me own bloody arm orf.'

'No need for that, Dulce, just talk to the Sarge. All right?'

'Sweet, darl. Fer Natalie an' Pepper anybloodythin', anythin' yer want. Yer can count on Dulcie,' she said proudly.

'What time is it?' I asked. 'Do you have a phone I can use?'

'Aw 's'about five-thirty, six,' she said. 'No, don't 'ave one. Bloody things only ring! There's one on the corner, but.'

I went to the phone box and called the Darlingston station. O'Malley wasn't there.

'How about Constable Hicks?' I asked.

'Yeah, 'ang on. 'Oo should I say is callin'?'

'Tell him it's the groundsman from Rushcutters Bay Park.'

'That you, Bill?' the constable's voice came down the line. 'Groundsman, eh? That's a bloody good one. What's doing?'

I told him about my conversation with Dulcie and asked him where the Sarge was.

'Shit! Joey and Jackie bloody Marsh! Look, he's popped down to see our friend in Bayswater Courts,' he half-whispered.

'Can't talk?' I asked.

'Yeah, just don't want to shout,' he answered, still whispering.

'Listen, constable, is there any chance you can come down and speak to Dulcie? Take her statement or whatever you need to do?'

'Sorry, Bill. The Sarge told me to stay here till he calls, but I tell you what. Can you bring her up to Monty's bar? The Sarge took you there one time. Do you remember it? I'm expecting the Sarge to call in any minute and I'll tell him to meet you there.'

'Great!' I said. 'Thanks.'

I hung up and immediately dialled Pepper.

'Hello, Natalie?' she answered.

'No, mate, it's me. Have you heard from her yet?'

'No, not a bloody word. I've spoken with Sergei a couple of times but he hasn't had any luck.'

'You OK?' I asked.

'Fine, mate.' She didn't really sound it. 'Where are you?'

'Still at Dulcie's. I'm taking her to meet the Sarge at Monty's. I'll call you then. Are you sure you're all right?'

'Yes I'm fine. Don't worry about me.'

In the few minutes I'd been in the phone booth it had got dark. Through the phone booth glass I could still see deep orange and blue in the sky above the buildings in the city. The door had opened once again and another night was upon us. The night! A million light years from the day. Just perfect for heinous acts, dirty doings and a murderer's plottings! This night could be bad times, bad times, bad times, here and now! A cab went by the phone booth and I stuck my head out, whistling him down. The cabbie screeched to a halt and reversed back to the phone booth. I ran over to his passenger window.

'You, you fuckin' bastard!' he shouted.

He jumped out of the cab and ran around to my side. Fuck me if it wasn't the cabbie I'd left sitting outside the Chevron, and this time he had flames coming out of his arse. He threw a huge king hit right at my head which I ducked and threw another with his left, which I managed to slip as well.

'Mate! Mate!' I shouted. 'I can explain. Calm down, it was an emergency.'

I danced around with the fat cabbie in the middle of the street, trying to keep him off me.

'Emergency my fuckin' arse!' he yelled, but he was

running out of puff. 'You fuckin' stitched me up, you bludger! I'm gonna kick yer fuckin' 'ead in and you'll 'ave a real bloody emergency.'

Enough of this shit, I thought and I hit him square in his fat gut with a short hard right. All the dance went out of him and he fell on his knees. I grabbed him by the arms and helped him up.

'Sorry, mate, but you've got to listen to me. It was an emergency then and it's an emergency now! If you don't believe me you can come and talk to Sergeant Brian O'Malley from the Darlingston division. That's who I'm going to meet, OK?' I pulled a ten pound note out of my pocket, tore it in half and gave him one of the pieces. 'Get me up to the Cross and you can have the other half of this. It'll more than cover both the fares. Sweet?'

'Sweet,' he mumbled, still trying to get his breath as we both got in his cab. I got Dulcie and we went up to Monty's where I gave the cabbie the other half of the ten. He was happy as a pig in shit. I went over to the bar and spoke to the barman. It was the same bloke as last time, Norm, and he remembered me.

'I'm here to meet the Sarge,' I said. 'Have you got a phone I can use?'

'No worries. There's one 'ere behind the bar.'

I called Pepper again but the line was engaged. *Maybe she's talking to Natalie*, I thought and hung up. I waited about a minute and called her again.

'Natalie?' she asked.

'No, mate, it's me. Have you heard from her?'

'Bill,' she said. 'Thank God. She was just on the phone.'

'Did you tell her?'

'I tried to, but she wouldn't let me get a word in

edgeways! As soon as I picked up the phone she started raving about how happy she was and said she had some great news for us. She had to go to Dulcie's and then the Silver Spade but said she'd be home with some champers in an hour. She hung up before I could tell her anyfing. She was bloody gone, Bill! It wasn't my fault. It wasn't,' she sobbed.

'I know, mate, I know. Just calm down,' I said. 'Now let's think. She said she was going to Dulcie's first, then to the Silver Spade?'

'Ri-hight,' Pepper sobbed

'OK,' I said. 'Jump in a cab and go around to the Chevron. See if you can see her. I'll go back to Dulcie's and wait there. When you get to the Chevron, go and wait by the front desk. And don't leave.'

'OK,' Pepper replied.

'If Natalie turns up, stay by the desk. I'll leave a message here for the Sarge and tell him what's happening. When he gets to Dulcie's I'll come and get you. OK?'

'OK,' she said, all tears gone now.

'One more thing. Before you go call the doorman at the Chevron. What's his name?'

'Brendan.'

'Yeah, Brendan. Call him and ask him to keep an eye out for Natalie. Tell him it's an emergency and to keep Natalie there if she comes. And phone for a cab. Don't go on the street and hail one! Get him to come around the back door, but don't wait on the street whatever you do.'

'All right,' she said. 'I'm sorry I cried. I'm togever now. I'll ring the Chevron and a cab right away. Bye.'

I told Dulcie to wait while I went and got a cab. 'Will you be all right here for a few minutes?' I asked her.

'I'd be a lot bloody better with a coupla scotches in me.'

'Norm, can I get a bottle of scotch for the lady?' I asked.

'Any particular brand?'

'Yeah, the brand in a bottle, darl.' Cackle, cackle, wheeeeeeze! Dulcie laughed cheekily.

'Get her a bottle of Cutty, Norm,' I said.

'No worries. How many glasses?'

'Oh just the one,' I said.

'No worries.'

Dulcie cracked the bottle and had two drinks down before I'd even got out the door.

'Ah that's better! Uuuurrrrpppp!' I heard her say as I left.

I sprinted up to Darlinghurst Road but there wasn't a vacant bloody cab in sight. I waited about five minutes, then ran back to the bar to call one. When I walked in the Sarge and Constable Hicks were there.

'We just found Manny,' the Sarge said as I sat down. 'Dead as a mullet with his throat cut.'

'Oh fuck!' The room started to spin.

'Yeah, he didn't show up this arvo like he was supposed to, so I got my mate down in Bayswater Courts to go and give him a nudge. When he got there he found the door open and Manny dead as a maggot with his throat slashed from ear to ear!'

'Whaaat!' I yelled. 'Jesus! Pepper!'

'I went straight over to your place,' O'Malley said. 'I knocked a couple of times but there was no answer so I let myself in. Pepper wasn't there.'

'Christ, she was probably downstairs waiting for a cab.'

'What cab?' he shot at me and I brought him up to date.

'Jesus, I must have missed her by seconds. What a pain in the arse! Look, do you want to go to Dulcie's or to the

Silver Spade? Either way, Constable Hicks goes with you. I've left my bloke at the Pagoda in case Natalie turns up, so what do you want to do?'

'I'll go to the Chevron, Sarge. You take Dulcie home and she can tell you what she told me. If Natalie doesn't show up I'll leave the constable there and bring Pepper round to Dulcie's. That OK?'

'Constable, do you know what Natalie looks like?'

He nodded.

'Good. Then let's do it. Ready, Miss Maysberry?'

'Not till I get me bottle of Cutty back I'm not,' she said stubbornly.

'I'll give it to you when we get there,' O'Malley told her.

'Pig's arse! I wanna carry it 'ome.'

'All right, all right! Here it is,' he said, passing it to her.

Dulcie took the bottle and nestled it gently in the crook of her right arm.

'Ready,' she laughed, and we all left.

I arrived at the Chevron with Constable Hicks about ten minutes later. Pepper was waiting for us and said that Natalie had already been and gone. She'd collected some back pay and left in a cab. Pepper had missed her by a matter of minutes and was beside herself with worry.

We got a cab around to Dulcie's and on the way I told her about Manny's murder and she burst into tears. I hugged her all the way and by the time we arrived she had cooled down a little but was still really freaked out about Natalie. We could hear the Sarge laughing loudly as we got out of the cab. Dulcie led us into her little parlour. Her attitude toward the Sarge had definitely changed in the time they'd spent alone. From the way she was talking to him, calling him 'darl' and all, he must have charmed the pants off her. She had practically finished her bottle of Cutty, but a bottle didn't even touch Dulcie's sides. Although she was a little louder, she seemed perfectly coherent. We told the Sarge about missing Natalie at the Chevron.

'We've got to find Natalie,' said Pepper. 'Oh God, we have to.' She started to cry again.

Dulcie put her arm around her. 'Don't worry, darl,' she said. 'Natalie'll turn up. She'll be sweet.' Dulcie's kindness seemed to calm Pepper.

'Darl, why dun yer tell 'em what we worked out,' Dulcie said to Senior Sergeant O'Malley. Constable Hicks and I looked at one another, both amused at the way Dulcie was talking to the Sarge.

'Well yes,' the Sarge said, clearing his throat. 'Dulcie has offered to let you two and Natalie stay here for a few days to keep you away from the flat and I think it's a bloody good idea. And Pepper, I don't think you should go to work for a few days either.'

'Fine with me if it's OK with Dulce,' I replied.

'Oh Dulce, I fink that's very sweet,' she said, giving her a hug.

'Thanks, Dulcie,' I chimed.

'Aw sweet,' said Dulcie.

'Sarge, I have to play at Surf City tonight but I'll have Ivan there and I'll be fine. I'll come here after I finish. OK?'

'Sure, but be careful, son.'

'We'll need to get some of our fings from the flat, though,' said Pepper, 'and someone should be there for a while in case Natalie calls or comes home.'

'I don't see any problem if there's two of you,' he replied. 'But be careful, eh?'

We were walking out of the elevator on the fifth floor of

the Pagoda. As we reached the door we heard the phone ringing. Pepper raced across the apartment and grabbed it.

'Hello, Pepper, it's Natalie. I'll be home soo . . .'

'Natalie, shut up and listen!' Pepper screamed into the phone.

'But . . .'

'No,' Pepper yelled, 'fucking listen to me! You're in real bloody danger. Half the town has been trying to find you all day!'

'What for?'

'Those girls who were murdered worked for Joey Szaso. Manny told the Sarge that he got his dope from Joey, and today Manny was found dead wiv his froat cut! . . . What? . . . No, I'm not bloody kidding! Where are you? We'll come and get you . . .'

'What!' said Natalie. From her tone Pepper realised it had only taken her a moment to know where she stood in all this.

'OK . . . OK . . . I'm down at . . .'

Pepper heard Natalie struggling.

'Natalie! Natalie!' Pepper shrieked as nothing but muffled screams came down the line. The screams got fainter, as if Natalie was being dragged from the booth.

'Naaaatalieee!'

A few seconds of silence, then click! The phone went dead.

23
Natalie's Surprise

WE were frantic! This was no longer a veiled threat of violence, it was happening, and we had no way of knowing what was coming next. No way to know where Natalie was or know who had cut her off. Pepper was convinced it was Joey and that seemed to be the logical conclusion given the events of the past twenty-four hours. I called the Sarge and told him what had happened. He said he'd put men on it immediately.

Pepper was all ready to round up a posse in the Cross and go on the hunt, but deep down we both knew this was both futile and dangerous. As I had to go to Surf City and play I told her I wanted her to go to Dulcie's until I finished.

'I'm not going anywhere except to look for Natalie,' she said defiantly.

'Look,' I told her. 'What are you going to do, start kicking fucking doors down and harassing Joey's molls? You'll create more problems for the Sarge than he needs. He's on the case now so let's give him a fair go.'

'I can't just sit around and not do anyfing.'

'What are you going to do then, mate? Come on, tell me! What?'

Pepper looked at me in stony silence, then tears welled up in her beautiful, sad green eyes.

'I don't know,' she said, 'but I'm not going to Dulcie's. I want to stay here.'

'Like hell!' I said. 'I've got to go to work in half an hour. Now you either come with me or go to Dulcie's, but you're not staying here alone. So make up your mind, but you're not staying here alone and that's that!'

'Bill, I'm not . . .'

'Pepper! I'm not giving you a choice! If you don't stop I'll call the Sarge and have him drag you to bloody Dulcie's. Stop acting ridiculously. There's nothing you can do right now other than put yourself in danger and create problems, so do the right thing, mate! Now what's it going to be?'

'Well I don't feel much like being at Surf City,' she replied. 'I'll go to Dulcie's if that's what you want.'

'That's what I want. That way I know you're safe. I'll come round as soon as I finish. I'll be there by one-thirty.'

'OK,' she said and we hugged.

I called a cab and told him to come to the back entrance. First I dropped Pepper at Dulcie's, then went to Surf City. Before going to the dressing-room, I went upstairs and told Ma Harrigan what was happening. As usual she was in control and suggested there was no point involving the band. I agreed. I knew bloody well that if I had, they'd have been off the stage and out the door trying to help, but like me, there was nothing they could do. There was also no point leaving 3000 Friday-night punters to wreck the place because the band had split, so I arrived backstage like everything was normal. Being with the band, surrounded by laughter and Bluey and Col's 'get fucked' helped take the edge off it a bit, but going on stage for that first set was tough. It was impossible to get Natalie and Pepper out of my mind and act like I was having a rocking good time when I was most decidedly having the worst fucking experience of my life! I kept looking around the room hoping to see them dancing away but it was a fantasy and only the crowd vibe and great music got me through the first show.

In the break I went to see if Ma Harrigan had heard anything. As I walked through the lobby I saw Constable Hicks, who'd come to take me up to the station. The Sarge wanted me to give a formal statement about Natalie's phone call in front of some detectives who were now on the case. He said Pepper had already been there about an hour before. Evidently she was back at Dulcie's, still upset but a lot better.

When I got to Darlingston the Sarge introduced me to three burly but friendly plain-clothes detectives. I told them everything I knew and a policewoman stenographer took it all down. They had already started rounding up Joey's girls but nothing concrete had turned up so far and they had a group of uniformed coppers combing the Cross, anywhere that Joey might be.

The Sarge knew I had to get back to work, so he OK'd it with detectives for me to come back first thing in the morning to sign my statement after it had been typed up. Constable Hicks drove me to Surf City and I got back only a few minutes late for the next set. The rest of the night was pretty much a blur. We finished the last song to a raucous response. I changed, said goodnight to the band and left. It was about 1.15 a.m. and Ivan was locking the front doors. He asked me if I needed any help. I thanked him and told him there was nothing he could do. It was now in the hands of the coppers. I grabbed a cab and went straight to Dulcie's, arriving to find her wandering nervously up and down the footpath outside her house, so I asked the cabbie to wait.

'What's the matter, Dulce?'

'Pepper bloody took off to your place! 'Bout forty-five minutes ago,' she said desperately. 'I couldn't bloody stop 'er! Said she couldn't stand sittin' round 'ere while Natalie was missin'. Said she 'ad ter go 'n' do somethin' 'erself. She'd gorn back ter see if she c'n find somethin' that'll give 'er an idea where Natalie is. Aw, Jeez I'm bloody worried!'

I couldn't believe my ears, but when I thought about it, I realised it was Pepper. No-one could stop her once she got an idea into her head.

'You stay here, Dulce. I'll go home and bring her back. OK, mate?'

'You sure, darl? Ya wan me ter come with ya?'

'Thanks anyway,' I said. 'You stay here in case she comes back.'

I took the cab to the Pagoda. There was a note stuck in the door and I grabbed it, hoping it might be from Pepper or Natalie. I opened the door to find all the lights were on but Pepper wasn't there. I read the note but could hardly decipher the scribble. It was signed with a Sergei and I realised it was from Natalie's brother. I could just make out, *Have had none luck Will call morning. If hear any call 45-2125.*

Pepper had obviously been there because a lot of Natalie's private papers and bits and pieces were spread out all over the floor. There was a note on the coffee table. It read: *Dear Bill, I've gone to ask around to see if anyone has seen Natalie. I had to do something. I'll be home soon. Don't worry I'll be fine. I love you, Pepper.*

The realisation that Pepper was now out running the streets alone at night trying to find Natalie made my brain race. I tried to make sense of it. What to do? Who to get to help?

What the fuck is happening? Natalie? Pepper? Joey Szaso? Manny? Murder? Heroin? What the fuck is going on? How in the hell did we all get caught up in this. I was unable to get my mind to rationalise so I called the Sarge. He was still there and when I told him about Pepper taking off he hit the roof and called her everything under the sun. When he cooled down I told him I'd stay where I was and wait for Pepper or Natalie's call. He said if he heard anything he'd call right away.

Just as I hung up the phone rang. 'Hello, Pepper?' I asked.

'No, Cool, it's Candy. Ready to party?'

'What?' I asked.

'Party, Cool! You know, eat, drink and be Mary,' he laughed. 'You not gonna let Natalie sail tomorrow without having a drink with ya old pals are ya?'

'Natalie? Sail where? I, I don't . . .' was all I could get out.

'You've not been smokin' anythin', have you, Cool? Me and Jimmy are up the Cross. Natalie came by today. Told me to call around now to set up a farewell drink. What's happening, kid?'

'What do you mean sail?' I asked in total disbelief. 'Sail where?'

'You mean she hasn't told you yet,' he said like he'd blown it. 'Oh shit, I wasn't supposed to say anything until she told you.'

'Told me what?' I asked, still lost as to what the fuck he was talking about.

'That she's sailing with us tomorrow, going all the way through to London. It will be a gas,' Candy said excitedly.

'What!' Then it hit me! 'Candy, Candy,' I said, relieved as my brain cleared and shot back into focus. Maybe Natalie was safe after all. 'Could Natalie still be there? Is there any way she could have gone back on board?'

'No way! She's not due to board until the morning and her tickets and passes aren't valid until then. Anyway, I saw her off the ship myself. Why, what's all the fuss about?'

'Listen, Candy. This could be a matter of life and death! Where are you?'

'Just near the Staccato. What the fuck ya'all talkin' 'bout, son?'

I quickly ran the scenario down and asked him and Jimmy to come to the apartment and tell me the whole story.

'I'll tell you what,' said Candy. 'Jimmy and me will duck back to the ship and ask around. See if anyone has seen her. Shouldn't take long. Then we'll come by.'

'Great,' I said. 'And thanks.'

I dialled Darlingston station again and asked for the Sarge or Constable Hicks. They weren't there but the desk sergeant said they'd probably be back in about an hour or so. I told him about the *Maracosa*.

'The *Mara*-what?' he asked like a dumb arsehole.

'The *Maracosa*! It's a liner docked down at the 'Loo. Listen, this is very important. It's about Joey Szaso and the girl who's disappeared. Tell him the girl went to the ship this evening. You've got to make sure you tell him she was there today. As soon as he comes in. Please write it down to be sure.'

'All right, all right! Keep yer britches on, lad! I'll tell 'im.'

Candy and Jimmy arrived about half an hour later. They'd checked the docks, even looked in the cabin Natalie had booked, but nobody had seen her. Then Candy told me the whole story of her visit to the boat. From his description of the meeting and the time frame, we were able to piece together Natalie's movements from the time Pepper had just missed her at the Chevron to her last phone call.

'What about her folks?' said Candy. 'Maybe she's gone to say goodbye or sumthin'. You never know. She might have got caught up there.'

I grabbed the phone and dialled the number on Sergei's note but there was no answer. As I hung up I realised that if Natalie had gone home they'd have contacted us by now. So that wasn't a possibility. Candy and Jimmy stayed for a while and we drank a couple of beers. They tried to cheer me up and we sat there hoping to see Pepper and Natalie come waltzing in at any moment, but they didn't. The boys left at around three-thirty and went back to the *Maracosa*, which was due to sail the next afternoon. They said they'd check it out again and have another look in the morning, and to make sure I spoke to them before they sailed. Let them know if anything had happened. Candy gave me a card with his rank and particulars on it, telling me to give it to the Sarge and that he'd be happy to speak to him. We hugged and they left.

'Don't worry, Cool. She'll turn up,' Candy said as he went out the door.

I must have fallen asleep because I woke up on the couch at about 5 a.m. with a blanket over me. Realising that Pepper must have covered me I went to the bedroom to see if she was OK. She was in bed asleep with the light from the hallway illuminating her sleeping form. I sat on the floor beside our bed, looking at her. Then it all hit me. The shock, fear, helplessness and anger all hit my brain at once. I began shaking and I sat there with my face on Pepper's hand, tears streaming. I felt her hand move and squeeze mine gently.

'Bill. Bill, is that you?' she half-whispered.

'Yes, mate. I'm right here.'

'Don't cry, baby,' she said softly. 'I'm OK, but Natalie . . .' Then she began to sob.

We held hands in silence, looking helplessly at each other, crying our eyes out, both realising just how much Natalie meant to us and that at best she was in grave danger and at worst . . .! Either way, life had changed. It was no longer fun and games. All the innocence had gone. It had taken just twenty-four hours for us to grow up. Neither of us would ever be kids again.

I got on the bed and took her in my arms and we held each other like helpless children. Pictures of Natalie and Candy on the *Maracosa* ricocheted around in my head. I could see her as clear as day, her dream about to come true. I started to doze and my subconscious took control, putting all the pieces of Candy's story together in a dream. Slow-motion images of Natalie leaving the Chevron in a cab and heading to the docks turned into a full-on technicolour movie in my head . . .

'Just drop me off here by the gates, mate,' Natalie said to the cabbie. She went straight to the security guard. 'I'm here to see chief steward Joshua Clemends on the *Maracosa*. He's expecting me.'

'No worries, love,' he said, eyeing her body. 'Just go along this wharf and you'll see the *Maracosa*. Can't miss her.'

Remembering the night on the *Maracosa* vividly, she walked straight to where she was berthed. Even though it was dark, large trucks sat next to the liner and wharfies and seamen were busily loading the ship with supplies. At the bottom of the gangplank was a security booth. Natalie went in and showed her pass. The guard gave her a visitor's badge and escorted her onto the huge ship.

She walked along the promenade deck, following the route she'd taken the night of the party and took the elevator down to F deck. Memories of the party filled her mind and she smiled to herself, remembering the last time she'd walked along this passageway wearing nothing but a garter belt and stockings under her dress. She remembered lifting it saucily a couple of times and flashing her naked arse at me and laughed out loud as the astonished look on my face came back to her. The thought sent a wave of sexual excitement through her body, ending in a jolt between her legs.

'Oh,' she sighed as it hit her. She reached cabin 801 and knocked softly on the door.

'Who 'dere?'

'It's me, Natalie,' she replied and Candy immediately opened the door.

'Sorry I'm a bit late,' she said. 'It all happened so fast today and I got caught up in the traffic on my way back from the city.'

'That's cool, babe.' He gave her a peck on the cheek. 'Come in, come in. I've got a few minutes before I go on duty. So you've got everything together, honey?'

'Yeah,' she said excitedly. 'I'm so happy. My visas have all come through so I'm all set. I sail with you on tomorrow's tide,' she giggled.

'Honey, you sounds just like a seaman already,' he laughed back, happy that he'd been able to help by holding a good cabin until the last minute. 'Have you told Pepper or Billy yet?'

'Not yet,' she replied. 'I want to surprise them tonight.'

'Suurrprise!' said Candy. 'They gonna shit when dey finds out, honey.' They both laughed. 'Why have you left it till the last minute to tell them?'

'Oh Candy, I know I've got a tough way about me sometimes, but I'm a real softie inside. I hate goodbyes, and if I'd told them weeks ago what I was planning we'd all be crying and stuff as the date got nearer. This way it will all happen quickly and we'll have one night to say goodbye. I love them both so much.' Tears were streaming down her face. 'See what I mean?' she said. 'Christ, if I'd told them what I was planning a month ago we'd all be blubbering wrecks by now and I'd never leave.'

'Cool, babe.' Candy gave her a fatherly hug. Candy had never come on to Natalie and she loved him for it. He was a real gentleman, and after some of the slimeballs she'd known in her time she really appreciated him.

Just then there was a tap on the door. Candy answered it and Laz and Jimmy walked in. They were both surprised to see Natalie and she excitedly told them about her big adventure.

'Oh tat's great, Natalie!' 'Ja, ve haff ein goot time togeser' they responded, genuinely happy for her. They all hugged.

'Don't call Billy or Pepper and say anything in case I haven't told them yet,' she said. 'I want it to be a surprise.'

'Fookin' surprise,' laughed Jimmy. 'Ya mean tey don't know yet? Tey'll fookin' croak!'

'Oh that won't be a problem,' said Candy. 'We've all pulled night duty. None of us are going ashore, so nobody gonna blow your cool, honey.'

'You mean you won't be able to have a drink with us later tonight? Billy's playing and I thought we could get together afterwards. Aw come on, you've gotta know a way off this boat to say goodbye.'

'Well, maybe we can work somethin' out,' Candy said. 'No guarantees, but we'll try! What time you figure?'

'Oh, late. I'm gonna have dinner with Pepper and Bill before they go to work and tell them the news. Then I've got to pack. Billy doesn't finish until one, so why don't you call at around one-thirty and we'll hook up from there.

'You've got the number, Candy?' He nodded his head.

'Bye, loov. Gotta go,' said Jimmy, giving her a big hug. 'See ya later, eh.'

'Jah,' said Laz and they both left.

Candy took Natalie to her cabin up on C deck, showed her around, and saw her to the gangway.

'Oh Candy,' said Natalie. 'I can never thank you enough for all your help. I'm so excited.'

'That's cool,' said Candy as he hugged her goodbye. 'It's my pleasure to help the people I love.'

'Bye, mate,' she said as she turned to walk down the gangway. She blew him a kiss from the wharf and Candy stood at the rail watching her disappear down the dock and melt into the shadows.

At the very moment the cab Pepper and I had taken from Dulcie's made its way up William Street, through the Cross and down Bayswater Road to the Pagoda, Natalie was walking to the end of the Woolloomooloo dock to get a cab home. Passing the last giant warehouse marked G12, she noticed a public phone and decided to call home and tell us she was on her way. As she put her coins into the phone we were walking out of the elevator on the fifth floor.

I heard a phone ring and saw images of Pepper and me as Natalie called . . .

Pepper screamed, 'Naaatalee!' and I shot out of the dream sweating bullets. I sat up in the bed and the phone was still ringing. It was our phone. I was awake and the phone was still ringing. I jumped out of bed and grabbed it like it was about to get away.

'Natalie?' I asked.

'No, Billy, it's Sergeant O'Malley here. Sorry to call you so early.'

'Did you get my message about the *Maracosa*?' I asked.

'Yes thanks, son, but I was already onto it. We chased down the cabbie that dropped Natalie down the 'Loo. I spent the night with a team combing the docks and the Cross for Natalie and Joey but we didn't come up with anything. We spent a couple of hours on the *Maracosa* and I spoke with your mate Candy this morning. He told me the whole story. Sorry I didn't call but I thought you both needed to get some sleep.'

'Did you come up with anything?'

'Listen,' he said. 'I'm really buggered and about to knock off. How about I come and see you for a minute on my way home?'

'We'll be here. We're not going anywhere.'

I went to check on Pepper but she was still sound asleep so I closed the door and left her in peace. She needed it. The Sarge arrived about fifteen minutes later.

'How are you, son?' he asked as I opened the door.

'Oh I'm OK, thanks.'

'I'm really bloody sorry Natalie's caught up in all this,' he said, patting me on the shoulder as we sat down. 'Jesus, I'm sorry. Are you sure you're all right?'

'Yep, thanks,' I said. 'I'll be OK. It's Pepper I'm worried about. What's going to happen with all this? What about Joey? Do you have any leads at all?'

'Not much at this stage, I'm afraid,' he said gravely. 'A security guard at the docks thinks he saw someone fitting Joey's description hanging around yesterday evening, but whoever it was was outside the gates and he didn't take that much notice. Drunks and mugs are always hangin' round down there so he didn't think anything of it.'

'That's it?' I asked.

'For the moment, yes. They've bloody vanished,' O'Malley's voice was full of frustration.

'The bludger got away, but he won't get very bloody far. We'll find the bastard, don't worry. We've got a full-scale search going and if he's about we'll get him. Fortunately there are also some real good blokes at Darlingston and they're out to prove that a couple of rotten apples haven't spoilt the whole bloody barrel. They're on the case with a vengeance. Joey's not going to come within a hundred miles of the Cross so don't worry. The whole bloody section is on it. There's a murderer loose because no-one would listen and they bloody know it. We've got rotten coppers and some smartarsed dicks with a lot of egg on their bloody faces. Everyone's either bloody embarrassed or shitting.'

I think he noticed the helpless look on my face because his voice changed from frustration to concern. 'How's Pepper doing, son?'

'As good as can be expected, thanks, Sarge.'

We sat and said nothing for a while and the Sarge seemed to drift off to some other place. I was tired and I'd had a sleep. O'Malley looked exhausted.

'Listen, Sarge, the *Maracosa*'s sailing this afternoon. Do you have any problems if Pepper and I go and say goodbye to our friends?'

'No, none at all,' he replied. 'The ship is clean. My ear didn't itch once. We've finished our investigations there.'

The Sarge left and I went back to bed. Pepper woke me about one-thirty with a cup of coffee. Evidently she'd been on a real rampage the night before. She went and asked Jean-Pierre for help and the two of them had hit every bar, strip club and joint in Darlinghurst, but to no avail. I told her everything that had happened and when I got to the bit about Natalie having a ticket on the *Maracosa* Pepper burst into tears.

'That was her surprise, Bill,' she sobbed. 'No wonder she was so excited. Oh the poor thing. Oh Natalie! She's dead, Bill. I know that bastard has killed her. I know he has. Natalie's dead.'

'Come on, Pepper, we can't know that for sure. She could be OK somewhere. Maybe Joey's just holding her,' I said, trying to comfort her and me. 'They were together for a while. Who knows, mate?'

'I know you're trying to cheer me up,' Pepper said, 'and I want to fink she's OK, but I can't! She's gone. This feeling is too big. She's gone! I know it.'

I had no reply because I could feel it too. It was as if something had been cut out of the universe. There was a piece of energy missing. Nothing I could pinpoint but a definite void. Something much greater than worry, fear, frustration or hope.

Something was gone. I'm not coming on here like I'm psychic, no such luck, but I felt it and knew exactly what Pepper was feeling.

'The *Maracosa*'s sailing in a couple of hours,' I said, trying to break the mood. 'I think we should go down and say goodbye to the boys. They really tried to help last night and I know they're terribly concerned for Natalie. Why don't we go down, mate? It's better than sitting around here moping all day.'

'Oh, OK,' she whimpered.

'Maybe we can have a bite at the Spaghetti Bar after. What do you think?'

'Anywhere but there, Bill. It'll only remind me of that night with Joey. I'd throw up!'

'How about Doyle's on the Rose Bay pier then?' I suggested. 'Some whiting and a nice cold bottle of white? Old Mrs Doyle's always friendly and she never lets us pay.'

'OK,' she said, unenthusiastically.

We got ourselves together and I called a cab to take us to the 'Loo. Neither of us said much on the way, both lost in our worst fears and private nightmares and the fact that it was now the next day and nobody had heard from Natalie.

The security guard at the gate took our names and in we went. The second I entered the gate I didn't feel right. Everything seemed familiar. Too familiar. At first I put it down to the night we'd come to the party but as I walked along the wharf I realised it was a lot more than that. There was the phone booth I'd seen Natalie call us from in my dream, and there was the building marked G12. I know bloody well I hadn't noticed them on the night of the *Maracosa* party and an eerie chill ran all over my body. My dream had been real. I started to feel faint and Pepper must have noticed the change come over me. There was no way to hide it. I was completely freaked.

'What's the matter, mate?' she asked. 'You look like you've seen a ghost.'

'I think I have,' I replied.

Pepper looked at me with an astonished look on her face. 'What do you mean?'

'Well, I couldn't get the image of Natalie out of my head after Candy and Jimmy left last night. I fell asleep thinking about her coming down here and I woke up this morning in the middle of a dream. I saw it all. I saw Natalie on the ship with Candy. Saw her leave, walk along this wharf and call us from that phone over there. I woke up to the sound of the phone ringing in my dream. You know, when Natalie called. It was real, mate, I swear it. I fucking saw all this as clear as we see it now. I thought it was just a dream but as soon as we got here it all came back. What I dreamed is exactly as it is here now. That phone. That building over there. The whole fucking thing. Shit, it's weird!'

'Did you see who grabbed her?' she shot at me.

'No I didn't. The phone rang and I woke up. It was the Sarge.'

'Oh shit,' she said and burst into tears.

We stood there and hugged for a minute, trying to shake it off, but it was all there. Natalie had been there the way I'd seen her and I don't doubt it to this day. The realisation had knocked me on my arse. I'd never had an experience like it before, but I know it was real and not just some fantasy brought on by the circumstances.

We made our way along the wharf to the *Maracosa*. Ten storeys tall, she looked gigantic and magnificent in her spotless white coat as she sat majestically in the afternoon sunlight as though she knew she was the centre of all attention. The area around the ship was a bustle of people and crew preparing to leave or people saying goodbye to loved ones. As we walked the thought that we would have been here today saying goodbye to a loved one hit us both and we walked along in a corridor of silence, lost in our private thoughts.

'Hey, Pepper. Hey, Billy,' I heard Candy shout. Looking up we saw both Jimmy and Candy in immaculate white uniforms and naval caps, waving and smiling at us from one of the decks high above the wharf. It occurred to me that all the time I'd known the boys I'd never seen them in uniform. Candy signalled to meet him at the gangway and I saw him shoot off. By the time we got there he came sprinting down to greet us.

'Hi, baby,' he said, hugging Pepper and kissing her cheek. 'Hi, Cool. How they hangin'?' He smiled, obviously trying to warm the cold air that surrounded Pepper and me. Jimmy hugged Pepper and kissed her cheek. 'Tanks fer coomin' lads. It's always nice ter av soomwun coom ta say farewell.'

'We just wanted to wish you a safe voyage and say thanks for the help last night.' I was just about to ask where Laz was when he came bounding down the gangway.

'Vos du leave visout saying gootbye to de Kraut?' he laughed and hugged us both.

'You want to come on board?' Candy asked. 'Can't stay long unless you want to sail, but ten minutes should be fine.'

All this time Pepper hadn't said a word and the boys had obviously seen that this was not the Pepper they knew. 'Oh no thanks,' she said. 'I don't think I could take it. Too many memories of good times wiv Natalie, you know?'

'I understand, darlin',' said Candy. 'Maybe next trip eh? Well, we gotta get on board or it'll be our asses. Keep safe you two and, Pepper, you keep your goddam chin up, it's much too pretty to be draggin' on the ground. Think good thoughts. She'll turn up.'

Pepper leapt into his arms and gave him a huge kiss and hug.

'I love you, Candy,' she said, fighting the tears, 'and Natalie loved you too. Fanks for everfing. And you too,' she said to Jimmy and Laz, hugging them. 'You're good friends. Please keep safe and look after Candy and write. We need to hear from you to know you're OK.' She turned to me and said, 'Bill, if you don't mind I'll go and wait by the gate. This place gives me the willies.'

'OK,' I said seeing the tears and she hugged me and headed back down the wharf.

'Pepper taking it hard, Cool?' Candy asked.

''Fraid so. She's convinced Natalie's dead and I honestly think she's gone too. I can feel it. Something's missing. We're hoping but it doesn't look good.'

'Well, Cool, you keep your chin up too and keep that great music comin'. The next trip I expect to be picked up in a big white limousine and treated with style.'

'You're on!' I smiled and shook his big friendly hand. We were all shaking hands when a voice from above shouted, 'Hey, Candy, get your black butt up here or we'll sail without ya!'

'Gotta go', 'See yous', 'Goot bye', they said and headed back on board.

I walked back down the wharf and we caught a cab home. We never made it to Doyle's. Just pottered around the apartment for the rest of the day trying to make happy conversation, but it didn't help. By the end of the day no sign of Natalie or Joey Szaso had turned up. Twenty-four hours is a long time and if Joey had killed Natalie or, as we hoped, only abducted her, he could be in another state by now and who knows how long it would be until we knew for sure? Or if we would ever know for that matter. Neither of us could get it out of our minds.

At 8 p.m. Pepper and I headed off to Surf City. Regardless of all the hassles, I was happy for the release that I knew a night of good music with the band and a rocking Surf City crowd would bring. As I walked in and smelt that old theatre scent, and felt the vibe, I realised what a great pleasure it was to be able to play in front of people every night and be able to enter that magic world of spotlights, music and good times seven times a week and pretty much switch off anything that existed outside the front doors. I could tell Pepper felt it too.

Our first record had been a big success in Sydney and NSW and radio stations in other states started to play it. In 1964 Melbourne and Sydney had this absurd rivalry that I guessed dated back to the early colonial days when Melbourne had been a free settlement and considered itself superior to that barbaric penal settlement in Sydney. The two cities seemed to hate one another, and I mean hate. This antagonism permeated everything, including the music business, and Melbourne radio stations rarely played Sydney acts and vice versa. It was ridiculous. So when we started to get airplay in Melbourne it was a major breakthrough for not just us but all Aussie bands. It seems that when a local Melbourne DJ by the name of Stan 'The Man' Rofe started to play us it had received a great reaction. The funny thing is that the station evidently thought we were an

American band, and by the time they found out we were a Sydney group it was too late. The record was already a hit.

The success of that first record catapulted us to a whole new level and we started to get offers to do national TV shows and tours, but the first thing we needed was a new record. The deal we had with Linda Lee was only for the first single and John Harrigan negotiated a fresh deal with a new label owned by Alberts Music, to be released through EMI, and we went into the studio to record again. We'd asked the crowd at Surf City what songs they'd like us to record and the overwhelming consensus was 'Poison Ivy', 'Zip-a-Dee-Doo-Dah', 'Sick and Tired', a song of Tony's, 'That I Love', and a ballad I'd sung since I was a child, originally recorded by Judy Garland, 'Over the Rainbow'. The response to these songs had been phenomenal and it was obvious that we would sell thousands of copies to just the Surf City crowds, which would guarantee us at the least a charting in Sydney.

We recorded them at the EMI studios in the city in one day, and this time we had the luxury of a three-track tape-recorder. This meant the band could be recorded on one track, vocal backing on another, and my lead vocal on the third. As usual, Col and Bluey were up to their old tricks, with Bluey taking every opportunity to crack us up. Knowing we could go back over vocal backing overdubs, he kept running into the studio and farting as loud as he could which not only got on tape and cracked us up, but infuriated the extremely straight recording engineer who'd never come across anything like us in his life. The Sydney Symphony was his idea of a wild bunch of guys. When he complained, Bluey's response was to run into the recording booth and rip off a horrendous fart, then run out holding the door closed, trapping a pong that was somewhere between rotting cabbage and dead dinosaur flesh in the booth. We stood around the mike in the studio crying with laughter as the engineer and his assistant desperately fanned the air. Overdubbing was a great new experience and it was such a luxury to be able to take the time to get vocal backing and harmony parts spot-on and spend the time to get the best possible lead vocal performance. By the end of the day we had all the songs recorded.

Somebody suggested it would be a great idea to add strings to 'Over the Rainbow'. We came back a couple of days later to find the string section from the Sydney Symphony set up ready to play. The arrangement had been done by a well-known arranger at that time named Franz Conde. It was generally known that Franz had written that classic song 'Sous les Ponts de Paris' (Under the Bridges of Paris) and sold it for fifty quid in England when he was bust. Franz later went on to be the musical director on my television show, 'It's All Happening'. The strings on 'Over the Rainbow' sounded fantastic and at the end of the session everybody in the EMI building came and listened. Their reaction was incredible and it was obvious we had a smash on our hands. That same week we did our first magazine cover shot for Australia's first new music magazine *Everybody's*. Resplendent in new suits specially made for the shot, we had it taken standing in front of the El Alamein fountain in the heart of the Cross. Given our beginnings, it seemed to be the perfect place.

Everybody's was run by two great journalists, Maggie McKieg and Jim Oram, and they both became great friends and staunch supporters of ours. They saw the importance of the new music and gave us coverage whenever they could. Their early belief and support was instrumental in our success, as it was for many of the other young bands like the Easybeats, Normie Rowe and the Playboys, Max Merritt and the Meteors, and Ray Columbus and the Invaders, that had started to emerge by late 1964 and early 1965.

The cover shot turned into a four-page article and other half-page photos of us with Jim Oram and Maggie McKieg taken in a recording studio. The response was fantastic and the magazine received thousands of fan letters, which resulted in *Everybody's* holding write-in competitions, etc. which received equal response. We were starting to roll seriously now.

On the one hand I had all these dreams coming true. On the other I was still trying to deal with Natalie's disappearance. A month had passed, and still no word of Natalie or Joey. I spoke to the Sarge regularly during this period, more for Pepper's sake than my own. I knew full well that the second the Sarge heard anything, no matter what it was, we'd be the first to know. He was incredibly sensitive to Pepper's state of mind and compassionate to a fault, never once telling me that he was too busy to talk or that he'd call me as soon as he heard. As time passed we all knew it was hopeless.

We never saw or heard from Natalie again. There was no question in anybody's mind that she was dead. All the hope in the world couldn't wash away the realities. Joey Szaso was a low-life murdering prick who had definitely killed Manny and probably Natalie. She was tough and smart. If she had been alive, somehow, some way, sooner or later, she would have contacted us and let us know she was OK. The call never came and we knew it wasn't coming.

This was the streets, not the movies. No romantic happy endings here. Much to the Sarge's fury and all our frustration, no trace was ever found of Natalie or Joey Szaso and for a long time we all thought the bastard had gotten away with it.

Then one night at Surf City I was told in no uncertain terms that he hadn't. A reliable and trusted friend told me that Joey Szaso now stands on the bottom of Sydney Harbour like a grotesque Statue of Liberty. His eyes gouged out. His arms and legs broken. His mouth glued shut and enough concrete on his feet to anchor the *Maracosa*. Evidently justice had been swift and he had been there since the night after Natalie disappeared.

I was also told that Joey had definitely murdered Natalie.

Promises were made and I will never know who avenged Natalie's death, but I know that the Cross had taken care of its own. My eternal thanks go to you, whoever you are.

24
The Call

CRIEF is a dark, lonely, private room with the curtains drawn, where cherished memories of laughter and tears dance with angels in the cathedral of the heart. No one may enter. None are welcome. No words penetrate its walls or ease the pain that fills it. The door remains locked until the will pries it open to allow the helpless, well-meaning, outside world to enter and interrupt its sanctity. Over and over the helpless voice asks 'Why didn't I . . .?' and sobs 'If only I'd . . .'—but you didn't and it's too late. Only private memories and ghostly images remain to forever give form, shape and testament to that which had been.

No more excited giggles and little girl talk when she became excited, or flicking her silky black hair with her fingers when she became nervous. No more excited conversations about a new life in Europe, of marrying earls and living in castles in a country far from the reality of her past, or plans for us all to meet one day in Paris. Gone forever the sound of practised elocution to conceal the Aussie roughness in her speech. The sound of her laughter, her style, scent, winks, long sensuous fingers, black lace, sweet breath, smiling black eyes, milk-white silky skin and generous, loving soul. No more! Natalie was dead!

Natalie was everywhere in the apartment. In the soap she'd bought for the bathroom, her favourite rug, wine, vases, pictures, scent, clothes, everything! For a while we tried to deal with it but neither Pepper nor I could stand to be there alone. Neither of us had realised it at the time but Natalie had been our teacher and main influence. Her life on the game had produced a sharp, hard, street grittiness that had changed into a soft, sophisticated wisdom and worldliness with us. Without our knowing it, she had helped shape us both in those short months. She had been an endless source of encouragement and support to me. Her loving, unselfish advice in dealing with the new world I found myself in had always been spot-on and like Pepper I missed her terribly. The intimate and happy relationship the three of us had shared was gone forever and nothing would ever take its place. But life must go on and it did.

Senior Sergeant O'Malley had become an unsung hero as a result of his investigation. Although he never found Natalie or Joey Szaso, in the course of the follow-up investigations he'd unearthed Joey's kick-back schemes, the dirty coppers at Darlingston, and the ineptness of some of the more senior detectives. And in searching the Cross for Joey, guess who turned up? Jackie Marsh. He also found her guns and plans of Surf City. After the Sarge threatened to implicate her in the heroin dealing, she finally admitted she planned to rob Surf City with Joey. Turns out that's why she'd been hanging in the Canberra Oriental Hotel.

She was casing the place from across the street. That's where she'd met Joey and together they'd hatched their plan. With all her back warrants for all I know she could be still knitting doilies for St Vincent de Paul out at Long Bay gaol. The Sarge was offered a promotion but decided to go out on a high and opted for retirement. Citizen Brian O'Malley said goodbye to the Cross forever and he and his wife Ginny moved to the beautiful NSW coastal town of Coffs Harbour.

'Poison Ivy' had been released and was an instant national number one smash. Our first. Overnight we were caught up in the whirlwind of success. Television appearances, concerts, interviews, photo sessions, PR appearances and mobbings in the street all hit in what felt like a week and there weren't enough hours in the day to fit them all in. Sometime around then we did our first appearance on the popular national television show hosted by Brian Henderson, 'Bandstand'. Along with Johnny O'Keefe's 'Sing Sing Sing' it was the most popular music television show in the country. That appearance more than any other solidified our grip on the number one spot and launched us formally as a national act. A number of other 'Bandstand' appearances followed and one day we received a call from Patti Mostyn, who was Johnny O'Keefe's personal assistant, inviting us on his show. Patti was the first person I'd met when I came down from Brisbane before making the permanent move. She's a great girl and a good mate. She later went on to write the book on promotion in Australia, doing PR for every international act under the sun and establishing herself as the undisputed Queen of Australian PR.

I was knocked out by her call. Johnny O'Keefe had always been a big hero of mine. I was lucky to have seen him perform in his prime when I was still a child performer and get to stand backstage and steal everything I could. In his prime J O'K was the best, and I mean the best, and I stood backstage and watched them all—from Chuck Berry and Little Richard to Jerry Lee Lewis. But J O'K was my hero. I didn't want to be Elvis or Jerry Lee. I wanted to be J O'K. He was my idol and although I'd met him many times before, the call to do his show was one of the biggest thrills I had at that time. Even though the new music scene was booming, there was still a reluctance on the part of some of the old guard to accept or legitimise it. We represented a new youth culture that was a threat to the old regime of which J O'K and Col Joye were the undisputed kings.

We'd heard that J O'K didn't want any of these young, scruffy, long-haired poofter bands on his show, but even he couldn't ignore the ratings, and the long-haired poofters were rating big time! Hence the call, and the date was set. We arrived at the Channel 7 studios in Frenchs Forest, where the show went live to air Sunday evenings, and were greeted with much respect by the producer who led us to the guest star dressing-room. He took us out to the studio and the band was formally introduced to J O'K. When he saw me he shook my hand warmly and gave me that squinty-eyed look of his. I guess he could see that look in my eye that said I'm going after your title, pal, and there's no stopping me. He was extremely friendly and we rehearsed two numbers, then went back to relax until our time came to perform. We were sitting around in the dressing-room waiting for the show to start when the producer arrived with a note for me from J O'K. I thought it was going to be a 'break a leg' note—you know, 'good luck with the show'—but not J O'K! He was defiant to the last, the bastard. The note read:

> Dear Billy and the band. Although it is my great pleasure to have you as my guests on Sing Sing Sing this week, due to the high standards we take great efforts to maintain I'm afraid I cannot allow you to be seen on the show with your long hair. If you wish to appear on my show this week you must get your hair cut. I have my personal barber ready and he will be happy to come down immediately and clean you all up.

It was signed 'Johnny O'Keefe'. I couldn't believe it. It was an ultimatum and a fucking insult to boot.

'Fuck 'im,' said Bluey.

'Fuck him's dead right,' I said. 'Why don't we ask him to come and tell us personally?'

They all agreed and the message was sent. About five minutes later there was a polite knock on the door and in swaggered J O'K, resplendent in his trademark black tuxedo and butterfly bow tie, white-coated barber in tow.

'Well, boys,' he said.

'Well what?' I asked.

'Have you decided to clean up your act or what?'

I looked at the boys. 'Well, what do you think?' I asked them.

Without hesitation a resounding 'Get Fuuucked!' hit the air.

'You can stick yer fuckin' show in yer arse as far as I'm concerned,' Bluey shouted.

'Me too!' echoed Col.

'Yeah, John,' I said. 'Shove it right up your arse and do a fucking tap dance in our two spots. See ya.'

We gathered up our things and left him standing there with his dick in his hand.

Believe me, in 1964 J O'K was God and very few performers if any had told God to stick his show in his fucking arse. He was dumbfounded. We were about to drive off when one of his assistants came puffing up to the van and told us, 'Er, Mr O'Keefe has decided to let you boys go on after all. Could you please hurry. We go to air in five minutes.'

We'd called his bluff and he'd backed down. I still admire his balls for trying. When we did our songs J O'K's vibe was great and he acted like nothing had happened. The bludger. Jesus, he could be a prick when he wanted to. The irony is that in late 1965 his show was cancelled due to low ratings and I was offered my own show, 'It's All Happening', which replaced it in 1966 on the same channel, in the same time slot, and went through the roof.

About half an hour before we were due to go to air on the third or fourth show I went to my dressing-room which was in the studio, just off the set. I'd got the door half open when it slammed back in my face and I caught a glimpse of who slammed it. It was fucking O'Keefe!

I could hear him rampaging around wrecking the place and 'fucking cunting' at the top of his lungs. He was as pissed as a fart. I didn't know what to do and neither did anybody else. He was obviously destroying the joint and we had to get him out before the show started or the sound of his rampage would be heard on TV sets across Australia. After much deliberation and several futile attempts from a number of the crew who'd worked with J O'K for years, the fire marshal was brought in to smash down the door with an axe, and a blind drunk J O'K was carried out of my dressing-room kicking and screaming and escorted from the building.

Everybody was stunned and we all felt sad to see this great man brought down to such a sorry state. J O'K had a history of breakdowns and this wasn't the first time that he'd pulled weird stunts. The inevitable had happened. The threat he saw in me to his position had materialised as fact and it flipped him out. The poor bastard. Years later we laughed about it together, both half-pissed sitting at the Checker's bar. He told me that the moment I went on that day on 'Sing Sing Sing' and he saw the crowd's response, he knew I'd take the title and he paid me the great compliment of saying that I'd done it with class and I deserved it. Johnny O'Keefe may have been many things, including a great performer and, at times, a raving maniac, but above all else, deep down, he was a gentleman to the end and I both respected and loved him deeply. He was one of a kind.

The little country tours we'd done in the past now turned into major events with us receiving almost royal welcomes when we arrived and playing to standing-room-only, sold-out shows night after night. As a result we started to tour on a regular basis and the inevitable started to occur.

I was on the road a lot and Pepper had to return home from the Pussycat to the empty apartment. We both knew this was going to happen one day, but had never included Natalie's horrible murder in the equation. The tragic haunted loneliness of the apartment was slowly destroying Pepper. Natalie's death had changed us both immeasurably and Pepper was never the same afterwards. She couldn't stand to go up the Cross and eventually quit her job at the Pussycat. Some days she didn't get out of bed and I'd come home after Surf City or a TV appearance to find her in the same T-shirt she'd been wearing when I left, her eyes swollen red from crying. Something had died in her with

Natalie and nothing I did or said could bring it back. The fire had gone out of her and it was breaking my heart. I think it had rekindled the awful memories of her own violent rape and she just couldn't let it go.

The band was offered some gigs in Melbourne and we went down to play our first interstate shows, which were incredibly successful, and it became obvious to everybody that Billy Thorpe and the Aztecs were destined to become a major force in Australian music. The night I arrived in Melbourne I called Pepper to see how she was but there was no answer. I called her two or three times a day that week but still no-one answered the phone. I was really worried so I called the Sarge, Wayne, Sammy, Jean-Pierre, anyone who might know where she was, but no-one had seen her. I came home a week later to find most of her things missing from the flat and knew she'd taken off.

I sat there in shock. Pepper was gone! I looked around the apartment. Everything was still there. Natalie, Pepper . . . us. All the bits and pieces of our lives together hit me. For the first time in my life I understood the feeling of being truly alone and I cried like a baby. A month or so after Natalie had disappeared Pepper and I had held a private ceremony. At midnight we picked up Dulcie and went down to the cliffs above the ocean on Dover Heights, not far from Camp Cove, which had been Natalie's favourite beach, where we'd spent so many happy hours together. Lighting one of Natalie's Russian Orthodox candles, we cried a prayer together and cast her photograph and precious Rolex into the Pacific Ocean crashing below us.

Two or three days after I got back from the Melbourne trip, I was sitting in the apartment in a lonely funk when the phone rang and I picked it up.

'Hello, Bill, it's me, mate,' Pepper said, then burst into tears. 'I had to get away, Bill. I just had to. I couldn't stand it any longer. It's killing meee.'

'Thank God you're safe. I've been worried sick. Everybody's been looking for you. The Sarge even put out a missing persons on you, mate. We thought you were dead! Where are you?'

'I'm wiv my parents, Bill,' she said. 'Oh Bill, Bill, I'm so sorry I just took off like that, but I had to get away! I had to! I couldn't face saying goodbye. It would've broken my heart. I can't stay in the Cross any more. Everyfing I look at reminds me of Natalie and it's killing me. Oh God it hurts so much.'

I didn't know what to say.

'My Mum called the night you went to Melbourne. Somebody from here saw me at Surf City wiv you a while back and that's how they tracked me down. They've been trying to find me for ages but didn't know where to start. My bruvver took off from home the night . . . the night they raped me! My parents didn't know where eiver of us went. Mum fort we'd run away togever. Oh Bill, they didn't find out what really happened until this year when Shirley told them and they've been trying to find me ever since. They were so happy to see me. They really do love me, Bill, and I need to be here wiv them for a while. I've got a lot of fings to fink out about my life and . . . and . . .' she said through her tears, 'I need to be alone for a while. Oh God I miss you!'

There was a long silence broken only by her gentle sobs. I was in tears too.

'Are you all right?' I managed to ask.

'Yes, I'm fine. Oh I miss you so,' she sobbed.

'God I miss you too, mate. When are you coming back?' I asked, trying hard not to lose it.

'Don't know, mate,' she said hesitantly. 'I've got a lot of fings to straighten out here and it may involve the coppers or somefing. My Mum and Dad said they'll stand by me no matter what. Bill, I've got to go now. I, I just wanted you to know I was all right. I can't talk anymore, Bill. I can't! I love you so much. I'll always love you no matter what. I want you to know that. I love you. Bye!'

'Pepper, Pepper! Wait, what's your phone number?' I yelled, but the line went dead.

Pepper never came back to the Cross. I received a couple of letters and postcards from different places from time to time but none of them had a return address or phone number. I tried to find her but had no idea where to start. The only time she'd ever talked about her past was that night after she nearly killed Joey. I'd asked her about it a few times, but she always brushed over it and I knew she wanted it kept hidden, even from me. I never even knew her real name. She'd never mentioned it and I'd never asked. She'd always been Pepper Walker to me. When the Sarge checked for me there was no report of the rape or of a missing person fitting her description, and he couldn't find any record of anyone by the name of Walker.

As time went by I realised it was over.

In 1964 we released four singles and had hit after hit. At one stage we had them all in the top twenty at the same time and we had one single or another in the charts for the entire year. One fantastic month we shared most of the top ten with the Beatles. That year we outdrew them in Melbourne when a phenomenal 60,000 came to the Myer Music Bowl for one show. The Beatles drew 50,000 over two shows around the same time. I'm not saying this for my own self-aggrandisement, but to simply point out our phenomenal and meteoric rise to success from playing to 250 punters a night during the week a mere twelve months earlier. We went from success to success and found ourselves being mobbed by fans wherever we went.

Around this time some of our most loyal fans, Sonia, Doris, Wendy, Deidre, Lynn Gilbert, Hazel Adair and Dulcie (not dear old Dulcie) organised and formed the first Billy Thorpe and the Aztecs Fan Club. They set up a small newsletter and a super-efficient mailing system for kids all over Australia to write and get information and photos. It produced instant results and before we knew it we were swamped with requests for T-shirts, autographs, locks of our hair, personal information on the members, like what we ate for breakfast, and offers to father children. The fan club did a terrific job for us and their tireless efforts were instrumental in spreading our fan base and popularity around the country.

The top-rating radio station in Perth in those days was 6PR and one of the jocks, Paul Gadine, was a big fan who'd been playing our records to death. As a result we got an offer to go and play there. Unbeknown to us, his enthusiastic support had turned our gig and arrival in Perth into the event of the decade. We arrived with Brian Henderson and the Channel 9 crew for our first Western Australian concert, which was to be filmed live for 'Bandstand', to find thousands of screaming fans waiting for us at the airport. After a police-escorted ride in the back of an ambulance, while being chased by hundreds of cars, we arrived at our hotel to find young girls under our beds, in the closets and climbing the fire escape to get in. It was insanity.

The Capitol theatre in Perth was an old-time music hall with two balconies. It held about 3000 people and was a great place to play. We were scheduled to do two back-to-back shows that night with a one-hour break in between. Both shows had sold out the day they were announced and along with 6000 or so ticket-holders there were an additional 2000 fans outside without tickets. We went on to the deafening screams of 3000 teenage girls. The second we started to play, groups of young girls leapt on the stage from all sides to hug and kiss us, only to be carried off by bouncers and instantly replaced by more crying, screaming girls. It was pandemonium. We loved it, of course, and beamed at each other as we rocked on and tried to get the music over the screaming.

Then all hell broke loose. Instead of rushing us in fives and tens, a sort of mass hysteria swept the crowd and waves of frantic, screaming girls hit the stage at once, knocked us flat on our arses and flattened all the gear. The house lights went up and a big copper came on stage and made an announcement that the concert would not continue until they quietened down. After about ten minutes we went back on and had no sooner started playing when another couple of hundred girls kamikaze'd us and the show was stopped again. Next minute the doors at the rear of the theatre behind the audience opened and down the aisles came a dozen or so coppers with police dogs who terrified the young girls back into their seats. The mobbing stopped but the hysteria didn't and we played the rest of the show with a copper on either side of the stage, while the dogs and their handlers patrolled the aisles like Nazi guards. It was ridiculous, but nothing could dampen the enthusiasm of the crowd and the first show was a great success.

We took a break while the next audience came in. The dressing-room was a hive of excitement. Nobody had expected this. It was our first experience as idols and none of us really had any idea how to act. They loved us and we honestly couldn't work out why. We were just a band after all, but they acted as if we were deities and that a touch or a kiss would heal all wounds or put them in a state of eternal bliss. I must say some of them were so beautiful that I was in a state of bliss myself. The thought of some of them sitting there quimming with no undies on, having tossed them on the stage, crossed my mind from time to time.

The second audience was seated and we went on again. The instant the curtain went up the same thing happened. Immediate mass hysteria and weeping young girls mobbing us and throwing their panties on stage. At one stage Bluey had about three pairs on his head and munched on the crutch of one pair as he played. About halfway through the show it was stopped again by the police and back they came with their dogs. We went back on again and the place continued to rage with the Nazis patrolling the aisles. I was standing dead centre of the stage when something caught my eye off in the wings to my right. The next second about twenty screaming girls covered in wet, gooey green slime hit the stage. Their wet feet slipped on the floor and they slid across the stage on their arses, heading straight at us like a runaway train. Some of them slid into the band and a pack of them came straight at me. I had nowhere to go and they hit me like the front row of the St George football team. I went off the front of the stage, fell about fifteen feet to the floor below, and landed on my face in the orchestra pit. As I hit I felt one of my fingers snap. Next thing about a hundred girls came over the edge of the orchestra pit like a herd of stampeding elephants and they landed right square on top of me. I felt a couple of my ribs break and I nearly passed out from the pain and suffocation. I couldn't breathe! A couple of bouncers jumped in to help me but a hundred to three ain't great odds and there was nothing much they could do. I'd just managed to get to my feet when some silly-arsed copper with his dopey fucking Alsatian guard dog jumped in and joined the fray and the first person the bloody dog bit was me.

I was trying to scramble back on stage with a busted finger and ribs. Here I am hanging off the stage with the band and some copper's trying to pull me back on while fighting off twenty slime-covered girls, when suddenly I've got a ninety-pound rabid police dog hanging off my arse in a death grip trying to drag me back into the pit and eat me. You might say I was in a predicament. It was then I saw Bluey swing the microphone stand over my head and hit the bloody dog smack between the eyes, killing it stone dead. It dropped off me like a swatted fly, taking a slice of my arse with it. The show was over!

I sat in the dressing-room with a towel filled with ice strapped to my ribs, a flannel on my torn arse, and gaffer tape around my fingers, feeling more like the losing end of a title fight than a pop star. The rest of the band and crew tried to get their heads around what had taken place. None of us had ever seen anything like what we'd just been through and it shook the shit out of us. I could easily have been killed. Nobody had any idea how the slime-covered girls got on the stage until a bouncer told us they had discovered a storm drain outlet somewhere at the back of the theatre and crawled through it to get inside. Now were these devoted fans or what? Unfortunately the film crew had feared for their lives and equipment during the first show and packed up in the intermission. Consequently only the first show was recorded for posterity, but I believe the police dogs are in it. One of the crew told me there was an ambulance waiting outside and I found out that it hadn't been sent for me. Evidently Brian Henderson had fainted halfway through the melee and they'd sent it for him. Poor old Brian. He's a great guy, and contrary to his squeaky clean TV image, loved a rage, but all this had terrified him. It was a long way from the prim and proper, family-style image that 'Bandstand' projected and I think he could see the headlines and his TV career passing before his eyes.

There was a big formal party in our honour after the gig, to be followed by another party at a private home in the exclusive Perth suburb of Dalkeith. The first party had an invitation-only guest list which included local music and media personalities, socialites and dignitaries. I arrived at the reception late, nursing my war wounds, to find Bluey up to his usual antics, dressed up as a waiter, serving hors d'oeuvres from a large silver platter. At first I just laughed with the rest of the band, amused at his antics, then nearly dropped dead when I saw he had his dick out on the tray amongst the canapés and sausages. He had carefully deco-rated it with whipped cream, lettuce leaves and olives, and there it sat in all its finery, a living Coquille Saint Bluey à la Mode. I caught sight of him just as he was offering the tray to the Lady Mayoress, who was laughing and joking with him as she delicately picked around Bluey's dick looking for the right snack. Fortunately she missed it and the escapade went down as one of the many events that only we knew about, to be filed away, cherished and laughed about for the rest of our lives.

Those concerts and the ensuing front-page publicity were the beginning of stardom for us and after Perth we sold out concerts all over Australia. The hysteria surrounding the Perth shows became pretty much par for the course from then on, and 1964 and 1965 were nothing short of a travelling rock 'n' roll, laugh and sex-filled lunacy that was incredibly successful, and without doubt the most exciting time of my life. The band and I went on to win every major music, radio and television award in the country, broke every sales and attendance record, and established ourselves as one of Australia's all-time most popular bands. Never had I imagined the phenomenal level of success and acceptance we achieved. From Surf City just two and a half years before, it had been a white-knuckle, magic-carpet ride that none of us will ever forget.

When I left home at sixteen I was ready to conquer the world, but had no idea what was waiting for me. By the grace of God every dream came true, and in my personal search for the grail I found so much more. I'm blessed to have been one of those fortunate riders on the crest of that unstoppable wave called change, and privileged to have felt first-hand the euphoria of the cosmically charged energy pumping directly from its core. I not only lived the myth, but experienced the very heart and soul of my generation as it led one of the most significant periods of sociological and cultural change ever to take place on this planet. All things must pass and sadly those times and the sense of innocence, freedom, challenge, love, and joy they evoked, are forever gone.

But the spirit lives!

Epilogue

IT was 1980, an unusually warm summer in London, and I'd been staying at the prestigious Savoy Hotel as a guest of Polygram Records. I'd moved to the USA in 1976 with my wife Lynn and four-year-old daughter Rusty and in 1979 the first American Thorpe from my branch of the family, my youngest daughter Lauren, was born. In November 1979 my first American-made album, *Children of the Sun*, had been released in the USA and had been a big hit, reaching the national top twenty and was followed by two more top-forty albums. From the release of *Children of the Sun* through 1980 I headlined my own sold-out tours all over the States, but unfortunately in the middle of it all my record label, Capricorn, had gone belly up, and in the screw-up I lost a genuine shot at a number one hit. The parent company Polygram International assumed the album rights and I now found myself in London on my way to Hamburg for the European release of the album.

I was standing at the front desk of the Savoy waiting to sign my account prior to my departure to Germany when I heard, 'Aw mate this is a bit bloody rich, isn't it? Ten bloody quid for a cup of tea!'

No mistaking that accent. It was an Aussie all right! I looked over to see the face and spotted him standing along from me at the reception desk haggling over his bill. He was five ten or eleven and about my age. Although it was a hot summer day he was dressed in the traditional Aussie cream twill R.M. Williams stock pants, a green plaid jacket, cream wool shirt, brown wool tie, brown Williams boots and a cream Williams hat. Definitely a cockey, born and bred. He turned, caught my stare, and an astonished look came over his face.

'Jeezus bloody Christ, it's not bloody Thorpie, is it?' he said at the top of his voice. 'Aw mate! I followed you for years! Saw you play a dozen bloody times. It's a pleasure to meet you, mate,' he said, walking over and shaking my hand. 'How the bloody hell are ya?'

'Great thanks, mate,' I said.

'Bob . . . Bob Galbraith from Moree,' he said. 'You been staying here long?'

'All week, Bob. Just checking out. I'm off to Hamburg in a couple of hours.'

'Ah shit! I'd have loved to have had a beer with you or something. Listen, have you got a minute? I'm with me missus and some friends. They're over in the tea room eating bloody cucumber sandwiches. Hate the bloody things! Would you mind coming over to say g'day? They're all old fans. My missus has got every bloody record you ever made. They'd shit if I brought you over. Would you mind having a photo with us and signing a couple of autographs, mate?'

'Not at all, mate. It would be my pleasure.'

We finished up at reception and headed into the famous Savoy tea room where the traditional afternoon British fare of tea and cucumber sandwiches was now being served. Bob waved to some people sitting near the window. I could tell right away they were Aussies. You can pick them a mile away in a snow storm. I saw a man and a woman sitting with a couple of young kids. Bob was smiling and pointing to me, nodding his head excitedly as they recognised me and big smiles came over their faces.

'These are my nippers, mate,' he said, nodding to a young boy and girl about eight and nine years old. They both had snowy white hair and the unmistakeable cheeky faces of Aussie kids. 'They're a bit young to remember you, mate.' He laughed. 'But they've heard your bloody records a thousand times.'

He introduced me to the couple sitting at the table and I was shaking hands with them when Bob gestured to the room behind me saying, 'and this is my wife Jan.'

I turned to meet her and saw a platinum blonde beauty. Then it hit me! I nearly died! Staring back at me through astonished, tear-filled green eyes was Pepper! I couldn't believe it and neither could she. We stood there in stunned silence, holding hands, staring at each other in disbelief. Her eyes closed slightly and with an almost imperceptible shake of her head she spoke to me the same way she had that night in the Spaghetti Bar so many years ago. Pepper's look told me Bob didn't know.

I raised her hand to my lips and kissed it gently. There was that unmistakeable scent. My head started to swim.

'Pleased to meet you, er, Jan,' I said, staring at Pepper in shock.

'Oh God! I can't fink of anyfink to say,' Pepper said, grinning that unmistakeable grin through her tears. 'Er, pleased to meet you too, Bill. Oh God.'

'See, I told you she'd shit herself when she met you,' Bob laughed, mistaking Pepper's tears.

'Listen, Thorpie, let me get a photo of you and Jan.' He picked up his camera from the table. 'Come on, mate, put your arms round her. That's it. Now Jan, put your arms round him and give him a big kiss on the cheek. Come on, love, he won't bite ya.'

Standing there in the tea room of the Savoy Hotel in London with Pepper hugging me, a million sounds, scents and images of her, Natalie and the Cross flooded my senses. It was overwhelming. Pepper squeezed me and kissed me tenderly on the cheek.

'Oh I've missed you, Bill,' she whispered. 'I fink I've peed my pants.' She giggled nervously.

'Eh listen, Thorpie,' Bob said as the shutter clicked. 'Do you remember Surf City?'

'Yes, mate. Sort of . . . sort of,' I replied.